Leveled Reader Resource Guide

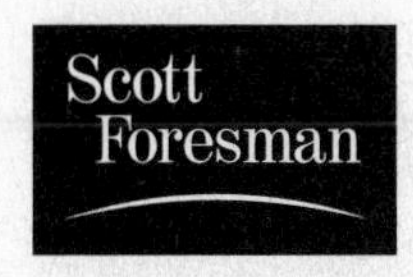

Editorial Offices: Glenview, Illinois • Parsippany, New Jersey • New York, New York
Sales Offices: Parsippany, New Jersey • Duluth, Georgia • Glenview, Illinois
Coppell, Texas • Ontario, California

ISBN: 0-673-59682-6

11 12 13 V039 10 09 08 07 06 05 04

Table of Contents

Unit 4 Time and Time Again

Unit 5 Traveling On

Unit 6 Think of It!

Introduction

The goal of *Scott Foresman Reading* is to help students not only become better readers in today's classroom, but also to build a love of reading that lasts a lifetime. Students who are having difficulty reading at grade level or reading fluently often develop negative attitudes about reading and themselves. Providing students with reading materials they can and want to read is the first step toward developing fluent readers. The Leveled Readers are a series of high interest, accessible materials that were developed to help students experience the joy of successful and meaningful reading. The Leveled Reader Resource Guide contains easy-to-use instructional plans, graphic organizers, Leveled Reader practice pages, the Scott Foresman Leveling System, and assessment forms that will help you select Leveled Readers appropriate for students' abilities; instruct and support students before, during, and after reading; and assess their performance level.

About the Leveled Readers

There are 360 Leveled Readers in the *Scott Foresman Reading* program that are written one to one and a half grades below grade level. Set A is Easy. Set B is Easy/Average. For each Student Edition selection, there is a corresponding Set A Leveled Reader and a Set B Leveled Reader. Each one focuses on the same target comprehension skill, tested selection vocabulary, and theme as the Student Edition selection. The Leveled Readers increase in difficulty within a grade and from grade to grade. As students' reading abilities develop, they can begin reading texts with longer and more complex sentences, more pages, fewer illustrations, and more challenging concepts.

Grade	Number of Pages Per Leveled Reader
Grades 1–2	8–16 pages
Grades 3–4	16 pages
Grades 5–6	16–24 pages

See the Scott Foresman Leveling System on pages 220–221 for more information about how the Readers are leveled and to help you select Readers that match students' reading abilities. (There are also Set C/Challenge Leveled Readers, which provide literature and activities for students reading at or above grade level. Each Set C Leveled Reader is linked thematically to a unit in the Student Edition and gives students additional opportunities to expand target comprehension, vocabulary, and critical thinking skills. Instructional plans for Set C Leveled Readers can be found in a separate Leveled Reader Resource Guide.)

Great care and attention were given to create Leveled Readers that are age appropriate and appealing to students for each grade level. The Leveled Readers provide students with a good mix of fiction and nonfiction texts in a variety of genres, such as fantasy, folk tale, realistic story, historical fiction, narrative nonfiction, biography, and how-to books. Many of the Leveled Readers for Grades 1–3 use predictable patterns of rhyme, rhythm, and sentence repetition to facilitate reading fluency. They include art on every page to ensure a good match between picture and text and to maximize comprehension. In all grades, there is a lively blend of humor, surprise, and novelty—characteristics that are very attractive to readers in Grades 1–6.

Using Leveled Readers

The Leveled Readers can be used to meet the diverse needs of your classroom in a variety of ways:

- as a means of developing fluency and reading skills and strategies for all students,
- as a substitute for the corresponding Student Edition selection for students who are reading below grade level,
- as a reinforcement of the corresponding Student Edition themes, tested selection vocabulary, and target comprehension skills for students reading at or below level,
- as a choice in Guided Reading groups,
- as a choice for self-selected reading,
- as a choice for shared reading,
- as a choice for a read aloud,
- as a choice for choral reading or to be performed as Reader's Theater,
- as a choice for take-home reading,
- as a choice to be used in conjunction with the Instructional Routine Cards,
- and as a text for assessment of oral reading and other reading skills and strategies.

Using Leveled Reader Practice Pages

Beginning on page 154, you will find Leveled Reader practice pages. There is one practice page for each Leveled Reader. These pages contain comprehension questions set in a test format that will help you assess students' understanding of the Leveled Reader and the target comprehension skill. At least two questions on each page are linked to the target comprehension skill. These pages will also provide test-taking practice with multiple-choice and short-response questions.

Use the Leveled Reader practice pages after students have read the Leveled Reader in conjunction with the after reading activities suggested in the instructional plans.

Guided Reading

The instructional plans in the Leveled Reader Resource Guide were developed to be compatible with a guided-reading approach. This approach can be used with small groups of students who are reading at a similar reading level. Use the following routine to guide children before, during, and after reading.

- Select and introduce an appropriate Leveled Reader to the group.
- Have each student read (softly or silently), while you listen, assess, and provide support as needed.
- After reading, reinforce reading skills and strategies, assess comprehension, and help develop fluency by having students reread the text.

The goal in the guided-reading approach is to have students read independently, silently, and, above all, read for meaning.

Managing the Classroom

When you are using the Leveled Readers with individual students or in small groups, you will need to keep the other students engaged in independent and meaningful learning tasks. Establish different work stations around the classroom where students can be working on different tasks simultaneously. Display a work board that indicates the work stations and tells which students should be at each work station. Explain what task or tasks are to be done at each station and give an estimate of how long students should work there. Alert students when they should rotate to new stations and change their station assignments on the work board. Develop a classroom routine regarding the work stations and the rotation among these work stations so students can read and work more independently.

Work stations you can create are:

- Listening Work Station
- Phonics Work Station
- Technology Work Station
- Writing and Language Work Station
- Independent Reading Work Station
- Cross-Curricular Work Station

Using the Leveled Reader Resource Guide

Each Leveled Reader has its own instructional plan in the Leveled Reader Resource Guide, but all plans follow similar before, during, and after reading routines.

At a Glance

1 Links to the Student Edition Each Leveled Reader is linked to a Student Edition selection and focuses on the same target comprehension skill, tested selection vocabulary (the group of tested words is divided between the A and B Leveled Readers), and unit theme.

Before Reading

2 Motivating the Reader Create interest in the Leveled Reader by building background and connecting to what students already know. Suggestions are given for using pictures, videotapes, classroom discussion, graphic organizers, writing, art activities, or simple science experiments.

3 Preview and Predict Preview the Leveled Reader by having students read the title and scan the cover, text, and illustrations. Have students make predictions about what happens in the story or what information they will find in the book. Then suggest a purpose for reading or have them set their own. Point out selection vocabulary and any unfamiliar words or expressions that might be important to understanding the book.

During Reading

4 Guiding Comprehension Have students read the Leveled Reader, either softly or silently, to a specific point in the book or the entire book. Then use the questions provided as needed to support and assess students' comprehension.

5 Ongoing Assessment Listen and watch for students to use effective reading strategies as they read. Use the If/Then statements provided to help students develop better reading strategies and build self-awareness and confidence about the good reading strategies they do use. Make notes about students' reading performance, using the Observation Checklist on page 222, or Taking a Running Record on page 223.

6 Model Your Thinking If students have difficulty with the target comprehension skill, then use the Think Aloud model provided to help students understand what the skill is, why it is a useful skill, and how this skill can be used to understand the Leveled Reader better.

After Reading

7 Revisiting the Text Students will better comprehend the text and develop fluency by rereading the Leveled Reader independently, with a partner, or in a small group. Activity suggestions are given to help students organize their thinking, respond to what they've read, and demonstrate their understanding. See also the Leveled Reader practice pages beginning on page 154.

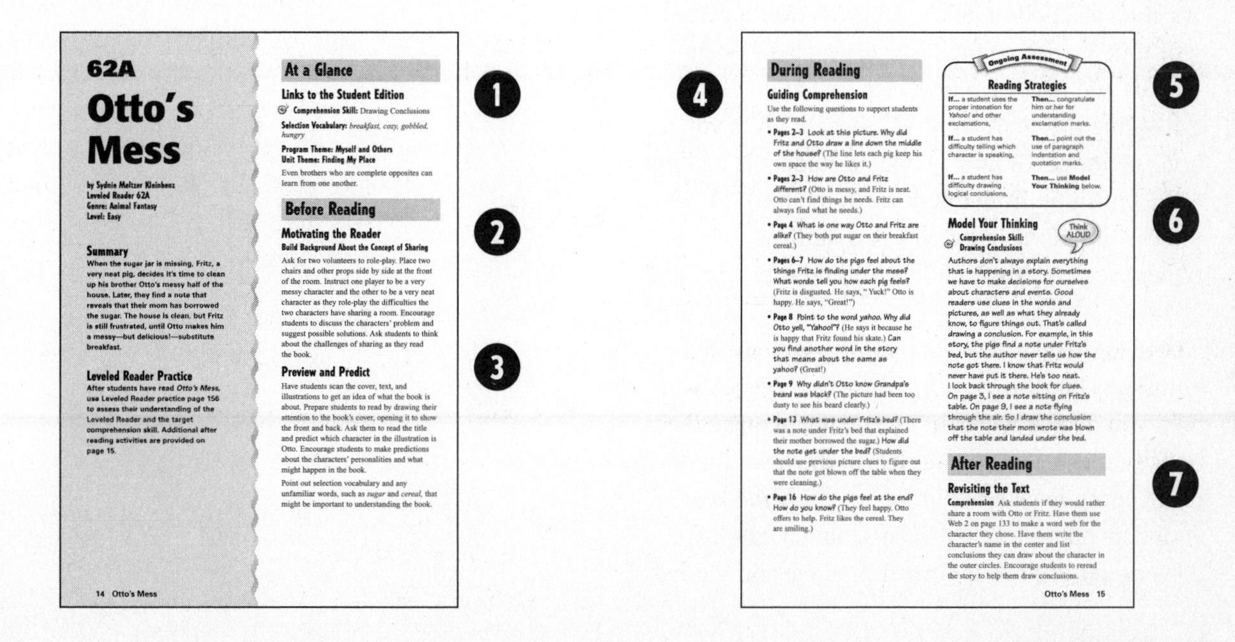

62A

Otto's Mess

by Sydnie Meltzer Kleinhenz
Leveled Reader 62A
Genre: Animal Fantasy
Level: Easy

Summary
When the sugar jar is missing, Fritz, a very neat pig, decides it's time to clean up his brother Otto's messy half of the house. Later, they find a note that reveals that their mom has borrowed the sugar. The house is clean, but Fritz is still frustrated, until Otto makes him a messy—but delicious!—substitute breakfast.

Leveled Reader Practice
After students have read *Otto's Mess*, use Leveled Reader practice page 156 to assess their understanding of the Leveled Reader and the target comprehension skill. Additional after reading activities are provided on page 15.

At a Glance

Links to the Student Edition
Comprehension Skill: Drawing Conclusions
Selection Vocabulary: *breakfast, cozy, gobbled, hungry*
Program Theme: Myself and Others
Unit Theme: Finding My Place
Even brothers who are complete opposites can learn from one another.

Before Reading

Motivating the Reader
Build Background About the Concept of Sharing
Ask for two volunteers to role-play. Place two chairs and other props side by side at the front of the room. Instruct one player to be a very messy character and the other to be a very neat character as they role-play the difficulties the two characters have sharing a room. Encourage students to discuss the characters' problem and suggest possible solutions. Ask students to think about the challenges of sharing as they read the book.

Preview and Predict
Have students scan the cover, text, and illustrations to get an idea of what the book is about. Prepare students to read by drawing their attention to the book's cover, opening it to show the front and back. Ask them to read the title and predict which character in the illustration is Otto. Encourage students to make predictions about the characters' personalities and what might happen in the book.

Point out selection vocabulary and any unfamiliar words, such as *sugar* and *cereal*, that might be important to understanding the book.

14 Otto's Mess

During Reading

Guiding Comprehension
Use the following questions to support students as they read.

- **Pages 2–3** *Look at this picture. Why did Fritz and Otto draw a line down the middle of the house?* (The line lets each pig keep his own space the way he likes it.)
- **Pages 2–3** *How are Otto and Fritz different?* (Otto is messy, and Fritz is neat. Otto can't find things he needs. Fritz can always find what he needs.)
- **Page 4** *What is one way Otto and Fritz are alike?* (They both put sugar on their breakfast cereal.)
- **Pages 6–7** *How do the pigs feel about the things Fritz is finding under the mess? What words tell you how each pig feels?* (Fritz is disgusted. He says, " Yuck!" Otto is happy. He says, "Great!")
- **Page 8** *Point to the word yahoo. Why did Otto yell, "Yahoo!"?* (He says it because he is happy that Fritz found his skate.) *Can you find another word in the story that means about the same as yahoo?* (Great!)
- **Page 9** *Why didn't Otto know Grandpa's beard was black?* (The picture had been too dusty to see his beard clearly.)
- **Page 13** *What was under Fritz's bed?* (There was a note under Fritz's bed that explained their mother borrowed the sugar.) *How did the note get under the bed?* (Students should use previous picture clues to figure out that the note got blown off the table when they were cleaning.)
- **Page 16** *How do the pigs feel at the end? How do you know?* (They feel happy. Otto offers to help. Fritz likes the cereal. They are smiling.)

Ongoing Assessment

Reading Strategies

If... a student uses the proper intonation for *Yahoo!* and other exclamations,	**Then...** congratulate him or her for understanding exclamation marks.
If... a student has difficulty telling which character is speaking,	**Then...** point out the use of paragraph indentation and quotation marks.
If... a student has difficulty drawing logical conclusions,	**Then...** use **Model Your Thinking** below.

Model Your Thinking
Comprehension Skill: Drawing Conclusions

Think ALOUD

Authors don't always explain everything that is happening in a story. Sometimes we have to make decisions for ourselves about characters and events. Good readers use clues in the words and pictures, as well as what they already know, to figure things out. That's called drawing a conclusion. For example, in this story, the pigs find a note under Fritz's bed, but the author never tells us how the note got there. I know that Fritz would never have put it there. He's too neat. I look back through the book for clues. On page 3, I see a note sitting on Fritz's table. On page 9, I see a note flying through the air. So I draw the conclusion that the note their mom wrote was blown off the table and landed under the bed.

After Reading

Revisiting the Text
Comprehension Ask students if they would rather share a room with Otto or Fritz. Have them use Web 2 on page 133 to make a word web for the character they chose. Have them write the character's name in the center and list conclusions they can draw about the character in the outer circles. Encourage students to reread the story to help them draw conclusions.

Otto's Mess 15

Using the Graphic Organizers

Graphic organizers can be found on pages 130–153. This set of twenty-four graphic organizers can be copied onto plastic transparency sheets and used on an overhead projector or copied onto paper for students to use as worksheets. Suggestions are given in the instructional plans for ways to customize and use these graphic organizers.

Assessing Performance

If/Then statements are provided in each instructional plan to help you assess and assist students as they read the Leveled Reader. The Leveled Reader practice pages provide comprehension questions set in a test format. Use the assessment forms that begin on page 222 to make notes about students' reading skills, strategies, and behaviors as they read.

- **Observation Checklist** (p. 222) Allows you to note the regularity with which students demonstrate their understanding and use of reading skills and strategies.
- **Taking a Running Record** (p. 223) Tells how to take a running record so you can calculate a student's reading accuracy and reading rate. (See also the sample Running Record on the next page.) Note: After Grade 3, some teachers do not take running records to assess oral reading.
- **Progress Report** (p. 224) Allows you to track a student's book-reading progress over a period of time by noting the level at which a student reads and his or her accuracy rate at that level. Reading the chart from left to right gives you a visual model of how quickly a student is making the transition from one level to the next. Share these reports with parents or guardians to help them see how their child's reading is progressing.

Use these assessment forms along with the Scott Foresman Leveling System on pages 220–221 to help you decide whether a student can make the transition to reading materials at the next, more challenging level (student consistently reads at an independent level with an accuracy rate of 98% or better), needs further practice and guided instruction with materials at the same level (student reads at an instructional level with an accuracy rate between 91–97%), or needs targeted instruction and intervention with materials developed for a lower level (student reads at a frustrational level with an accuracy rate below 90%). See the Assessment Handbook for further ideas and forms to help you assess students.

Taking a Running Record

The sample on the next page shows the miscues a student made while reading aloud. See page 223 for more information on taking a running record and assessing the results. Use the notations in the sample to identify the kinds of miscues the student makes while reading. Count the number of errors and subtract them from the total number of words to find the number of words the student read correctly. Divide the number of words read correctly by the total number of words to find the student's accuracy rate. If the student makes the same error more than once, such as mispronouncing *exactly* twice, count it as one error. If possible, tape-record the student reading so you can check your running record. Calculate the reading rate by dividing the total number of words by the number of seconds the student took to read the text. Multiply by sixty to find how many words per minute the student can read. End by having the student retell or summarize the text, so you can assess his or her comprehension of it. Note: After Grade 3, some teachers do not take running records to assess oral reading.

Running Record Sample

Fritz and Otto drew a line down the middle of their (cozy) house. Fritz lived on the right. ^side Otto lived on the ~~left.~~ Fritz kept his things neat. Otto's things were not ~~exactly~~ very neat.

Fritz kept his things clean. /klen/ Otto's things were not exactly clean. Fritz could always find what he needed. Otto could never find what he needed.

But Fritz and Otto did one thing the same. They both made their breakfast <u>cereal</u> H sweet with sugar. (sc) That was how their mom always fixed it. So Fritz and Otto shared the sugar jar.

—From *Otto's Mess,*
Leveled Reader 62A,
Grade 3

Total Number of Words: 93

Number of Errors: 5

Accuracy Percentage Score: 95%

Reading Time: 70 sec

Reading Rate: 80 wpm

Miscues

Omission The student omits words or word parts.

Insertion The student inserts words or parts of words that are not in the text.

Substitution The student substitutes words or parts of words for the words in the text.

Mispronunciation/Misreading The student pronounces or reads a word incorrectly.

Hesitation The student hesitates over a word and the teacher provides the word. Wait several seconds before telling the child what the word is.

Self-correction The student reads a word incorrectly but then corrects the error. Do not count self-corrections as actual errors. However, noting self-corrections will help you identify words the student finds difficult.

$$\frac{93-5}{93} = \frac{88}{93} = .946 = 95\%$$

$$\frac{93}{70} \times 60 = 79.7 = 80 \text{ words per minute}$$

121A

Robo-Police

by Meish Goldish
Leveled Reader 121A
Genre: Humorous Story
Level: Easy

Summary

Carla and Juan are upset by the mess in the school cafeteria. Juan builds a remote-controlled robot using a shop vac. A few days later, Juan and Carla try out the robot at school. To their surprise, not only does it "eat" trash on the cafeteria floor, but it eats students' food off their plates!

Leveled Reader Practice

After students have read *Robo-Police*, use Leveled Reader practice page 154 to assess their understanding of the Leveled Reader and the target comprehension skill. Additional after reading activities are provided on page 11.

At a Glance

Links to the Student Edition

Comprehension Skill: Sequence

Selection Vocabulary: *demonstration, cafeteria, racket*

Program Theme: Myself and Others
Unit Theme: Relating to Others

Two friends build a robot to try to solve an irritating problem: how to get other students to clean up their messes in the cafeteria.

Before Reading

Motivating the Reader

Build Background About Inventions

If possible, display pictures of such household inventions as a vacuum cleaner, a dishwasher, a laundry machine, and a food processor. Invite volunteers to act out how to use each invention. Draw a robot on the chalkboard. Discuss how a robot could do the same work as one of the inventions. Have students name the advantages and disadvantages of robots. Students can work together to draw pictures of a robot they would like to have. They can label the robot's parts to tell what their robot can do.

Preview and Predict

Have students scan the cover, text, and illustrations to get an idea of what the book is about. Have students use word and picture clues to predict what a robo-police robot does and what events might happen in the book. Encourage students to read to find out if their predictions are correct.

Point out selection vocabulary and any unfamiliar words, such as *remote control* and *genius,* that might be important to understanding the book.

During Reading

Guiding Comprehension

Use the following questions to support students as they read.

- **Page 2** **Why is the cafeteria a mess?** (Students have dropped straws, wrappers, and other trash on the floor.)
- **Page 3** **What does Carla mean by *police* in this sentence? How might teachers police the cafeteria?** (Students should recognize that *police* is used as a verb to mean "to patrol or look for problems or to make sure problems don't occur.")
- **Page 5** **Why does Juan make a Robo-Police?** (He thinks a robot will get students to clean up their mess.)
- **Pages 6** **What does the word *racket* mean in this sentence? What other word might make sense in this sentence?** (It means "a noise." Possible synonyms: noise, sound.)
- **Page 6** **Describe the steps in Juan's demonstration.** (First he tips over a garbage can. Next he turns on the machine. Then he runs the vacuum's hose across the floor to suck up the garbage. Lastly, he turns the vacuum off.)
- **Pages 8–9** **Look at the picture on page 8. Explain how the robot "eats" with its feet.** (The hose for the shop vac is near the bottom of the robot. The hose sucks up, or "eats," trash.)
- **Page 10** **Why does Juan think Carla is a genius?** (She thinks of making the robot work by remote control.)
- **Page 14** **What surprising thing happens when Juan brings the robot to school?** (It "eats" students' lunches off the table.)
- **Page 16** **Do you think the robot has solved the problem? Why or why not?** (No. Although the robot cleaned the floor, it created a new problem by "eating" students' lunches.)

Ongoing Assessment

Reading Strategies

If... a student has difficulty with such compound words as *remote control* (page 10),	**Then...** help the student use the meanings of the two smaller words to decode the larger word. (*remote control:* a control, such as a radio signal, used to operate an object from a distance)
If... a student has difficulty understanding why the robot still needs work,	**Then...** suggest the student reread page 14 and describe the illustration.
If... a student has difficulty following the sequence of events,	**Then...** use **Model Your Thinking** below.

Model Your Thinking

Think ALOUD

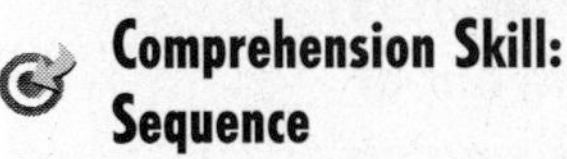

Comprehension Skill: Sequence

I know that story events happen in a certain sequence, or order. As I read, I follow the sequence of events to help me understand what is happening in the story. I look for sequence clue words such as *first, while,* and *next.* I also use the words and illustrations to picture the order of events in my mind. For example, on page 6, I read about Juan's demonstration with the shop vac. First he tips over the trash, and then he turns on the vacuum cleaner. Then he runs it along the floor to clean up the mess. Finally, he shuts off the vacuum. Following this sequence helps me understand how the robot will be able to clean up the mess in the cafeteria.

After Reading

Revisiting the Text

Comprehension Have pairs reread pages 12–16 and list the sequence of events. Then have them create a comic strip showing what happens when Juan and Carla bring the Robo-Police to the cafeteria.

121B

Rusty's Song

by Milo Mason
Leveled Reader 121B
Genre: Humorous Story
Level: Easy/Average

Summary

Old Cowboy, who never speaks, enjoys a simple life with Rusty, a talented singing dog. When they run out of food, Old Cowboy enters a singing contest. When Old Cowboy freezes on stage, Rusty starts singing. Even though dogs aren't allowed in the contest, Rusty's singing is so moving that he wins the cash prize.

Leveled Reader Practice

After students have read *Rusty's Song,* use Leveled Reader practice page 155 to assess their understanding of the Leveled Reader and the target comprehension skill. Additional after reading activities are provided on page 13.

At a Glance

Links to the Student Edition

Comprehension Skill: Sequence

Selection Vocabulary: *switch, triggered, diary*

Program Theme: Myself and Others
Unit Theme: Relating to Others

Two friends discover that music is an important way to make each other happy.

Before Reading

Motivating the Reader

Build Background About Cowboys

If possible, display and discuss pictures of cowboys. Invite volunteers to role-play being a cowboy. Ask them questions about how animals like horses and dogs are good company on the lonely trail. Encourage students to think about how dogs can be good friends.

Preview and Predict

Have students scan the cover, text, and illustrations to get an idea of what the book is about. Ask them to read the title and to predict which character is Rusty. Have students use word and picture clues to predict what will happen to Rusty and Old Cowboy. Encourage students to set their own purpose for reading, such as finding out how Rusty's song is important to the story.

Point out selection vocabulary and any unfamiliar words or phrases, such as *it's the singing that counts,* that might be important to understanding the book.

During Reading

Guiding Comprehension

Use the following questions to support students as they read.

- **Pages 2–3** What is Old Cowboy like? (He never talks, but he thinks a lot and enjoys life.)
- **Page 4** What is special about Rusty? (She is a dog that yelps, howls, and whines sad songs better than humans do.)
- **Pages 6–7** What problem do Rusty and Old Cowboy have? (They have no money, so they can't buy any beans.)
- **Page 7** What does the word *triggered* mean in the sentence? Restate the sentence in your own words. (The word *triggered* means "caused." Possible sentence: The sign caused Old Cowboy to think of an idea.)
- **Page 7** What do you think Old Cowboy's plan is? How do you know? (He will enter Rusty in the contest. He reads the sign and then looks at Rusty. The contest is a singing contest, and Rusty can sing very well.)
- **Page 9** Why does Old Cowboy think "it's the singing that counts"? (He thinks that the best singer should win the contest, even if the singer is a dog.)
- **Page 9** What do you think will happen next? (Possible predictions: Old Cowboy will find the courage to sing. Old Cowboy won't be able to sing.)
- **Page 11** Why does the audience begin to laugh and boo? (They are laughing at and booing Old Cowboy because he isn't able to sing.)
- **Page 15** How does Rusty win the contest? (Her song is so sad and beautiful that the judge changes the rules to allow dogs in the contest.)

Ongoing Assessment

Reading Strategies

If... a student has difficulty with such figurative expressions as *drifted to you like a cloud*,	**Then...** help him or her use self-sticking notes to rewrite the phrases in words he or she understands.
If... a student reads the judge's dialogue with expression,	**Then...** praise him or her for bringing a character's words to life.
If... a student has difficulty following the sequence of events,	**Then...** use **Model Your Thinking** below.

Model Your Thinking

Comprehension Skill: Sequence

Sequence is the order things happen. As I read, I look for clue words such as *first*, *next*, and *then* to figure out the order of events. For example, on pages 6 and 7, I read about the events that lead up to Old Cowboy entering the contest. The words *first day*, and *day after that* tell me that Old Cowboy and Rusty go hungry for two days. On the third day, Old Cowboy sees the sign. He studies the sign, looks at Rusty, and comes up with the plan to enter Rusty in the contest. Following this sequence of events helps me understand why Old Cowboy needs money and how he comes up with a plan to get it. As I keep reading, I continue to look to see what happens next.

After Reading

Revisiting the Text

Comprehension List the book's title and write a beginning event *(Old Cowboy and Rusty look at scenery)* in the Beginning box of the Plot/Story Sequence organizer on page 137. Have students reread the book and complete the organizer by listing the most important events in the beginning, middle, and end of the story. Then have students meet in small groups and use their organizers to discuss their favorite parts of the story.

122A The Visitor from Space

by Susan McCloskey
Leveled Reader 122A
Genre: Science Fiction
Level: Easy

Summary

Carrie is trying to contact her dad, who is looking for life on the distant planet Artemis. One night, a spaceship lands near Carrie's house, and a man leaves behind a box. The next day, Carrie finds a dog—a present from her dad. She learns that the dog was probably brought to Artemis by ancient Egyptian space travelers.

Leveled Reader Practice

After students have read *The Visitor from Space*, use Leveled Reader practice page 156 to assess their understanding of the Leveled Reader and the target comprehension skill. Additional after reading activities are provided on page 15.

At a Glance

Links to the Student Edition

Comprehension Skill: Character

Selection Vocabulary: *anticipation, darted, retraced, withdrew*

Program Theme: Myself and Others
Unit Theme: Relating to Others

A search for life on other planets leads to a surprise visitor and an unusual pet.

Before Reading

Motivating the Reader

Build Background About Space Travel

Draw a spaceship on the chalkboard and ask students to discuss space travel, both real and imaginary. Have pairs of students role-play a discussion between an astronaut on a faraway planet and a scientist on Earth or between two space explorers discovering a new planet. As students prepare to read the book, ask them to think about what astronauts might find on distant planets.

Preview and Predict

Read aloud the title and ask students to look at the illustrations. Tell students that this book is science fiction. Discuss the characteristics of science fiction. Have students use word and picture clues, as well as what they know about science fiction, to predict what will happen in the book and who the visitor from space might be.

Point out selection vocabulary and any unfamiliar words, such as *theory, evidence,* and *structures,* that might be important to understanding the book. You may also wish to list and discuss space-related terms, such as *planet, solar system, spaceship,* and *galaxy.*

During Reading

Guiding Comprehension

Use the following questions to support students as they read.

- **Page 2** What is Artemis? (a planet)
- **Page 4** What does Carrie's dad hope to find? (He wants to find life on the planet Artemis.)
- **Page 5** How do you think Carrie feels? What words and picture clues tell you this? (She is nervous and excited. Story clues include: "jerked awake"; "heart pounded in anticipation"; "darted to the window." In the picture Carrie looks as if she has woken suddenly.)
- **Page 5** What does the word *darted* mean in the sentence? How does the word help you know how Carrie might be feeling? (The word *darted* means "rushed or moved quickly." It helps show that Carrie is curious and excited.)
- **Page 9** How does the animal feel? How do you know? (It's afraid. *Frightened* is a clue, and it moves away from Carrie.)
- **Page 10** Look at the picture. What is a food dispenser? (It is a machine that gives you food when you push its buttons.)
- **Page 11** What does Carrie think the dog looks like? (a dog from ancient Egypt)
- **Page 13** Read what Carrie thinks. What do you think is going on? (Answers will vary, but students should recognize that Carrie's dad had something to do with the sudden appearance of the dog.)
- **Page 14** Carrie's dad says, "You're quite a detective." What does this tell you about Carrie? (She is smart.)
- **Page 16** What did Carrie's father find on Artemis? Is it an important discovery? (He found some dogs that are like those that were in ancient Egypt. The dogs help prove that ancient Egyptians traveled to outer space.)

Ongoing Assessment

Reading Strategies

If... a student has difficulty understanding the significance of finding the dogs,	**Then...** have the student reread pages 3–4. Ask whether the dogs are good evidence.
If... a student has difficulty with some space-related terms and other scientific vocabulary,	**Then...** help the student use self-sticking notes to label or draw illustrations that show what the words mean.
If... a student has difficulty drawing conclusions about characters,	**Then...** use **Model Your Thinking** below.

Model Your Thinking

Comprehension Skill: Character

Characters are the people or animals in a story. Sometimes an author tells me what a character is like. Other times I can figure this out by looking at what the character does, says, or thinks. I can also look at how other characters act toward the character and what they say about him or her. For example, on page 13 of this book, Carrie is talking to her dad on the phone. By her words, I can tell that she is a caring person who is worried about her dad. When her dad tells Carrie, "You're quite the detective" and he tells her an important secret, I can tell he thinks Carrie is smart and a person he can trust.

After Reading

Revisiting the Text

Comprehension Use Web 2 on page 133. Have students reread the book and make a word web listing what Carrie is like and how they know. Then have students imagine they are Carrie. Have them write a diary entry that tells about important events in the story and how Carrie feels about them.

122B

Chiapas

by Chris Angelilli
Leveled Reader 122B
Genre: Realistic Story
Level: Easy/Average

Summary

Carlos is visiting Chiapas, Mexico, with his uncles Gabino and Ino. He thinks he will not like seeing old buildings, but finds himself fascinated by Mayan and Spanish history. He likes scary stories, so his uncles take him to a scary place: the underground tomb of Pacal, a Mayan king.

Leveled Reader Practice

After students have read *Chiapas,* use Leveled Reader practice page 157 to assess their understanding of the Leveled Reader and the target comprehension skill. Additional after reading activities are provided on page 17.

At a Glance

Links to the Student Edition

Comprehension Skill: Character

Selection Vocabulary: *cemetery, scent, alternating, faith*

Program Theme: Myself and Others
Unit Theme: Relating to Others

Learning about how others once lived can help us better understand ourselves. Carlos's uncle teaches him that the past can be as exciting (and scary) as modern-day entertainment.

Before Reading

Motivating the Reader

Build Background About Mexico

Display a map of Mexico and help volunteers identify the Chiapas region near the southeastern border by Guatemala. Encourage any students who have been to Mexico to share their experiences. The ruins described in the book are real. If possible, show students photographs of Mayan ruins so they can get a sense of the enormous size of some of these ancient cities and structures.

Preview and Predict

Have students scan the cover, text, and illustrations to get an idea of what the book is about. Explain that the book is realistic fiction, which means that the characters and events are similar to those in real life. Ask students to use story clues to predict what the main character does and what Chiapas is like.

Point out selection vocabulary. Model how to use the pronunciation guides to pronounce Spanish words such as *Chiapas* (page 3) and *San Cristóbal* (page 5). You may also wish to point out architectural terms, such as *mansions, pyramid, temples, palace,* and *tomb.*

During Reading

Guiding Comprehension

Use the following questions to support students as they read.

- **Pages 2–3** **What does Carlos think he will like and dislike about his vacation?** (He wants to meet his Uncle Gabino, but he misses his home and friends. He thinks Chiapas will just have old buildings and no video game arcades, movie theaters, or comic books.)
- **Page 4** **Look at Gabino's words and actions. What is this character like?** (He is friendly and is pleased to see his brother and nephew. He is a bit daring, since he likes to drive fast.)
- **Page 5** **What does "Have a little faith in your brother" mean?** (It means that Gabino wants Ino to trust that he will be a safe driver.)
- **Pages 6–7** **How are Carlos's feelings about his trip changing?** (He is beginning to enjoy the trip. He thinks San Cristóbal is beautiful. He enjoys eating the tamales.)
- **Page 7** Point to *scent.* **When you come across a word like this, how can you figure out how to say it?** (Answers will vary. Encourage students to use other words they know, such as *scene* and *bent,* to help them figure out how to pronounce the word.)
- **Pages 8–9** **What can you tell about Carlos from these pages?** (He likes scary things, such as scary books and cemeteries.)
- **Page 13** **Why are Carlos's feelings alternating between fear and excitement?** (He is excited to be in an ancient, underground cemetery, but it is a little scary too.)
- **Page 15** **What lesson does Carlos learn?** (He learns that he was wrong to think the trip would be boring. He had a great time. He discovered that looking at old buildings could be exciting.)

Ongoing Assessment

Reading Strategies

If... a student says the Spanish words correctly,	**Then...** praise the student for correctly using the pronunciation guides.
If... a student has difficulty drawing conclusions about characters,	**Then...** use **Model Your Thinking** below.

Model Your Thinking

Comprehension Skill: Character

Characters are the people or animals in a story. This book tells about a main character, Carlos, who goes on a vacation in Chiapas, Mexico. To understand the book better, it is important to know what Carlos is like and how his feelings change from the beginning of the book to the end. I can look for clues in what Carlos says, thinks, and does. For example, on page 3, Carlos thinks Chiapas won't be much fun. However, on page 10, Carlos says, "Wow! Are those pyramids?" These words and the exclamation point show Carlos is now excited about visiting the ancient buildings. I can also look for clues based on what his uncles say to him. On page 11 of this book, Gabino asks Carlos if he is ready to see Pacal's tomb. From this clue, I can guess that Gabino thinks Carlos is a curious person who is looking forward to exploring the tomb.

After Reading

Revisiting the Text

Comprehension Have pairs reread the book and use Web 1 on page 132 to record details about Carlos. Then have pairs pretend they are Carlos and a friend from home. Encourage them to use their word webs to help them role-play a conversation about Carlos's vacation.

123A

Lilah's Gift

by Lynn Cullen
Leveled Reader 123A
Genre: Realistic Story
Level: Easy

Summary

Lilah is sad because she must give away Lolly, her smart dachshund pup. One day she sees how a hearing-ear dog alerts a hearing-impaired woman that her child is hurt. Lilah knows that Lolly would make a great hearing-ear dog and decides to give Lolly to a special trainer.

Leveled Reader Practice

After students have read *Lilah's Gift*, use Leveled Reader practice page 158 to assess their understanding of the Leveled Reader and the target comprehension skill. Additional after reading activities are provided on page 19.

At a Glance

Links to the Student Edition

Comprehension Skill: Generalizing

Selection Vocabulary: *awe, horrified, panicked, select*

Program Theme: Myself and Others
Unit Theme: Relating to Others

By donating a beloved pup to help the hearing impaired, Lilah finds a way to lessen her own hurt and help others.

Before Reading

Motivating the Reader

Build Background About Dogs

Write the word *dogs* on the chalkboard and invite volunteers to list the qualities that make a dog a good pet. Then ask students to share what they know about working dogs. As needed, prompt students by asking how dogs help ranchers, police officers, and people with physical disabilities. Encourage students to think about the different roles dogs have in our lives as they read the book.

Preview and Predict

Have students scan the cover, text, and illustrations to get an idea of what the book is about. Have a volunteer read page 2 aloud. Then ask students to describe Lilah's problem and make predictions about how she will solve it. Encourage students to set their own purpose for reading, such as reading to find out what Lilah's gift is.

Point out selection vocabulary and any unfamiliar words and phrases, such as *lollipop, shelter,* and *hearing-ear dog,* that might be important to understanding the book.

During Reading

Guiding Comprehension

Use the following questions to support students as they read.

- **Page 2** **What problem does Lilah have?** (She can't keep her puppy.)
- **Page 3** **What does the sentence "The puppy thought the world was his lollipop" mean?** (The puppy likes to lick.)
- **Page 5** **What does the word *convinced* mean in the sentence?** (It means "knew for sure.")
- **Page 6** **Look at the sentence "Lolly might look like that someday." Who is thinking that? Why?** (Lilah is thinking about what Lolly might be like when he grows up.) Ask similar questions as students read to help them focus on Lilah's thoughts.
- **Page 9** **Look at the word *panicked*. What clue words in nearby sentences can help you figure out its meaning?** (The words and phrases "horrified," "girl fell," "yelled," and "popping out of the chair" are clues that *panicked* means "felt a sudden fright.")
- **Page 9** **What does the dog do when the girl falls?** (He barks at the mother and then runs to the girl.) **Why do you think the dog acts like this?** (He barks to get the mother's attention and then runs to the girl to show the mother what the problem is.)
- **Pages 10–11** **Why do you think Mrs. Goodman has a look of awe on her face?** (She must think it is wonderful that the dog alerted the hearing-impaired woman about her fallen child.)
- **Pages 14–15** **What kinds of dogs do you think make the best hearing-ear dogs, based on what you have learned?** (The best hearing-ear dogs are small to mid-sized dogs that can jump and like to lick.)
- **Page 16** **What is Lilah's gift?** (Her gift is to give Lolly to a special program to be trained as a hearing-ear dog.)

Ongoing Assessment

Reading Strategies

If... a student has difficulty identifying Lilah's thoughts,	**Then...** have the student ask himself or herself "Is this someone's thoughts? If so, who is thinking this?"
If... a student cannot identify generalizations or make generalizations,	**Then...** use **Model Your Thinking** below.

Model Your Thinking

Comprehension Skill: Generalizing

Authors often make generalizations, which are statements that tell what several things or people have in common. A valid generalization is supported by facts and logic. A faulty generalization is not. On page 14, Lilah's mother says, "The trainers only select the smartest pups." This statement tells me about the kinds of pups that become hearing-ear dogs. It seems to be a valid statement, since the author supports it by giving facts about the important tasks these dogs must do. Good readers can also make their own generalizations that tell about the facts, ideas, or characters in a book. After reading pages 14 and 15, I can make the generalization that some puppies can be trained as hearing-ear dogs. Note that I said *some puppies*. It would be a faulty generalization to say *all puppies*, since I read that only the smartest puppies are chosen.

After Reading

Revisiting the Text

Comprehension Write a valid generalization that is based on the book in the center of Web 1 on page 132, such as *Hearing-ear dogs are smart.* Work with students to find examples from the book or from their own experiences that support the generalization.

123B

The Lion and the Ant

retold by Jan M. Mike
Leveled Reader 123B
Genre: Folk Tale
Level: Easy/Average

Summary

In this folk tale, jungle animals line up to honor Lion, the king of the beasts. Ant and Worm are told they are too small and unimportant to bow to Lion. The next day, Lion is in a lot of pain. Ant solves the problem when she finds Worm sleeping in Lion's ear. Lion rewards Ant by saying ants may live wherever they choose.

Leveled Reader Practice

After students have read *The Lion and the Ant,* use Leveled Reader practice page 159 to assess their understanding of the Leveled Reader and the target comprehension skill. Additional after reading activities are provided on page 21.

At a Glance

Links to the Student Edition

Comprehension Skill: Generalizing

Selection Vocabulary: *bitter, determined, suspicious*

Program Theme: Myself and Others
Unit Theme: Relating to Others

The lesson of this folk tale is that no one is ever too small to be important, not even ants and worms.

Before Reading

Motivating the Reader

Build Background About Jungle Animals

If possible, display pictures of the jungle animals mentioned or illustrated in the book, such as a lion, a macaw, an elephant, a leopard, a cobra, an ant, and a worm. Invite volunteers to tell what they know about each animal, such as what it looks like, what sounds it makes, and how it acts. Encourage students to point to similarities and differences among the animals. You may wish to share some basic facts about these animals. As students prepare to read, encourage them to compare the characteristics of the fictional animals with the behaviors of real-life animals.

Preview and Predict

Have students scan the cover, text, and illustrations to get an idea of what the book is about. Encourage students to use what they know about folk tales to make predictions about what will happen in the book and what the animal characters are like. For example, they might predict that Ant will help Lion in some way. Suggest students read to find out what happens when Lion and Ant meet.

Point out selection vocabulary and any unfamiliar words, such as *patient, respectful,* and *celebration,* that might be important to understanding the book.

During Reading

Guiding Comprehension

Use the following questions to support students as they read.

- **Pages 2–3** *Why do you think Queen Ant thinks that Lion might ignore her daughter?* (Ants are small, and lions are large and powerful.)
- **Page 5** *What causes Ant to fly into the air?* (Leopard swishes his tail in front of her.)
- **Page 6** *How do the other animals treat Ant?* (Macaw laughs when Ant lands in a puddle, and Cobra tells her she is unimportant.)
- **Pages 8–10** *Why do you think Ant and Worm feel bitter?* (Both were sent by their parents to greet Lion, yet they are told they are too unimportant to meet him.) *Would you feel the same way?* (Answers will vary.)
- **Page 11** *What problem does Lion have?* (He has a terrible pain in his ear that no one can fix.) *What do you think will happen next?* (Predictions may vary, but students should recognize that Ant will find a way to help Lion.)
- **Page 12** *Why does Lion hold out his paw?* (so Ant can use it to crawl up to his ear)
- **Page 12** *What is another word for spied that makes sense in this sentence?* (saw)
- **Page 14** *Why does Lion's pain go away?* (Worm was causing the pain. Once he left, the pain stopped.) *Why couldn't the other animals make the pain go away?* (None of them were small enough to get inside Lion's ear.)
- **Pages 14–15** *How does Ant prove that ants can be powerful friends?* (Ant wakes up Worm, who is sleeping in Lion's ear, so Lion's pain disappears. Only Ant is able to make the pain go away.)
- **Pages 15–16** *What lesson do Lion and the other animals learn?* (No one is ever too small to be important.)

Ongoing Assessment

Reading Strategies

If... a student has trouble explaining why the other animals can't help Lion,	**Then...** have him or her imagine Cobra or one of the other animals trying to get inside Lion's ear.
If... a student has difficulty following the sequence of events,	**Then...** have him or her complete the Story Sequence organizer on page 139 and use it to retell the story.
If... a student cannot identify generalizations or make generalizations,	**Then...** use **Model Your Thinking** below.

Model Your Thinking

Comprehension Skill: Generalizing

Authors often make generalizations that tell what several people or things have in common. Good readers look for such clue words as many, some, never, none, and all to help them recognize generalizations. For example, on page 5, I read "None of the others would even look at her." This statement tells me how the other animals treated Ant. I can also make my own generalizations. For instance, a valid, or accurate, generalization would be: Most of the animals were very rude to Ant. Notice that I use most instead of all. Since Worm was not rude to Ant, it would be a faulty, or inaccurate, generalization to say all of them treated her rudely. Valid generalizations are supported by facts and logic. Faulty generalizations are not.

After Reading

Revisiting the Text

Comprehension Write several generalizations based on the book (both valid and faulty) on the chalkboard, such as *No one is ever too small to be important.* Have students use details from the book and their own experiences to decide whether each generalization is valid.

124A Great Talents

The Story of Negro League Baseball

by Mark Spann
Leveled Reader 124A
Genre: Photo Essay
Level: Easy

Summary

From the late 1800s until 1947, African Americans could not join major league baseball. In this photo essay, readers learn about some of the heroes of the Negro Leagues, such as home run king Josh Gibson, pitcher Satchel Paige, and baseball legend, Jackie Robinson.

Leveled Reader Practice

After students have read *Great Talents: The Story of Negro League Baseball*, use Leveled Reader practice page 160 to assess their understanding of the Leveled Reader and the target comprehension skill. Additional after reading activities are provided on page 23.

At a Glance

Links to the Student Edition

Comprehension Skill: Cause and Effect

Selection Vocabulary: *cut, valuable*

Program Theme: Myself and Others
Unit Theme: Relating to Others

Despite prejudice that barred them from major league teams, African American baseball players found success in the Negro Leagues.

Before Reading

Motivating the Reader

Build Background About Prejudice

Invite volunteers to role-play a situation where talented athletes are trying out for a sports team but the coach (played by you) keeps rejecting the players for reasons other than how well they play, such as wearing the wrong color shirt, having hair that is too short or too long, and so on. Then discuss how the athletes feel and whether the coach's decisions were fair. Encourage students to think about how an African American athlete would feel if he or she were not allowed to be on a team because of race. Discuss situations or experiences where someone was treated unfairly because of someone else's prejudices.

Preview and Predict

Have students scan the cover, text, and photographs and make predictions about what kinds of information will be in the book. Then have them fill in the first two columns of the K-W-L Chart on page 135 with what they know about the Negro Leagues and what they want to find out. After they read, they can fill in the third column with what they have learned.

Point out selection vocabulary and any unfamiliar words, such as *major leagues, talented,* and *all-star,* that might be important to understanding the book. You may also wish to explain the historical use of *negro* and *colored.*

During Reading

Guiding Comprehension

Use the following questions to support students as they read.

- **Page 3** Who is the greatest home run hitter? (Josh Gibson) Why don't most people today know about Josh Gibson? (Even though he hit 962 home runs, he never played for the major leagues.)
- **Pages 4–8** This photo essay is not told in time order. What clues help you follow the sequence of events? (dates such as "1947" and "1885" and phrases such as "150 years ago")
- **Page 5** What does *cut* mean in this sentence? What other word or phrase would make sense in this sentence? (asked to leave, kicked out, let go)
- **Page 5** Why were African Americans cut from regular teams? (Some people felt that players with different skin colors should not play on the same teams.)
- **Page 8** Who were the Cuban Giants? (They were the first baseball team made up of African American players.)
- **Page 13** Why was Satchel Paige a valuable player? (He was a pitcher who could throw the ball harder and faster than anyone else.)
- **Pages 14–15** How did Satchel Paige's team cause baseball to change? (People saw how good the players were, and eventually the major leagues invited African American players to join.)
- **Page 16** What happened to the Negro Leagues once African Americans began playing in the major leagues? (They became less popular. They stopped playing.)

Ongoing Assessment

Reading Strategies

If... a student has difficulty understanding and recalling information,	**Then...** encourage the student to pause while reading to restate the information in his or her own words.
If... a student cannot recognize cause-and-effect relationships,	**Then...** use **Model Your Thinking** below.

Model Your Thinking

Comprehension Skill: Cause and Effect

As they read, good readers think about how events in a story are connected. An effect is what happens. A cause is why it happens. Clue words such as *because*, *therefore*, and *since* can help readers figure out causes and effects. For example, the word *therefore* on page 5 signals a cause-effect relationship. I ask myself, "Why were African Americans cut from regular teams?" I reread the paragraph and I see that one cause is that some people felt players with different skin colors should not do things together, such as play baseball. Sometimes an effect will have more than one cause or a cause will have more than one effect. Two effects of African Americans being cut from the major leagues were that the major leagues lost valuable players and African Americans could no longer play big-league baseball.

After Reading

Revisiting the Text

Comprehension Use the Cause and Effect organizer on page 145. Depending on students' abilities, have them identify cause-and-effect relationships from the book on their own, or provide students with a partially completed organizer with some causes and/or effects given. Students can fill in the missing information.

124B

What Are Friends For?

by Catherine Murphy
Leveled Reader 124B
Genre: Realistic Story
Level: Easy/Average

Summary

Carol is training for a race with her best friend, Yumiko, but she then begins training alone when she finds out Yumiko has been running extra laps without her. Before the race, Yumiko helps Carol by pointing out her untied laces. During the race, Carol helps Yumiko when she trips. Yumiko tells Carol to win the race for both of them, and Carol does.

Leveled Reader Practice

After students have read *What Are Friends For?*, use Leveled Reader practice page 161 to assess their understanding of the Leveled Reader and the target comprehension skill. Additional after reading activities are provided on page 25.

At a Glance

Links to the Student Edition

Comprehension Skill: Cause and Effect

Selection Vocabulary: *corridors, custodian, challenging*

Program Theme: Myself and Others
Unit Theme: Relating to Others

Two girls learn the importance of friendship when they compete against each other in a race.

Before Reading

Motivating the Reader

Build Background About Competition

Write the word *competition* on the chalkboard. Discuss with students the good and bad things that can come from competeting against someone. Use a T-Chart to list students' ideas. Invite students to describe or act out any problems they've had when they competed against a friend. Have other students suggest ways these problems can be avoided or resolved.

Preview and Predict

Have students scan the cover, title, and illustrations to get an idea of what the book is about. Read aloud page 2, and ask students to make predictions about what the Dover Dash is, who the narrator is, and what problem the narrator has. As they read, encourage students to think about how characters other than Carol might be feeling.

Point out selection vocabulary and any figurative phrases, such as *wings on my feet,* that might be important to understanding the book.

During Reading

Guiding Comprehension

Use the following questions to support students as they read.

- **Page 3** What problem does Carol have? (Her best friend, Yumiko, has been practicing running without Carol.)
- **Pages 3–4** How does Carol feel? What clues help you figure this out? (She is upset. She speaks grumpily and snarls. She looks angry in the pictures.) Do you think Carol is right to feel the way she does? Why or why not? (Encourage well-supported answers.)
- **Page 5** What happens to the person who wins the Dover Dash? (The winner gets a trophy and a ride on a float in the Fourth of July parade.)
- **Page 7** What happens when Carol finds out Yumiko was running extra laps? (Carol quits practicing with her and stops being her friend.)
- **Page 8** Why do you think Yumiko warns Carol about her untied shoe? (Yumiko still wants to be Carol's friend.)
- **Page 9** What do you think "Take your marks" means? (It means "get ready at the starting line.")
- **Page 10** Why does Yumiko fall? (She trips on a stick.)
- **Page 11** Why do you think Carol turns around? (She decides helping a friend is more important than winning.)
- **Page 15** What does the expression "wings on my feet" mean? How is Carol feeling? (It means Carol feels she could fly. She feels great when she sees her friends cheering for her. It helps her run faster.)
- **Page 16** Why do you think the author keeps repeating the phrase "What are friends for?" When is this phrase used? (She is showing what it means to be a good friend. The phrase is used each time one friend helps the other friend.)

Ongoing Assessment

Reading Strategies

If... a student has difficulty with the figurative expression "wings on my feet" on page 15,	**Then...** ask the student to imagine its literal meaning and tell whether having wings would make a person go faster or slower.
If... a student cannot recognize cause-and-effect relationships,	**Then...** use **Model Your Thinking** below.

Model Your Thinking

Comprehension Skill: Cause and Effect

A cause is why something happens and an effect is what happens. Sometimes a cause has more than one effect. Sometimes an effect has more than one cause. Clue words such as *therefore, as a result,* and *since* can help me figure out a cause-and-effect relationship between events. If there are no clue words, I have to figure it out myself. For example, on page 16, I find out that Carol wants to share the trophy with Yumiko. I ask myself, "Why does she want to do this?" I recall that Yumiko pointed out Carol's untied shoe and that she told Carol to keep running to win the race for both of them. These are two reasons why Carol wants to share the trophy.

After Reading

Revisiting the Text

Comprehension Use the Cause and Effect organizer on page 145. Have pairs work together to identify cause-and-effect relationships in the story. If students have difficulty getting started, point out an effect and ask students to find out why this effect happens. Have students use the organizers to act out their favorite part of the story.

125A

Aisha's New Look

by Catherine Murphy
Leveled Reader 125A
Genre: Realistic Story
Level: Easy

Summary

Aisha doesn't like how she looks with eyeglasses, though she loves seeing things at a distance clearly. At her cousin Danay's house, her glasses help Aisha notice a small child walking into the street and Aisha rescues her. Danay is impressed by Aisha's improved eyesight. When Danay shows Aisha her new braces, both girls realize they look just fine.

Leveled Reader Practice

After students have read *Aisha's New Look,* use Leveled Reader practice page 162 to assess their understanding of the Leveled Reader and the target comprehension skill. Additional after reading activities are provided on page 27.

At a Glance

Links to the Student Edition

Comprehension Skill: Author's Purpose

Selection Vocabulary: *community, resident, in-between*

Program Theme: Myself and Others
Unit Theme: Relating to Others

Aisha and her cousin Danay help each other overcome their worries about how they look.

Before Reading

Motivating the Reader

Build Background About Self-Image

Have students draw a self-portrait. Under the portrait have them list five words that tell who they are. Invite volunteers to show their drawings and read their descriptive words. Discuss the kinds of words people used. Ask whether they were words that described physical appearance, skills and abilities, hobbies, personality traits, and so on. Talk about how often people worry about how they look.

Preview and Predict

Have students scan the cover, text, and illustrations to get an idea of what the book is about. Ask students to predict what Aisha's new look might be and how she might feel about this new look. Encourage students to check their predictions as they read, revising them as needed.

Point out selection vocabulary and any unfamiliar words, such as *reflected* and *adjust,* that might be important to understanding the book.

During Reading

Guiding Comprehension

Use the following questions to support students as they read.

- **Page 2** **Who is the "I" telling the story?** (Aisha) **What problem does Aisha have?** (She just got new eyeglasses, and she thinks they make her look funny.)
- **Page 3** **Why doesn't Aisha want to visit Danay?** (She doesn't want Danay to see her with her new eyeglasses.)
- **Pages 4–5** **Why does Aisha say there are parts of her community she hasn't seen?** (Things such as leaves or birds looked blurry before she got glasses. She sees things around her much more clearly with her glasses.)
- **Page 7** **How do you think Danay will react when she sees Aisha's glasses?** (If she is a good friend, then she probably won't say anything mean to make Aisha feel bad. She might be surprised if she didn't know Aisha was getting glasses.)
- **Page 9** **What do you think is wrong with Danay?** (Predictions will vary.)
- **Pages 10–13** **How do Aisha's glasses help her save a child?** (She is able to see a little girl walk into the street and rescue her in time.)
- **Page 12** **Look at the words *yelled, dashed,* and *pounded.* How do these words help you picture what is happening?** (They are action words, so they help me picture what Aisha is doing.)
- **Pages 14–16** **What is the overall feeling or mood at the end of the book? Why?** (It is a happy feeling because Aisha saved the little girl, Aisha now likes her eyeglasses, and Danay is no longer embarrassed about her new braces.)
- **Page 16** **Why do you think the author wrote this book?** (to share a message about not worrying so much about how we look; to entertain readers with a good story)

Ongoing Assessment

Reading Strategies

If... a student has difficulty understanding the change in feelings for the two girls,	**Then...** have the student compare the illustrations on pages 8 and 15.
If... a student has difficulty explaining why the author may have written the book,	**Then...** use **Model Your Thinking** below.

Model Your Thinking

Comprehension Skill: Author's Purpose

Authors often have more than one purpose, or reason, for writing. As I read, I think about whether the author might be writing to persuade, to inform, to entertain, or to express. As I read the book, I ask myself, "Why do I think the author wrote the book? Why do I think that way?" I think one reason is to share an important lesson about not worrying so much about how we look. I also think the author wrote this book to entertain. I thought Aisha was a very interesting character, and, as I read, I was eager to find out what would happen to her. Good readers know they can adjust their reading rate once they have figured out an author's purpose. Since this book is entertaining I read it faster than if it were full of facts.

After Reading

Revisiting the Text

Comprehension Have students use Web 1 on page 132. Have them write the author's purpose or purposes in the center and list supporting reasons around the outside of the circle. Have students use the webs to help them role-play being the author of the book. Students should explain to readers why he or she wrote the book.

125B

The Fifth Act Players

by Susan Blackaby
Leveled Reader 125B
Genre: Realistic Story
Level: Easy/Average

Summary

Some fifth graders start a drama club called the Fifth Act Players. At first the group makes up a silly play, but then the students write a play based on their experiences. They perform the play to help raise funds for a Sidewalk Sweep at a housing project.

Leveled Reader Practice

After students have read *The Fifth Act Players,* use Leveled Reader practice page 163 to assess their understanding of the Leveled Reader and the target comprehension skill. Additional after reading activities are provided on page 29.

At a Glance

Links to the Student Edition

Comprehension Skill: Author's Purpose

Selection Vocabulary: *applied, council, project*

Program Theme: Myself and Others
Unit Theme: Relating to Others

Some fifth graders learn the importance of sharing their talents to help their community.

Before Reading

Motivating the Reader

Build Background About Theater

Invite students to share any experiences they have had of putting on a play or watching one. Have students brainstorm ideas of things associated with putting on a theatrical play. Work together to create a list of what the class would have to do to put on a play.

Preview and Predict

Have students scan the cover, text, and photographs to get an idea of what the book is about. You may wish to point out that even though the book is illustrated with photographs, it is a realistic story—not nonfiction. Have students use word and picture clues to make predictions about who the Fifth Act Players are and what they will do. Encourage students to read to find out if their predictions are correct, revising them if necessary.

Point out selection vocabulary and any unfamiliar words, such as *volunteered, housing project, graffiti,* and *fundraiser,* that might be important to understanding the book. You may also wish to preview some of the slang or ideomatic expressions in the dialogue, such as: *Do you read me, man?* or *break a leg.*

During Reading

Guiding Comprehension

Use the following questions to support students as they read.

- **Page 2** Who are the Fifth Act Players? (They are a drama club made up of fifth graders from King School.)
- **Page 2** What is the difference between the words *elected* and *volunteered*? (*Elected* means someone is voted to a position, and *volunteered* means someone says he or she will do the job.)
- **Page 5** What are Kenny, Jojo, and Liza doing? (They are pretending to put on a play.)
- **Page 5** What does the slang word *yo* mean? (*Yo* means "hey.") Why do you think the author uses slang in the students' dialogue? (She wants the characters to seem like real students.)
- **Page 9** What is a Sidewalk Sweep? (It is a city clean-up plan to paint over graffiti at a housing project.)
- **Pages 9–10** What is Dolly's proposal? (to have the Players put on their play to raise funds for a Sidewalk Sweep)
- **Page 10** How does Kenny feel about putting on a play? How do you know? (He is excited about the idea. He says, "This is great!" He slaps hands with Dolly and Liza. The exclamation mark shows he feels strongly about it.)
- **Pages 12–14** How do the students get ready for the play? (They help with publicity, make the scenery, get the props ready, go over their lines, and review a checklist.)
- **Page 15** What is the students' play about? (It is about some students who are sad that their teacher is leaving.)
- **Page 16** Why do you think the author wrote this book? (to entertain readers with an interesting story; to tell about what it takes to put on a play)

Ongoing Assessment

Reading Strategies

If... a student doesn't understand some of the slang words or words based on Shakespearean English,	**Then...** help him or her rephrase the words into more standard English.
If... a student has difficulty explaining why the author may have written the book,	**Then...** use **Model Your Thinking** below.

Model Your Thinking

Comprehension Skill: Author's Purpose

An author's purpose is the reason or reasons an author writes something. As I read, I think about whether the author might be writing to persuade, to inform, to entertain, or to express. I ask myself, "Why did the author write the book? Why do I think that way?" I think the author wrote this book to entertain readers, since it is about students who do and say interesting things, just like students in real life. I also learned a lot about what it takes to put on a play, so perhaps the author is also writing to inform readers about drama clubs and plays. I can adjust my reading rate once I have figured out an author's purpose. For instance, if I'm reading a funny story, I might read more quickly than if I'm reading an encyclopedia article.

After Reading

Revisiting the Text

Comprehension Use the Four-Column Chart on page 152, and write these heads across the top of the chart: *to inform, to persuade, to entertain, to express.* Work together to decide which purpose or purposes suit this book. Have students fill in the book title in the appropriate column(s). Then have students fill in the other columns with examples of a type of writing or specific titles. Have students include reasons to support their examples.

126A

Turtles of the Sea

by Diane Hoyt-Goldsmith
Leveled Reader 126A
Genre: Informational Article
Level: Easy

Summary

This nonfiction book provides interesting facts about what sea turtles look like, how they survive in the water, what they eat, and how they reproduce. Detailed photographs give readers a close-up view of these amazing sea creatures.

Leveled Reader Practice

After students have read *Turtles of the Sea,* use Leveled Reader practice page 164 to assess their understanding of the Leveled Reader and the target comprehension skill. Additional after reading activities are provided on page 31.

At a Glance

Links to the Student Edition

Comprehension Skill: Steps in a Process

Selection Vocabulary: *communicate, cooperate*

Program Theme: The World Around Us
Unit Theme: My World and Yours

By learning more about creatures such as the sea turtle, we can help figure out ways to protect them.

Before Reading

Motivating the Reader

Build Background About Sea Turtles

Show students pictures of different kinds of turtles, including sea turtles. Draw a word web on the chalkboard and write *Turtles* in the center. Have students use the pictures and what they already know to list details about turtles in the outer circles. Have students draw a picture of a turtle and write a caption stating one fact about it. After they've finished reading the book, students can create additional pictures with new facts.

Preview and Predict

Have students scan the cover, text, and photographs. Students can use word and picture clues to predict what the book is about and what kinds of information it will give. Have students write two or three questions of inquiry about sea turtles. Encourage them to look for answers to their questions as they read.

Point out selection vocabulary and any unfamiliar words, such as *abilities* and *destroyed,* that might be important to understanding the book. Draw students' attention to the labels on pages 6 and 7, and remind them to compare the pictures with text nearby.

During Reading

Guiding Comprehension

Use the following questions to support students as they read.

- **Pages 2–3** How do the photographs help you understand the text? (They show what a sea turtle looks like and how it swims with its flippers.)
- **Page 4** What does the author find surprising about sea turtles? (Sea turtles do not need to eat often, and they can stay underwater for a long time.)
- **Page 5** What is an *Archelon?* (It is a large sea turtle that lived long ago, like the dinosaurs.)
- **Pages 6–8** What kind of information is given on these pages? (These pages tell about different kinds of sea turtles.) How do the photographs help you understand this information? (The photographs show each turtle described.)
- **Page 9** State the main idea of this page in your own words. (Turtles may talk to one another by making sounds or by moving.)
- **Page 10** What is unusual about the place where sea turtles choose to hatch their eggs? (They often travel back to the place where they themselves were hatched. They sometimes travel hundreds of miles.)
- **Page 11** What is the first step a female sea turtle will do to build her nest? (She uses her flippers to brush away loose sand and twigs.)
- **Page 13** Why do baby sea turtles "scurry" to the ocean after hatching? (They are in danger of being eaten by birds and other animals.)
- **Page 15** What is one way people have worked together to protect sea turtles? (People in Hawaii put up "Turtle Crossing" signs near places where sea turtles cross the road to lay their eggs.)

Ongoing Assessment

Reading Strategies

If... a student has difficulty differentiating among the five different kinds of sea turtles,	**Then...** suggest the student read the text first and then match it to a labeled photograph.
If... a student has difficulty following steps in a process,	**Then...** use **Model Your Thinking** below.

Model Your Thinking

Comprehension Skill: Steps in a Process

Steps in a process are the order of steps taken to make or do something. Clue words such as *first, then,* and *next* help me figure out the order. If there are no clue words, I picture the steps in my mind to figure out the order. Pictures or diagrams can also help you understand these steps better. For instance, pages 10 through 12 describe how a female sea turtle lays her eggs. Although there are no clue words on page 10, I can use common sense to know that she must first travel to dry land before she can build a nest. The word *first* on page 11 tells me that brushing away loose sand and twigs is the first step in building a nest. The picture helps me understand what the nest looks like after the eggs are hatched.

After Reading

Revisiting the Text

Comprehension Have small groups use the Steps in a Process organizer on page 148 to show the most important steps of laying sea turtle eggs. Have students reread pages 10 through 12. Help them fill in the first step in the first box. (Female turtles often swim to where they were hatched.) Students can renumber a second chart, if needed, depending on how they break down the process.

126B

The Big What-If

by David Neufeld
Leveled Reader 126B
Genre: Realistic Story
Level: Easy/Average

Summary

While beach-combing alone on Brighton Beach, Austin finds a stranded dolphin. It doesn't seem injured, just tired. He talks to the dolphin and tries to keep it moist with sea water. The tide comes in, but not far enough. Eventually his mother and friends find him, and they work with others to dig a channel to the sea. The dolphin swims to safety.

Leveled Reader Practice

After students have read *The Big What-If*, use Leveled Reader practice page 165 to assess their understanding of the Leveled Reader and the target comprehension skill. Additional after reading activities are provided on page 33.

At a Glance

Links to the Student Edition

Comprehension Skill: Steps in a Process

Selection Vocabulary: *doomed, dolphins, hovered, injured, desperate*

Program Theme: The World Around Us
Unit Theme: My World and Yours

A clever boy figures out how to get a stranded dolphin back to its own world—the sea.

Before Reading

Motivating the Reader

Build Background About Problem-Solving

Describe a problem beginning with the words *What if*. . . . For example, ask them what they would do if they found a dolphin stranded on the beach. Have volunteers tell or show what they would do to solve the problem. List the steps described or demonstrated on the chalkboard. Discuss whether these steps make sense, revising steps if suggested by students.

Preview and Predict

Have students scan the cover, text, and illustrations to identify the story problem and to make predictions about how it might be solved. Have students complete the Story Prediction organizer on page 130. Suggest students read to find out if their predictions are correct. They can complete their Story Prediction organizers after they finish reading the book.

Point out selection vocabulary and any unfamiliar words and phrases, such as *tide, living daylights,* and *canal,* that might be important to understanding the book.

During Reading

Guiding Comprehension

Use the following questions to support students as they read.

- **Pages 2–3** **How does Austin's skill at the "what-if" game help him with the dolphin?** (The "what-if" game is a game about solving problems. Austin thinks about how he solves problems in the game, and then thinks about how he can solve the dolphin's problem.)
- **Page 4** **How does Austin get the dolphin's skin wet?** (He pours seven buckets of sea water on the dolphin.)
- **Page 4** **Why is Austin thinking about time?** (He wonders how long the dolphin can survive out of the water. He wonders how long it will be before his mother will begin looking for him.)
- **Pages 6–7** **Is the mood on these pages happy, serious, or funny? How can you tell?** (The mood is serious because Austin is very worried about the dark clouds and the dolphin's safety.)
- **Page 9** **Why do you think Austin starts to ask himself these "what-if" questions?** (He is trying to figure out what his mom might do, since he is late getting home.)
- **Page 12** **What do the boys do first to help the dolphin?** (They begin digging a canal.)
- **Page 12** **Why does Austin's mother talk to the dolphin?** (Austin thinks it will make the dolphin feel less scared.)
- **Page 13** **What does *desperate* mean? What other word or words would make sense in this sentence?** (very worried, anxious)
- **Pages 14–15** **What happens that helps move the dolphin through the canal?** (People help push and lift the dolphin. Austin keeps its head pointed toward the sea. A big wave fills the canal with water, shooting the dolphin forward.)

Ongoing Assessment

Reading Strategies

If... a student has difficulty understanding Austin's different "what-if" scenarios,	**Then...** have him or her work with a partner to answer each "what-if" question.
If... a student has difficulty organizing steps in a process,	**Then...** use **Model Your Thinking** below.

Model Your Thinking

Comprehension Skill: Steps in a Process

Figuring out the steps in a process means telling the order of steps taken to make or do something. Paying attention to these steps helps me understand how things happen and what might happen next. Good readers look for clue words, such as *first, after,* and *then,* to help them figure out the order of the steps. If there aren't any clue words, good readers look at illustrations or try to picture the steps in their minds and then think about what order makes the most sense to them. For example, on page 4, I read the first two sentences and picture Austin running to the sea, filling his bucket, and pouring it on the dolphin. He repeats these steps seven times to get the dolphin's skin wet, and then he rests in the sand.

After Reading

Revisiting the Text

Comprehension Use the Steps in a Process organizer on page 148. Write above the flowchart: *How do Austin and his friends save the dolphin?* Have pairs reread pages 12–15 and complete the flowchart. Depending on how pairs organize the steps, they may need more than one chart. Pairs can then use their flowcharts to role-play an interview about the rescue between Austin and a TV reporter.

127A

Condor Morning

by Kana Riley
Leveled Reader 127A
Genre: Realistic Story
Level: Easy

Summary

Before dawn, Jemma goes with her Aunt Connie to witness the release of some California condors. Jemma thinks her aunt's bird-watching journal is just a boring list of numbers. After she sees a condor take flight and looks at her aunt's recorded data and drawings, she decides that bird-watching is much more than numbers.

Leveled Reader Practice

After students have read *Condor Morning,* use Leveled Reader practice page 166 to assess their understanding of the Leveled Reader and the target comprehension skill. Additional after reading activities are provided on page 35.

At a Glance

Links to the Student Edition

Comprehension Skill: Graphic Sources

Selection Vocabulary: *recovered, identify, ecology, pressure*

Program Theme: The World Around Us
Unit Theme: My World and Yours

Numerical data and observation can help us learn more about endangered animals such as the condor.

Before Reading

Motivating the Reader

Build Background About Endangered Animals

Ask students to think of an animal and to imagine how our world would be different if there were no more animals of that type left on the planet. Use an almanac to share statistics about endangered species with students, such as the fact that there are more than 1,600 endangered species and only about 700 recovery plans. Brainstorm with students things people could do to help endangered species. Encourage students to think about these ideas as they read the book.

Preview and Predict

Have students scan the cover, text, and illustrations to get an idea of what the book is about. Point out that the *I* in the story refers to Jemma, the girl pictured on page 2. Explain that the story is told from Jemma's point of view. Encourage students to make predictions about what the title means and what events will happen in the story. Suggest students read to find out what the title *Condor Morning* means.

Point out selection vocabulary and any unfamiliar words that might be important to understanding the book. If possible, show a photograph of a condor so that students have a sense of its large size. Show photographs of the other birds mentioned in the book as well.

During Reading

Guiding Comprehension

Use the following questions to support students as they read.

- **Pages 2–3** Is Jemma excited about seeing the condors? (No, it is cold and dark outside, and she would rather be asleep.)
- **Page 4** How does Jemma think she and her Aunt Connie are different? (Aunt Connie thinks in numbers. Jemma says she is more of a poet, so she probably thinks in words and images.)
- **Pages 5–7** Why is the number thirty-nine important to Aunt Connie? (When she was twelve, she learned there were only thirty-nine condors left. She then became interested in ecology and later became a scientist.)
- **Page 7** What does *recovered* mean in this sentence? (It means the condor population increased in number.)
- **Pages 8–9** What does the picture show? (a page of Aunt Connie's journal) How does Jemma feel about the journal? (She thinks it is just a boring list of names, dates, and times.)
- **Page 10** Why do you think Jemma is holding her breath? (She is excited to see what the condors might do.)
- **Page 13** How does Jemma feel when Aunt Connie opens her journal? (She can't believe her aunt is thinking about numbers when watching these big birds fly.)
- **Page 14** Why is Jemma surprised by the notebook? (Her aunt drew pictures in it.)
- **Page 15** Why does Aunt Connie think numbers are important? (Scientists keep track of the condors by putting numbers on them.)
- **Page 16** How have Jemma's feelings about numbers changed? How do you know? (She begins to see why they are important. She calls the condor "number twenty-seven.")

Ongoing Assessment

Reading Strategies

If... a student cannot interpret the journal on page 9,	**Then...** have the student read down one column at a time to see how the entries are alike.
If... a student has difficulty interpreting graphic sources,	**Then...** use **Model Your Thinking** below.

Model Your Thinking

Comprehension Skill: Graphic Sources

A graphic source shows information visually, such as pictures, charts, graphs, maps, diagrams, and schedules. Before I read, I look through the book for graphic sources. They are clues to what the story will be about. As I read, I compare the graphic source to the text to see how they are related. For example, I can compare Jemma's description of her aunt's bird journal on page 8 with the illustration of the journal on page 9. Jemma says the journal is *just* a list of names, dates, and times, but I can tell from this list the different birds Aunt Connie has seen and the locations and dates of trips she took. The journal also helps me understand a bit more about what kinds of data bird-watchers may record. Later, I could use the illustration to create my own bird journal.

After Reading

Revisiting the Text

Comprehension Use the Three-Column Chart on page 151. Above the chart, write *The Condor.* In the first row, write the heads: *What It Looks Like, Where It Lives,* and *How It Moves.* Have students reread the book and complete the chart. Then have students use their charts to write a scientific description or a poem about the condor. You may wish to provide students with additional reference material about condors.

127B

Disaster Super Heroes

The Red Cross

by Phoebe Marsh
Leveled Reader 127B
Genre: Informational Article
Level: Easy/Average

Summary

In 1859, a Swiss man named Jean Henri Dunant was horrified by the sight of wounded soldiers in Italy. His organizing efforts led to the formation of the International Red Cross in 1864. Clara Barton founded the American branch in 1881. Today the American Red Cross assists veterans, organizes blood drives, and provides relief services after disasters, such as hurricanes, floods, and earthquakes.

Leveled Reader Practice

After students have read *Disaster Super Heroes: The Red Cross,* use Leveled Reader practice page 167 to assess their understanding of the Leveled Reader and the target comprehension skill. Additional after reading activities are provided on page 37.

At a Glance

Links to the Student Edition

Comprehension Skill: Graphic Sources

Selection Vocabulary: *damage, hurricane, mightiest, predict*

Program Theme: The World Around Us
Unit Theme: My World and Yours

More than a million volunteers show they care about others by donating their time and skills to the American Red Cross.

Before Reading

Motivating the Reader

Build Background About Disaster Relief

Discuss the effects of natural disasters, such as tornadoes, floods, hurricanes, and earthquakes. Explain that volunteer groups such as the Red Cross come to victims' aid. Ask students to describe the kinds of help people might need after surviving a disaster. Answers might include food, shelter, medicine, and clothing. Record their ideas on the chalkboard.

Preview and Predict

Have students scan the cover, section heads, text, and photographs. Encourage them to use picture and word clues to make predictions about what they will learn about the Red Cross. Have students suggest questions of inquiry that they think the book will answer, such as: How did the Red Cross start? Who is Clara Barton? What does the Red Cross do? Suggest students read to find out the answers to their questions.

Point out selection vocabulary and any unfamiliar words, such as *relief* and *humanitarian,* that might be important to understanding the book.

During Reading

Guiding Comprehension

Use the following questions to support students as they read.

- **Pages 2–3** Why do you think the author calls the Red Cross a "lifeline"? (It gives help to people who might otherwise have trouble surviving.)
- **Pages 4–6** How did the Red Cross start? (In 1859, Henri Dunant was shocked by the sight of wounded soldiers. He asked European governments to organize volunteer groups to help wounded and sick soldiers. In 1864, twelve governments started the International Red Cross.) Ask other questions based on the section heads.
- **Page 6** What does this map show? (cities in Switzerland and the borders of nearby countries)
- **Page 6** What does this symbol on the lower right corner of the map represent? How do you know? (It is Switzerland's national flag. The text tells what the flag looks like.)
- **Page 7** How did Clara Barton change the role of the Red Cross in America? (She added disaster relief service.)
- **Page 10** What does the Biomedical Services do? (It helps get blood and organ donations for hospitals to use.) Ask similar questions for the other two divisions.
- **Page 10** How does the photograph help you understand what donating blood is like? (It shows a nurse collecting blood from a woman who is smiling and looks relaxed, which tells me it doesn't hurt when you give blood.) Ask similar questions about other photographs.
- **Page 15** What does *mightiest* mean? What other word makes sense in this sentence? (biggest, greatest)
- **Page 16** How does the author feel about the Red Cross? How do you know? (She is very impressed by the organization. She calls them "super heroes" and says that "people can always depend on the Red Cross.")

Ongoing Assessment

Reading Strategies

If... a student has difficulty telling the main idea of a section,	**Then...** point to the section head and have the student tell how the text relates to this head.
If... a student has difficulty interpreting graphic sources,	**Then...** use **Model Your Thinking** below.

Model Your Thinking

Comprehension Skill: Graphic Sources

Graphic sources, such as pictures, charts, graphs, maps, diagrams, and schedules, show information visually. Before I read, I look through the story or article for graphic sources. I use them to help me predict what the text will be about. As I read, I compare what I've read to the graphic sources. For example, on page 5, I read about the First Treaty of Geneva, and on page 6 I see that Geneva is a city in Switzerland, near France. The map and the flag help me better understand the history of the start of the Red Cross. After I read, I can create my own graphic source to help me organize the information that I've read, such as a time line showing the history of the Red Cross or a table listing the services the Red Cross provides.

After Reading

Revisiting the Text

Comprehension Use the Four-Column Chart on page 152. In the first row, write: *Armed Forces Emergency Services, Biomedical Services, Health and Safety Services,* and *Disaster Services.* Have pairs review the book to list details about each service. Then have them pick a service in which they would like to be a volunteer and explain why they chose that service.

128A

One Hundred Houses

by Steven Otfinoski
Leveled Reader 128A
Genre: Informational Article
Level: Easy

Summary

Habitat for Humanity is a group that builds homes for needy people. Volunteers and new homeowners work together to construct these homes. In 1998, hundreds of volunteers went to Houston, Texas, to build one hundred houses. In addition to building homes, people can volunteer to cook for other workers, provide medical help for anyone injured, and pick up garbage and recycle materials.

Leveled Reader Practice

After students have read *One Hundred Houses,* use Leveled Reader practice page 168 to assess their understanding of the Leveled Reader and the target comprehension skill. Additional after reading activities are provided on page 39.

At a Glance

Links to the Student Edition

Comprehension Skill: Fact and Opinion

Selection Vocabulary: *organized, donate, advised*

Program Theme: The World Around Us
Unit Theme: My World and Yours

People can make the world a better place when they work together to help others. Habitat for Humanity volunteers show they care by helping build homes for people in need.

Before Reading

Motivating the Reader

Build Background About Houses

Display photographs of different types of homes, such as a brick apartment building, a wooden house, and an adobe house. Have students compare and contrast each building and list the materials used to make each house. Use local housing examples to illustrate that building materials are often chosen for their availability or function. The thick walls of adobe-brick houses, for instance, keep people who live in warm climates cool during hot summers. Invite students to describe or draw pictures of their dream homes.

Preview and Predict

Have students scan the cover, text, and photographs for clues that this book is an informational article. Ask students to predict what the book will be about and suggest they read to find out what the title means.

Point out selection vocabulary and any unfamiliar words, such as *habitat, humanity, bonding,* and *dedicated,* that might be important to understanding the book.

During Reading

Guiding Comprehension

Use the following questions to support students as they read.

- **Pages 2–3** **What does this photograph show?** (It shows people from Habitat for Humanity traveling to Houston to build houses for needy families.)
- **Pages 4–5** **How does the author support the statement that Habitat for Humanity is not a charity?** (He explains that each homeowner must work to build a home in order to get it.)
- **Page 4** **What does Betty Polk mean when she says, "And every drop of sweat was worth it"?** (She means that having a home is worth the hard work it takes to build it.)
- **Pages 6–7** **How does Jimmy Carter feel about being a volunteer?** (He thinks it's a wonderful experience.)
- **Page 7** **What does *bonding* mean in this sentence? Restate the sentence in your own words.** (It means "friendship or close relationship." The house owner and the volunteer workers develop a close relationship.)
- **Pages 8–9** **What kind of information is given on these pages?** (The pages tell about three different volunteers and how they feel about working for Habitat for Humanity.)
- **Pages 11–12** **Which part of the work force would you want to join? Why?** (Encourage well-supported answers.)
- **Pages 15–16** **How does Habitat for Humanity help people?** (It helps them learn how to build homes, take pride in their work, and feel part of a community.)
- **Page 16** **How do you think the author feels about Habitat for Humanity? How does he support his opinion?** (He thinks the group does a lot of good work for people. He provides facts about the kinds of work that people do and includes quotes from homeowners and volunteers about what great experiences they have had.)

Ongoing Assessment

Reading Strategies

If... a student recognizes the author's positive opinion of the organization,	**Then...** praise the student for drawing conclusions about what he or she has read.
If... a student has difficulty distinguishing statements of fact and opinion,	**Then...** use **Model Your Thinking** below.

Model Your Thinking

Comprehension Skill: Fact and Opinion

A fact tells something that can be proved true or false. I can check a statement of fact by looking in a reference book, asking an expert, and so on. An opinion tells someone's ideas and feelings and may begin with clue words such as *I believe* or *In my opinion*. A statement of opinion cannot be proved true or false, although it may be supported or explained. As I read, I ask myself: "Can this statement be proved true or false?" For example, on page 4, Mrs. Polk's comments express her beliefs about the value of the work she did. Her statements can't be proved true or false. However, the statement that she and her husband worked 300 hours could be proved true or false by checking with someone who worked on that project.

After Reading

Revisiting the Text

Comprehension Use the T-Chart on page 150. Write *Facts* on the left side and *Opinions* on the right. Have pairs review the book and record at least two facts and two opinions. Then invite volunteers to read aloud statements from their charts. Have the other students tell whether each statement is a fact or opinion and explain their choices.

128B

Fast and Forever

by David Neufeld
Leveled Reader 128B
Genre: Informational Article
Level: Easy/Average

Summary

The starlight we see at night has been traveling to Earth for a long time. Fantastic stories have been passed down through generations about figures formed by some clusters of stars, such as the Big Dipper, the Pleiades, and Orion. People have been interested in studying the night sky for a very long time. The Great Pyramids of Egypt may even have been the first star observatories.

Leveled Reader Practice

After students have read *Fast and Forever,* use Leveled Reader practice page 169 to assess their understanding of the Leveled Reader and the target comprehension skill. Additional after reading activities are provided on page 41.

At a Glance

Links to the Student Edition

Comprehension Skill: Fact and Opinion

Selection Vocabulary: *unfortunate, deliveries*

Program Theme: The World Around Us
Unit Theme: My World and Yours

We can look to the stars to get a sense of the vastness of the universe.

Before Reading

Motivating the Reader

Build Background About Stars

Have students close their eyes and try to picture the following passage as you read it aloud:

> Thousands of years ago, a huge star exploded. The bright light from the explosion traveled millions of miles through space. Tonight, if you look up at the stars, you may see the light from that long-ago explosion.

Then have students draw a sketch of themselves viewing the night sky and write a caption about what they see.

Preview and Predict

Have students scan the cover, text, and pictures. Encourage them to use picture and word clues to predict what kinds of information they will find in the book. Have them complete the first two columns of the K-W-L Chart on page 135 by telling what they already know about stars and what they would like to know about them. Suggest students read to find the answers to the questions they wrote in the second column. They can complete the third column after reading the book.

Point out selection vocabulary and any unfamiliar words, such as *evidence, astronomer,* and *observatories,* that might be important to understanding the book. Draw their attention to the labels naming the stars and constellations. Model how to use the pronunciation guides to say these names.

During Reading

Guiding Comprehension

Use the following questions to support students as they read.

- **Page 3** **To whom is the author of the book speaking? How do you know?** (He is speaking to the reader. He uses the pronoun *you*.)
- **Page 3** **What is a light-year?** (It is how far light travels in one year—six trillion miles.)
- **Pages 4–5** **What are the "deliveries from the past" mentioned by the author?** (The light we see from stars comes from the past.) ***Give an example of one of these deliveries.*** (Answers should be based on the text.)
- **Page 5** **Look at the letters in parentheses. How do you say this word?** (Students should use the pronunciation guide to help them pronounce *Polaris* correctly.) **What is another name for Polaris?** (the North Star)
- **Page 7** **What does this illustration show?** (It shows the names and shapes of stars and star groups seen in the winter sky.) **When you look in the night sky, do you see these connecting lines? Why or why not?** (No. The lines are shown here to help readers see the shape of the star group better.)
- **Page 8** **How does the author support his belief that using binoculars is more fun than using just your eyes?** (He explains that you can see more stars if you use binoculars and then he gives two examples.)
- **Pages 10–13** **How can you use Orion to identify other stars? Give an example.** (You can use a star in Orion as a starting point and then look for others from this point. Examples will vary but should be based on the text.)
- **Page 14** **What are star observatories? Think about the base word *observe* in *observatories*.** (These are places where people can look at stars.)
- **Page 15** **What do these pictures show?** (They show how the size and position of the pyramids are like the stars in Orion's belt.)

Ongoing Assessment

Reading Strategies

If... a student is confused by the reference to Orion's belt,	**Then...** sketch the star group and include arms, head, and legs so the student can better visualize it.
If... a student has difficulty distinguishing between statements of fact and opinion,	**Then...** use **Model Your Thinking** below.

Model Your Thinking

Comprehension Skill: Fact and Opinion

A statement of fact tells something that can be proved true or false. To check a statement of fact, I can look in a reference book, ask an expert, and so on. A statement of opinion tells someone's ideas and feelings and may include clue words such as *I believe* or *In my opinion.* A statement of opinion cannot be proved true or false. For example, on page 8, the author states that it is "even more fun to look up at space using binoculars." Because this statement cannot be proved true or false, I know it is a statement of opinion. The statement that "the Pleiades is a star cluster with about four hundred stars in it" is a statement of fact because I could use an encyclopedia or a science textbook to prove whether it is true or false.

After Reading

Revisiting the Text

Comprehension Have students complete the K-W-L Charts they started before reading the book by telling what they have learned about stars. Encourage them to include both statements of fact and opinion. Have students write *F* after statements of fact and *O* after statements of opinion. Invite volunteers to share their charts with the other students.

129A

The Trees

by Alice Cary
Leveled Reader 129A
Genre: Narrative Nonfiction
Level: Easy

Summary

In the mid-1800s, Potwisha Chief Chappo takes rancher Hale Tharp to visit the majestic sequoias high in the California mountains. Tharp and other white settlers move into this area. As a result, many Potwisha die from diseases caught from these settlers, and many sequoias are cut down. The Potwisha leave the area. Tharp fears that all the sequoias will be cut, until naturalist John Muir convinces the government to protect these trees.

Leveled Reader Practice

After students have read *The Trees*, use Leveled Reader practice page 170 to assess their understanding of the Leveled Reader and the target comprehension skill. Additional after reading activities are provided on page 43.

At a Glance

Links to the Student Edition

Comprehension Skill: Author's Viewpoint

Selection Vocabulary: *pondered, prospered, seeped*

Program Theme: The World Around Us
Unit Theme: My World and Yours

Humans can sometimes cause others and the environment great harm. The creation of the Sequoia National Park helped save many sequoia trees.

Before Reading

Motivating the Reader

Build Background About Sequoias

Show students pictures of giant sequoias, and share some of the following facts to give them a sense of the tremendous size of these trees. The world's largest known living tree is a giant sequoia that weighs almost 6,200 tons. This is roughly the equivalent of 41 blue whales or 740 elephants. A National Champion sequoia has a girth measuring more than 83 feet, a height of 275 feet, and a crown spread of 107 feet. Measure the arm span on one student and help students figure out how many students it would take to encircle this National Champion tree. Repeat for the tree's height.

Preview and Predict

Have students scan the cover, text, and pictures to get a sense of what the book is about. Draw students' attention to the illustrations that show humans next to sequoias, and ask students to make predictions about what might be special about the trees in this book. Have them set their own purposes for reading, such as reading to find out how the author feels about the trees.

Point out selection vocabulary and any unfamiliar words, such as *Potwisha, sequoias, lumber mill, livestock, graze, naturalist,* and *stump,* that might be important to understanding the book.

During Reading

Guiding Comprehension

Use the following questions to support students as they read.

- **Page 2** Where and when does this story take place? (in California in the mid-1800s)
- **Page 3** What is special about sequoias? (They are very old and very large.)
- **Pages 4–5** Why does Tharp spend summer in the Giant Forest? (There isn't enough food or water for his horses in the valley.)
- **Page 7** What are some of the effects that result from the white settlers moving into the forest? (Many Potwisha get sick and die. The Potwisha lose their land. Many sequoias are cut down.)
- **Page 7** How does the author feel about what happened to the Potwisha? What emotional words help you figure this out? (The author feels very bad about what happened to the Potwisha. The words *deadly, horrible, taking, killing,* and *sadly* show the author's strong feelings.)
- **Page 8** What is the mood on this page? How can you tell? (The mood is sad because the two friends will never see each other again. Chappo cries.)
- **Pages 10–11** Why do you think John Muir wants to look at the sequoias? (He is a naturalist. He wants to study the trees because they are unusually old and large.)
- **Pages 12–14** What did John Muir do? (He studied the sequoias, took notes and wrote about them, and helped people understand that these trees must be protected.)
- **Page 14** Why do you think Congress created Sequoia National Park? (They realized that these trees needed to be protected, so they created a park to stop others from cutting down these trees.)
- **Page 15** What does the map show? (It shows the area set aside for national forests.)

Ongoing Assessment

Reading Strategies

If... a student has difficulty identifying the emotionally loaded words on page 8,	**Then...** restate the sentences using other, less-loaded words. Have the student explain how the choice of words changes the meaning of the sentences.
If... a student has difficulty explaining the author's viewpoint,	**Then...** use **Model Your Thinking** below.

Model Your Thinking

Comprehension Skill: Author's Viewpoint

An author's viewpoint is the way an author feels about the subject he or she is writing about. Good readers look at the words an author uses and the opinions an author expresses to figure out what the author's viewpoint is. For example, on page 14, the author says "thanks to Muir and others" the sequoias were protected in a national park. That language tells me that the author is grateful that the trees are saved and that she probably thinks it is a good idea that national parks were created to protect these ancient trees. Balanced writing presents both sides of an issue equally. Unbalanced, or biased, writing presents only one viewpoint. Since the author of this book only presents the viewpoint that cutting the trees down is wrong, this book is an example of biased writing.

After Reading

Revisiting the Text

Comprehension Have small groups reread the book and use Web 1 on page 132 to list words and phrases that reveal the author's viewpoint. Then have students pretend they are the author. Ask them questions about events in the book and how they feel about these events. Remind students to express the author's opinions.

129B

A Walk Through a Salt Marsh

by Steven Otfinoski
Leveled Reader 129B
Genre: Narrative Nonfiction
Level: Easy/Average

Summary

A salt marsh is mostly mud, grass, and water. Or is it? This book takes readers on a walk through a salt marsh, pointing out the interesting plants and animals that abound there. It also explains how marshes purify water and protect nearby land from flooding.

Leveled Reader Practice

After students have read *A Walk Through a Salt Marsh,* use Leveled Reader practice page 171 to assess their understanding of the Leveled Reader and the target comprehension skill. Additional after reading activities are provided on page 45.

At a Glance

Links to the Student Edition

Comprehension Skill: Author's Viewpoint

Selection Vocabulary: *brim, miraculous, quantities*

Program Theme: The World Around Us
Unit Theme: My World and Yours

The first step toward caring for an environment, such as a salt marsh, is to observe it carefully and learn more about it.

Before Reading

Motivating the Reader

Build Background About Environments

If possible, show pictures of different types of environments, such as an urban city, a beach, a desert, a tropical rainforest, and a marsh. Invite volunteers to describe each environment. Use Web 1 on page 132. Have students write the words *Salt Marsh* in the center. Have them add words to the web that describe a salt marsh. Invite volunteers to share their webs.

Preview and Predict

Have students scan the cover, text, and illustrations. Then ask them to make predictions about what they might learn about salt marshes from reading the book. Have them write a few questions of inquiry about salt marshes, such as: What kinds of animals live in a salt marsh? Encourage them to look for answers to their questions as they read.

Point out the selection vocabulary and any unfamiliar words, such as *habitats, tide, environments, nursery,* and *nutrients,* that might be important to understanding the book.

During Reading

Guiding Comprehension

Use the following questions to support students as they read.

- **Page 3** Why is a salt marsh underwater sometimes? (The tides bring salt water from the ocean in and out of the marsh.)
- **Page 4** What does the author mean when he says the marsh is "one of the richest environments on Earth"? (Many different kinds of plants and animals live there.)
- **Page 6** How is the word *nursery* used in this sentence? Restate the sentence in your own words. (Many of the fish we eat begin life in the salt marsh.)
- **Page 7** What important role does salt cord grass have in the salt marsh? (Its roots keep soil from washing away. It is food for ducks, geese, and muskrats.)
- **Pages 8–9** How does this picture help you understand the text? (It shows the four kinds of salt marsh plants described. It helps the reader better visualize and evaluate the author's descriptions of these plants.)
- **Pages 10–11** If you saw a fiddler crab with a big left claw and small right claw, what conclusion could you draw about that crab? (Somehow, perhaps in a fight, the crab lost its original big right claw.)
- **Page 12** Why does a salt marsh snail climb to the top of the marsh grass? (The snail can only live underwater for an hour, so it climbs to the top of the grass to stay above the water that rushes in during high tide.)
- **Page 13** Why do egrets shake their feet in the marsh water? (The shaking scares tiny fish into moving, and egrets can then catch them.)
- **Page 16** How do you think the author feels about salt marshes? Which words help show how he feels? (He thinks they are wonderful places that need to be protected. He uses the words *miraculous wonders* to describe life in the salt marsh.)

Ongoing Assessment

Reading Strategies

If... a student has difficulty comprehending how tides affect a salt marsh,	**Then...** draw a sketch of a marsh and have the student add and label lines for high tide and low tide.
If... a student has difficulty explaining the author's viewpoint,	**Then...** use **Model Your Thinking** below.

Model Your Thinking

Comprehension Skill: Author's Viewpoint

An author's viewpoint is the way an author thinks about the subject he or she is writing about. Good readers look at the words an author uses and the opinions an author expresses to figure out what the author's viewpoint is. For example, on page 16, the author says, "The salt marsh is full of miraculous wonders." He tells us that it is unfortunate other people don't see it that way— which is his opinion. This author definitely has a strong viewpoint about the salt marsh. He loves it and wants it to be protected. Balanced writing presents both sides of an issue equally. Unbalanced, or biased, writing shows only one viewpoint. In this book, the author presents only one viewpoint about salt marshes, so his writing can be considered biased.

After Reading

Revisiting the Text

Comprehension Use Web 1 on page 132. In the center, write: *Why should a salt marsh be preserved?* Have students reread the book and list all the reasons that the author gives for why a salt marsh should be preserved. Discuss the author's viewpoint and identify words and phrases that reveal it. Then have students pretend they are at a town meeting. They can use their word webs to help them explain to their audience why salt marshes are important.

130A

The California Gold Rush

by Deborah Bruss
Leveled Reader 130A
Genre: Informational Article
Level: Easy

Summary

In January 1848, James Marshall discovered gold in a river near Sutter's mill. The following year, thousands of people rushed to California, hoping to strike it rich. San Francisco's population grew from eight hundred to twenty-five thousand in a few short years. Few people, however, became wealthy. Many miners died from disease or accidents.

Leveled Reader Practice

After students have read *The California Gold Rush*, use Leveled Reader practice page 172 to assess their understanding of the Leveled Reader and the target comprehension skill. Additional after reading activities are provided on page 47.

At a Glance

Links to the Student Edition

Comprehension Skill: Drawing Conclusions

Selection Vocabulary: *jewelry, sapphire, indicates*

Program Theme: The World Around Us
Unit Theme: My World and Yours

In the mid-1800s, people rushed to California to search the rivers and underground for glittering nuggets of gold. While few struck it rich, the face of California changed forever.

Before Reading

Motivating the Reader

Build Background About the Gold Rush

Give students a brief description of the California Gold Rush. Have students imagine what it would have been like to be in San Francisco at that time. Ask students to think about how a discovery like this could change a town and its people. Have students describe events that might occur and act them out. One student can role-play James Marshall, the man who first discovered the gold. Other students can choose roles such as miner, shopkeeper, banker, and boardinghouse owner.

Preview and Predict

Have students scan the cover, text, pictures, and map to get an idea of what the book is about. Encourage students to make predictions about the setting and what will happen in the book. Suggest they set their own purposes for reading, such as to find out what happened when people rushed to California or how many people actually got wealthy from finding gold.

Point out the selection vocabulary and any unfamiliar words, such as *nugget, overrun, shifted, blasted,* and *collapsed,* that might be important to understanding the book.

During Reading

Guiding Comprehension

Use the following questions to support students as they read.

- **Pages 2–3 How did James Marshall decide that his glittering nugget was real gold?** (First, he bit it to make sure it was soft like real gold. Next, he hammered it to make sure it wouldn't break. Finally, he boiled it in lye to see if it stayed unmarked. Since his nugget passed all three tests, he knew it was real gold.)
- **Pages 2–3 What do you think fool's gold is?** (It is something that glitters like gold, but it is not valuable. People might be fooled by its glitter into thinking it is real gold.)
- **Pages 4–5 Why do you think the author concludes that Sam Brannon was selfish?** (He wanted to make money off of the miners, even if it meant that the area around Sutter's mill might be ruined.)
- **Pages 8–10 What does the map show?** (It shows the three main routes to California from the East.) **Which route would you choose? Why?** (Answers will vary but should reflect information in the text.)
- **Pages 11–14 Did miners have easy lives? Explain.** (No. A few got rich, but most did not. Many died from disease or accidents.)
- **Page 12 How did women earn money during the California Gold Rush?** (A few became miners, but most earned money by cooking, running boardinghouses, or doing laundry for the miners.)
- **Page 12 Do you think Levi Strauss was a smart businessman? Explain.** (Yes. He sold jeans to miners instead of trying to find gold.)
- **Page 14 How did California change after the Gold Rush?** (Thousands of people came to California. San Francisco became a big city. Miners damaged the land, and many lost their lives. Many Native Americans lost their lives and their land.)

Ongoing Assessment

Reading Strategies

If... a student can describe the effects of the Gold Rush,	**Then...** praise him or her for summarizing important details.
If... a student has difficulty drawing logical conclusions,	**Then...** use **Model Your Thinking** below.

Model Your Thinking

Comprehension Skill: Drawing Conclusions

When I form an opinion about something I've read, I am drawing a conclusion. To draw a conclusion, I think about the facts and details that I've read and what I already know. For example, on pages 2 and 3, I read about the steps that James Marshall takes to test whether he has fool's gold or real gold. One conclusion I can draw from these details is that James Marshall was a careful man, since he checked to be sure he had real gold. This conclusion makes sense, since I know a careful person would take his time before deciding whether his nugget was real gold.

After Reading

Revisiting the Text

Comprehension Use the Three-Column Chart on page 151. Across the top, write the heads *People/Events, Evidence,* and *Conclusions.* List key people and events from the book in the first column. In the second column, pairs can list facts and details and what they already know about these people and events. In the last column, pairs record the conclusions they can draw about the people and events based on the evidence. Invite students to share their conclusions and explain how they reached them.

130B

Why the Spider Has a Tiny Waist

retold by Jan M. Mike
Leveled Reader 130B
Genre: Fable
Level: Easy/Average

Summary

Anansi, a greedy spider, has invitations to two feasts that take place at the same time, and he wants to eat at both of them. He wraps a vine around his waist and has an elephant in each village pull on an end when the feasts begin. When the elephants pull at the same time, Anansi's big stomach is squeezed tight. This fable explains why, to this day, spiders have such tiny waists.

Leveled Reader Practice

After students have read *Why the Spider Has a Tiny Waist,* use Leveled Reader practice page 173 to assess their understanding of the Leveled Reader and the target comprehension skill. Additional after reading activities are provided on page 49.

At a Glance

Links to the Student Edition

Comprehension Skill: Drawing Conclusions

Selection Vocabulary: *smudge, counter*

Program Theme: The World Around Us
Unit Theme: My World and Yours

Fables often seek to explain the world around us and teach important lessons. This fable explains why spiders today have such tiny waists and what can happen if you get too greedy.

Before Reading

Motivating the Reader

Build Background About Spiders

Show students photographs or labeled diagrams of different types of spiders. Have students use Web 1 on page 132. They should write *Spiders* in the center and list common characteristics of spiders. Point out that the bodies of spiders are divided into three main parts.

Preview and Predict

Have students scan the cover, text, and pictures to get an idea of what the book is about. Draw their attention to the book's title, and ask students to think of other fables or folk tales they have read that explain something about our world. Ask them what they think this fable may explain. Encourage students to make predictions about what they think will happen to Anansi in the story. Have them set their own purposes for reading, such as reading to find out why the spider has a tiny waist.

Point out selection vocabulary and any unusual food words that might be important to understanding the book.

During Reading

Guiding Comprehension

Use the following questions to support students as they read.

- **Pages 2–3 What does the author mean by the sentence "Every counter groaned under the weight of all that food."? Were the counters talking? Explain.** (No. It is an expression that means the counters were covered with a lot of food.) Ask similar questions about other figurative phrases.
- **Page 4 What problem does Anansi have?** (He has been invited to two feasts that are both held at the same time. He wants to go to both feasts.)
- **Page 4 What does Anansi's reaction to his problem tell you about him?** (He is greedy because he wants to eat at both places. He is cheap and lazy because he is excited that he doesn't have to work or pay for the food.)
- **Pages 6–8 What happens when Anansi visits the village in the east?** (He tries to sneak some food, but an elephant stops him. He tries to trick the elephant, but it doesn't work.) **What does this tell you about these characters?** (Anansi is sneaky. The elephant is polite but firm.)
- **Page 9 What do you think Anansi will do next?** (Students will probably say that Anansi will try to trick the elephant into letting him taste the food.)
- **Pages 12–15 What is Anansi's idea?** (Anansi believes the feasts won't begin on time. He wants to know when each feast actually starts, so he can eat at both feasts. He ties a vine around his waist and has the elephants at each village tug it to let him know when each feast starts.)
- **Pages 15–16 Did Anansi's plan turn out as he'd hoped? Why or why not?** (No. He didn't expect that the elephants would pull at the same time. He ends up missing both feasts.)
- **Page 16 What lesson do you think Anansi might have learned?** (Don't be so greedy.)

Ongoing Assessment

Reading Strategies

If... a student has trouble figuring out Anansi's plan,	**Then...** wrap string around the student's finger to model it.
If... a student can tell what lesson Anansi learns,	**Then...** praise him or her for figuring out the theme of the book.
If... a student has difficulty drawing logical conclusions,	**Then...** use **Model Your Thinking** below.

Model Your Thinking

Comprehension Skill: Drawing Conclusions

When I form an opinion about something I've read, I am drawing a conclusion. To draw a conclusion, I think about the facts and details I've read and what I already know. On pages 6 through 8, Anansi tries to trick the elephant into letting him taste the food. Based on Anansi's words and actions and what I know about good behavior, I draw the conclusion that he is a sneaky and greedy character with poor manners. This conclusion makes sense because it seems that only a greedy and sneaky person would act the way Anansi does. Drawing conclusions about characters and events helps me figure out more about them.

After Reading

Revisiting the Text

Comprehension Use the T-Chart on page 150. Write *How Anansi Acts* on the left side and *What I Know About Good Manners* on the right side. Students can complete the charts using details from the book and their own understanding of what it means to be a good dinner guest. Then have students write a poem about Anansi, using their charts to help them draw conclusions about this character. Students can draw pictures to illustrate their poems.

131A The Secret Fort

by Juanita Havill
Leveled Reader 131A
Genre: Realistic Story
Level: Easy

Summary

Changing schools is difficult for most boys and girls. It is especially hard for Emily since she is the only deaf student in her new classroom. She seeks comfort by creating a special place where she can think and be alone. It is there that she makes new friends and begins to feel at home.

Leveled Reader Practice

After students have read *The Secret Fort,* use Leveled Reader practice page 174 to assess their understanding of the Leveled Reader and the target comprehension skill. Additional after reading activities are provided on page 51.

At a Glance

Links to the Student Edition

Comprehension Skill: Character

Selection Vocabulary: *interpreter, gestured, conversation*

Program Theme: Learning and Working
Unit Theme: A Job Well Done
Emily has fun working on her own private fort. She soon learns it is even more fun to work with others and to build friendships through teamwork.

Before Reading

Motivating the Reader

Build Background About Secret Places

Discuss how many people have a special place to be alone and think. Encourage students to recall places they have used as private getaways. Invite them to draw a picture of a place they go to be alone or a place they dream about creating for themselves. Have students write a description of this place and tell why it is special.

Preview and Predict

Have students scan the cover, text, and illustrations to get an idea of what the book is about. Ask them to point out details of the secret fort and use the details to guess where the fort is located. Have students read the first two paragraphs and predict why Emily might want a secret place. Suggest students read to find out more about the secret fort and how it makes Emily feel.

Point out selection vocabulary and any unfamiliar words, such as *sign, e-mail,* and *shelter,* that might be important to understanding the book. Be sure students understand that people who are deaf communicate with others through signing, lip reading, and interpreters.

During Reading

Guiding Comprehension

Use the following questions to support students as they read.

- **Page 2** **Why doesn't Emily feel comfortable at her new school?** (She has been there only one week. She is the only deaf student. Neither the teacher nor students sign. She left her best friend behind.)
- **Pages 2–3** **How does Emily communicate with people? How can she communicate with people who don't understand sign language?** (She can sign, read lips, and write e-mail. If people can't understand sign language, Emily can use an interpreter who can tell others what Emily is signing.)
- **Page 4** **Why does Emily like running by the cornfield?** (She likes it because she doesn't have to keep an eye out for city traffic.)
- **Pages 6–7** **How does Emily make her fort?** (She leans dried cornstalks against a large broken tree branch and ties the stalks together with corn leaves.)
- **Pages 8–9** **What has happened to Emily's fort?** (A storm tore it apart.) **What does Emily do next?** (She builds a better one out of wood.) **What does this action tell you about Emily?** (She doesn't give up. She is a determined person.)
- **Page 10** **Why does Emily like to go to the fort?** (She isn't feeling comfortable at school, but she feels comfortable at the fort.)
- **Page 12** **What is Emily's first reaction when she sees the two girls and her ruined fort?** (She is angry and thinks they destroyed it.)
- **Pages 14–15** **How do Sally and Karen let Emily know they want to be friends?** (They tell their names, touch her shoulder, offer help, and invite her to join the track team.)
- **Page 16** **How have Emily's feelings about her new school changed?** (She has made friends and is looking forward to trying out for track. She is cheerful and excited rather than lonely and frightened.)

Ongoing Assessment

Reading Strategies

If... a student confuses *sign* (verb) with *sign* (noun),	**Then...** give examples of both meanings. Have the student use context and syntax clues to figure out which meaning makes the most sense.
If... a student has difficulty drawing conclusions about characters,	**Then...** use **Model Your Thinking** below.

Model Your Thinking

Comprehension Skill: Character

Characters are the people or animals in stories. I can learn about them by their words, actions, and how others act toward them. I also think about real people I know who are like these characters. I can use Emily's actions and the way she faces problems as clues to her personality. For example, on page 8, Emily doesn't give up when her fort is destroyed. Instead she builds a new, stronger fort. This tells me she is a strong, determined girl. It helps me understand how she gets along so well in a hearing world. People who don't give up easily are usually people who are successful in life. I believe Emily will get along fine at her new school.

After Reading

Revisiting the Text

Comprehension Have students reread the book and list details about Emily in Web 1 on page 132. Then have volunteers use their webs to introduce Emily (played by another student) to her new classmates.

131B Grounding Grandma

by Sharon Fear
Leveled Reader 131B
Genre: Fantasy
Level: Easy/Average

Summary

Burt's family is worried that Grandma Wingfield is getting forgetful. When he and his sister go to check on Grandma, Burt learns an amazing family secret — most of the Wingfields can fly!

Leveled Reader Practice

After students have read *Grounding Grandma,* use Leveled Reader practice page 175 to assess their understanding of the Leveled Reader and the target comprehension skill. Additional after reading activities are provided on page 53.

At a Glance

Links to the Student Edition

Comprehension Skill: Character

Selection Vocabulary: *dribbling, volunteers, skied*

Program Theme: Learning and Working
Unit Theme: A Job Well Done

When Burt Wingfield discovers he might have a surprising talent, he learns he must use it wisely. He finds that a special skill can bring new responsibilities.

Before Reading

Motivating the Reader

Build Background About Senior Citizens and Aging

Display pictures of seniors doing work and recreation. Ask students to draw a picture or write about an elderly friend or family member. Then have students share their efforts. Discuss what contributions elderly people make to their family, friends, and communities. Talk about negative stereotypes that some people may have about senior citizens. Encourage students to compare their friend or relative to Grandma Wingfield as they read the book.

Preview and Predict

Have students scan the cover, text, and illustrations to get an idea of what the book is about. Have them use word and picture clues to make predictions about the characters and what they are like. Suggest students read to find out what the book title means.

Point out selection vocabulary and any unfamiliar words, such as *hysterical, vertical, grounded, dunked,* and *descend,* that might be important to understanding the book. Discuss how both planes and people can be grounded.

During Reading

Guiding Comprehension

Use the following questions to support students as they read.

- **Page 2** **What do you think *slam-bamming* means? Why do you think the author chose to use this word?** (It means "bouncing hard." It helps to describe the action and sound of a basketball hitting the floor.)
- **Page 4** **What problem is Grandma having? How do the Wingfields learn of Grandma's problem?** (A letter from neighbors says that Grandma is forgetful and that she is doing activities she shouldn't do.)
- **Page 5** **How does Burt feel about going to stay with his Grandma? What word is a clue to help you figure this out?** (He doesn't want to go. The word *whine* helps describe how he feels.)
- **Page 6** **As he enters Mount Airy, what does Burt find unusual?** (A windsock shows wind direction, but there is no airport. An elderly man is working up on a roof.)
- **Pages 9–10** **Look at the picture. What does it mean to dunk a basketball? Why do you think Burt is so amazed that Grandma can dunk?** (To dunk is to jump up high and stuff the ball through the hoop. Most elderly people probably couldn't jump that high.)
- **Pages 10–12** **What is the Wingfield secret? Think back to what you read. What were clues that the author gave that hinted at this secret?** (Some Wingfields can fly. Clues include the family name of Wingfield, the town name of Mount Airy, windsocks and weather vanes, a cousin on the roof, Grandma climbing up on the roof, Grandma dunking a basketball, and Grandma dusting near the ceiling.)
- **Page 15** **Why does Burt need to learn the rules of flying?** (He can't use it unfairly. He needs to keep it a secret.)
- **Page 16** **What questions are left unanswered?** (Should Grandma be grounded? Will Burt be able to fly?)

Ongoing Assessment

Reading Strategies

If... a student does not connect flying with the words *Wingfield, Airy,* and *windsock,*	**Then...** help that student use word parts to see the connection.
If... a student guesses the fantastic element of the book before it is actually revealed,	**Then...** congratulate him or her for using word and picture clues to predict events.
If... a student has difficulty drawing conclusions about characters,	**Then...** use **Model Your Thinking** below.

Model Your Thinking

Comprehension Skill: Character

Characters are the people or animals in stories. Good readers think about what a character says, thinks, and does to learn more about that character. They also look at the way other characters treat the character and think about what they know about real people. The Wingfields do not use their flying ability to take advantage of people, show off, or get rich. On page 15, Grandma says that to fly during a basketball game would be cheating. From these actions and words and what I know about people like the Wingfields, I can tell that the Wingfields are honest and caring.

After Reading

Revisiting the Text

Comprehension Use Web 2 on page 133. Ask pairs to choose a character and write the character's name in the center. Have each pair reread the story to look for something that: (1) their character says, (2) their character does, or (3) is said about their character. Have them (4) make their own judgment about the character. Have students record their findings in the four outer circles. Invite them to share their webs.

132A The Impossible Rescue

by Mark Spann
Leveled Reader 132A
Genre: Informational Article
Level: Easy

Summary

In 1996, a freight train derailed and crashed into a Minnesota railroad yard. Engineer Richard Vitek was trapped under the wreckage. Heroic emergency teams turned what seemed like an impossible rescue into a success story.

Leveled Reader Practice

After students have read *The Impossible Rescue,* use Leveled Reader practice page 176 to assess their understanding of the Leveled Reader and the target comprehension skill. Additional after reading activities are provided on page 55.

At a Glance

Links to the Student Edition

Comprehension Skill: Graphic Sources

Selection Vocabulary: *locomotives, dispatched, heroic, rescuers*

Program Theme: Learning and Working
Unit Theme: A Job Well Done

Some workers must make life-and-death decisions every day. They may even put their own lives on the line.

Before Reading

Motivating the Reader

Build Background About Heroic Rescues

Provide news clippings or videos about rescues. Have groups discuss rescues they've seen, been part of, or heard about. (These can be as simple as freeing a cat from a tree.) Ask each group to select a rescue event and write a headline about it. To expand the activity, invite volunteers to role-play being TV reporters and have them report the rescue.

Preview and Predict

Have students scan the cover, text, and illustrations to get an idea of what the book is about. Ask them to predict what problem the book shows and how it will be resolved. Direct their attention to the book title. Suggest that students read to find out if the rescue is really impossible.

Point out selection vocabulary and any unfamiliar words, such as *engineer, wreckage,* and *paramedics,* that might be important to understanding the book.

During Reading

Guiding Comprehension

Use the following questions to support students as they read.

- **Pages 2–3** Why did the train speed out of control? (The brakes didn't work.) Why weren't people at the train yard worried? (They knew that the train would slow down to a stop when it started up the next hill.)
- **Pages 3–4** What mistake turned the problem into a disaster? (Switches set in the wrong position sent the train onto the wrong track where it wouldn't be stopped.)
- **Page 4** What does this illustration show? (It shows the inside parts of a diesel electric locomotive.)
- **Pages 5–6** What happens when the runaway train reaches the train yard? (It crashes into the other locomotives, knocking them off track. Wood and metal from the wrecked trains and office fly everywhere. Eight people are injured, and Richard Vitek is missing.)
- **Page 6** What is another word that means almost the same as *dispatched?* (sent)
- **Pages 8–9** What has happened to Richard Vitek? (He is trapped under the wreckage.)
- **Page 10** What made the rescue seem impossible? (Workers were afraid if they moved the heavy wreckage, it could fall and crush Richard Vitek.)
- **Page 11** How did rescuers deal with the fire danger from leaking fuel? (Since sparks from electrical tools could start a fire, they used air-powered chisels.)
- **Pages 12–14** How do the rescue workers free Richard Vitek? (They dig a hole next to Richard. He slides into it, and then the workers pull him out from under the wreckage.)
- **Page 16** According to the author, what special quality does a rescue worker have? (A rescue worker has a strong desire to help people.)

Ongoing Assessment

Reading Strategies

If... a student cannot follow the sequence of events,	**Then...** have him or her use the Steps in a Process organizer on page 148.
If... a student has difficulty interpreting graphic sources,	**Then...** use **Model Your Thinking** below.

Model Your Thinking

Comprehension Skill: Graphic Sources

Graphic sources, such as pictures, maps, diagrams, or graphs, show information in a way that is easy to read and understand. Before I read, I look at the book's graphic sources to find out what the book is about. As I read, I compare the text to the pictures and diagrams to help me better understand the book's main ideas. For example, the diagram on page 4 makes it easier to picture the locomotives that pulled this train. I can see where the fuel must have seeped from the tank and where the engineer sat. The diagram helps me imagine the huge locomotive that trapped Richard Vitek and understand better what made the rescue so difficult.

After Reading

Revisiting the Text

Comprehension Have student take turns leading a book walk of this book. Students can point to one of the illustrations in the book and explain how it helps them better understand something in the book.

132B

These Old Shoes Remember

Colonial Life in America

by Caren B. Stelson
Leveled Reader 132B
Genre: Narrative Nonfiction
Level: Easy/Average

Summary

The author takes readers on a journey from a present-day historical museum back in time to colonial New England. By walking through a village and spending time on a family farm, readers get a close up look at colonial life in America.

Leveled Reader Practice

After students have read *These Old Shoes Remember*, use Leveled Reader practice page 177 to assess their understanding of the Leveled Reader and the target comprehension skill. Additional after reading activities are provided on page 57.

At a Glance

Links to the Student Edition

Comprehension Skill: Graphic Sources

Selection Vocabulary: *downpour, rugged, schedules*

Program Theme: Learning and Working
Unit Theme: A Job Well Done

Every member of a colonial family had jobs to do to keep the home and farm running smoothly.

Before Reading

Motivating the Reader

Build Background About Colonial America

Ask students how they picture the American colonists. Prompt them to share what they already know and display pictures from history references. Write *The Colonists* in the center of Web 2 on page 133. Near the four outer circles, write: *Clothing, Daily Life, Work,* and *Fun.* Have students suggest ideas for each circle. Discuss what students think they would or would not like about living in America at this time.

Preview and Predict

Have students scan the cover, text, and illustrations to get an idea of what the book is about. Suggest they use the story subtitle and pictures to make predictions about the setting. Prompt them to set purposes for reading by asking:

> What would you like to find out about Colonial America?

Point out selection vocabulary and any unfamiliar words, such as *museum* and *cooperate,* that might be important to understanding the book.

During Reading

Guiding Comprehension

Use the following questions to support students as they read.

- **Page 2** *What does this picture show?* (It shows a pair of boy's shoes from New Hampshire in 1748 that are now in a museum.)
- **Pages 2–3** *Whom is the narrator addressing?* (the reader)
- **Page 4** *How does the picture help you better understand what stocks are?* (Stocks were used to lock up law-breakers. The picture shows holes where a person's head and hands would go. It helps you understand how uncomfortable and embarrassing it would be to be locked up in stocks.)
- **Page 6** *Who are Ezra and Charity? What tasks do they have to do?* (They are a brother and sister who lived long ago in Colonial America. Ezra feeds the chickens. Charity gathers the hens' eggs.)
- **Pages 8–9** *What was a colonial farmhouse like?* (It had one room, a sleeping loft, a large stone fireplace, and a long table.)
- **Page 12** *Why are people willing to work hard without complaining?* (They know everyone must do their share in order to survive.)
- **Page 13** *What does this picture show?* (a horn book)
- **Page 14** *What lessons does Grandma think boys and girls need to learn?* (She says boys must learn to farm and girls must learn to keep house.)
- **Page 16** *What does the author mean by "Change is in the wind too"?* (She means that changes to the family's way of life will soon happen, such as war and new inventions.)
- **Page 16** *Would you like to live in Colonial America? Why or why not?* (Encourage well-supported answers.)

Ongoing Assessment

Reading Strategies

If... a student does not understand the time shift back in history,	**Then...** have the student reread the first two pages. Help him or her find words and phrases that give clues to time. ("After 250 years," "back into history," "Colonial America")
If... a student relates sites on the map on page 4 to story text,	**Then...** compliment the student for using a graphic source to visualize setting.
If... a student has difficulty interpreting graphic sources such as a map,	**Then...** use **Model Your Thinking** below.

Model Your Thinking

Comprehension Skill: Graphic Sources

Good readers know they can use graphic sources, such as pictures, maps, charts, and diagrams, to help understand the text better. They compare the graphic source to the information in the text. I see a simple map on page 4 that can help me better understand the description of the village. As I read about each part of the village, I find it on the map. I can see the meeting house and the stocks. Some buildings, such as the general store, are not on the map, but I can picture where they would be. I use both the book's words and pictures to get a sense of what life was like in Colonial America.

After Reading

Revisiting the Text

Comprehension Have pairs redraw a larger version of the map on page 4. Have them reread page 5 and expand their map by adding sites outside of town. Have them then use the map to give a tour of the village, restating information about what life was like in Colonial America.

133A

Head First

by Mike Dion
Leveled Reader 133A
Genre: Realistic Story
Level: Easy

Summary

Cindy would like to dive, but she has a big problem. She hates putting her head underwater. Since diving means going in head first, Cindy has to overcome her fear. After lots of practice, she not only learns to dive but also joins the swim team to compete in the Girls' Diving Championship.

Leveled Reader Practice

After students have read *Head First,* use Leveled Reader practice page 178 to assess their understanding of the Leveled Reader and the target comprehension skill. Additional after reading activities are provided on page 59.

At a Glance

Links to the Student Edition

Comprehension Skill: Plot

Selection Vocabulary: *trophy, championship, opponent*

Program Theme: Learning and Working
Unit Theme: A Job Well Done

It takes courage to set aside fears and learn something new. That courage plus hard work usually equals success!

Before Reading

Motivating the Reader

Build Background About Diving

Show pictures and videotape, if possible, of divers in action. Draw a diagram of a diving board and the water's surface. Have students describe or demonstrate the position of a diver's hands, legs, and feet at the point of entry into the water. Point out that the ideal dive is one in which the diver enters the water in a vertical position, creating the smallest amount of splash.

Preview and Predict

Have students scan the cover, text, and illustrations. Direct their attention to the cover illustration and the illustration on page 15. Prepare students for reading by asking:

> How do you think the character feels in this first picture? How do you think she feels in this picture near the end of the book?

Encourage students to make predictions about what problem the main character has and how it will be resolved. Students can set their own purposes for reading, such as reading to find out more about diving.

Point out selection vocabulary and any unfamiliar words, such as *wimp, strive, ordeal,* and *competing,* that might be important to understanding the book.

During Reading

Guiding Comprehension

Use the following questions to support students as they read.

- **Page 3** What problem does Cindy have? (She would like to learn how to dive, but she hates putting her head underwater.)
- **Page 3** What does "head first" mean? (It means that when you dive, your head goes into the water before the rest of your body does.)
- **Pages 4–5** What do Cindy's actions tell you about Cindy? (She is willing to try something, even if she is scared. She doesn't give up.)
- **Page 6** What three things does Ellen say Cindy needs in order to learn how to dive? (practice, a coach, and a good opponent)
- **Pages 6–8** Why does the diving teacher suggest that Cindy find a good opponent? Who does Cindy consider to be the best diving opponent? (A person works harder against a good opponent. Cindy thinks Laura Hale is the best diving opponent.)
- **Page 9** Why do you think Ellen spends so much time with Cindy? (Ellen probably sees Cindy's abilities and considers her a possible member of the diving team.)
- **Page 10** How does Cindy feel her first time on the diving board? (She is both scared and excited.)
- **Pages 12–16** What happens at the competition? (Susan is sick, and Cindy takes her place. Even though she is scared, Cindy makes a good dive.)
- **Page 15** Read the second sentence. How does it help you picture Cindy's dive? (The comparison to an arrow of light tells me that her dive was good. She dove fast and straight like an arrow.)
- **Page 16** How does Cindy react when she doesn't win her first meet? (She doesn't mind. She is happy about her first correct dive and looks forward to another meet.)

Ongoing Assessment

Reading Strategies

If... a student cannot use the similes on page 11 to visualize the dives,	**Then...** suggest the student draw pictures of a bent elbow, bow, and hinge to visualize the dives.
If... a student has trouble describing the book's plot,	**Then...** use **Model Your Thinking** below.

Model Your Thinking

Comprehension Skill: Plot

A plot includes the important events of a story. The conflict is the story's main problem. The rising action is the series of events in which the character tries to solve the problem. The climax is the high point of the story, where the character faces her problem. The resolution is how the story ends or how the problem is solved. At the beginning of the book, I learn that Cindy wants to be a diver but is afraid of diving into water head first. This is the story's conflict. In the middle, she tries to solve her problem by getting a coach and practicing. The climax comes when Cindy dives in a swim meet. At the end, Cindy successfully dives with the team, and her conflict is resolved.

After Reading

Revisiting the Text

Comprehension Have groups reread the book and use the Plot Structure organizer on page 138 to identify the plot elements. Have groups use their story maps to retell the story in their own words to you or to another group.

133B

What Isn't Possible!

by David Neufeld
Leveled Reader 133B
Genre: Historical Fiction
Level: Easy/Average

Summary

When coal fires heated homes, young boys, called chimney sweeps, were hired to keep the chimneys clean. Otis and Carl are chimney sweeps. Since Carl is too big to fit inside the chimney stacks, Otis does the dirty work. Otis feels unlucky, but when he finds a bracelet in a chimney, his luck changes. When Otis returns the bracelet to the owner, he is rewarded with a new bicycle. Now Carl and Otis can get safer jobs as messengers.

Leveled Reader Practice

After students have read *What Isn't Possible!*, use Leveled Reader practice page 179 to assess their understanding of the Leveled Reader and the target comprehension skill. Additional after reading activities are provided on page 61.

At a Glance

Links to the Student Edition

Comprehension Skill: Plot

Selection Vocabulary: *strengthen, swollen*

Program Theme: Learning and Working
Unit Theme: A Job Well Done

Before child labor laws, children often did hard and dangerous work to help their families survive. Because they could fit down chimney stacks, young boys risked their lives and health cleaning chimneys.

Before Reading

Motivating the Reader

Build Background About Child Labor

Ask students to describe household chores or tasks that they do. Then ask them what they know about jobs children did 100 to 150 years ago. If possible, display pictures of child workers of the late 1800s and early 1900s. Explain that during this time children often did dangerous jobs. Give the examples of pony express riders, chimney sweeps, and factory workers. Explain that in 1916 labor laws began regulating the work children could do. Encourage students to think about what it would be like to be a chimney sweep suspended on a rope scrubbing the inside of a chimney.

Preview and Predict

Have students scan the cover, text, and illustrations to predict what the book is about. Encourage students to make predictions about the story's setting, characters, and events. You may wish to explain that historical fiction combines fictional characters with an historical setting. Invite students to read to learn how children lived and worked during the late 1800s.

Point out selection vocabulary and any unfamiliar words, such as *mansion, hearth,* and *pauper,* that might be important to understanding the book.

During Reading

Guiding Comprehension

Use the following questions to support students as they read.

- **Pages 2–3** Why is Otis panicking? (Someone has lit a fire while he is cleaning the chimney.)
- **Page 3** What does a chimney sweep do? (He cleans the inside of chimneys.) Why does Otis take Carl's place? (Carl has grown too big to fit inside the chimneys.)
- **Page 4** What do you think a lighter is? Restate Pinkie's statement in your own words. (I heard you got caught in a chimney where someone lit a fire in it.)
- **Page 5** What words would you use to describe Otis? (unlucky, hard working)
- **Page 6** When Otis and Carl go to the mansions, why does the author say, "They seemed to have crossed into another country?" (The boys are poor. The lifestyle of the rich is so different from their own that it seems as if they are going to a foreign country.)
- **Pages 9–10** When Otis finds the gold bracelet, what decision do the brothers face? (Should they keep the bracelet or return it?) What would you do if you were Otis? (Answers may vary.)
- **Page 12** Why does Mr. Pope use the phrase "what isn't possible" when speaking about aircraft, automobiles, dirigibles, and the discovery of the long-lost bracelet? (These are all things people thought would be impossible, but flying and finding the bracelet have now been accomplished.)
- **Pages 11–14** Do you think the boys made the right decision about the bracelet? Why or why not? (Students will likely say yes. It was the honest thing to do, and Otis got a bicycle as a reward.)
- **Pages 15–16** How will the boys' lives now change? (With a bicycle, they can now become messengers. This is a much safer job.)

Ongoing Assessment

Reading Strategies

If... a student does not recognize that Mr. Pope is the maker of Pope bicycles,	**Then...** return to sections that describe white bicycles with POPE written on them (pages 5 and 15).
If... a student has trouble describing the book's plot,	**Then...** use **Model Your Thinking** below.

Model Your Thinking

Comprehension Skill: Plot

A plot includes the conflict, or problem that a character has; the rising action where the problem builds; the climax, or high point, where the character confronts the problem; and the resolution, where the problem is solved. This plot revolves around two problems facing Otis. A personal problem is that he sees no way to get a bicycle. A larger problem is that he must do risky work for very little money. The events leading up to the bracelet's discovery are the plot's rising action. The climax is when the boys return the bracelet. This event leads to the resolution, where both problems are solved—Mr. Pope gives Otis a bicycle, which allows the boys to be messengers instead of chimney sweeps.

After Reading

Revisiting the Text

Comprehension Ask pairs to map out the important events in the book. Depending on students' abilities, assign or allow them to self-select one of the organizers on pages 137–139. Then have pairs use their organizers to draw a cartoon strip retelling the story.

134A Amazing Ants

by Janet Buell
Leveled Reader 134A
Genre: Informational Article
Level: Easy

Summary

Their great numbers, variety, enormous strength, fierce loyalty, and industrious nature make ants the wonders of the insect world. This book describes different types of ants and the jobs they do.

Leveled Reader Practice

After students have read *Amazing Ants*, use Leveled Reader practice page 180 to assess their understanding of the Leveled Reader and the target comprehension skill. Additional after reading activities are provided on page 63.

At a Glance

Links to the Student Edition

Comprehension Skill: Text Structure

Selection Vocabulary: *colony, producers, venom, emerge*

Program Theme: Learning and Working
Unit Theme: A Job Well Done

No creature sets a better example of hard work than the ant. Each member does a task that contributes to the well-being of the colony.

Before Reading

Motivating the Reader

Build Background About Ants

A real, live ant farm would certainly spark students' interest. If that is not possible, display pictures or a nature videotape of ants. Then use the T-Chart on page 150 to explore students' attitudes. Label the first column *WOW!* and the second *YUCK!* Have students record ant features they find interesting and amazing in the first column and traits they find gross or frightening in the second column. Encourage students to add to the chart as they read the book.

Preview and Predict

Have students scan the cover, text, and photographs. Encourage them to make predictions about what information will be in the book. Suggest students read to find out what makes ants so amazing.

Point out selection vocabulary and any unfamiliar words, such as *fierce, queen, larvae,* and *cooperate,* that might be important to understanding the book. Remind them to compare the text to the photographs to help them figure out the meanings of unfamiliar words.

During Reading

Guiding Comprehension

Use the following questions to support students as they read.

- **Page 2** Are ants strong or weak? How do you know? (They are strong, since they can lift loads ten times their weight.)
- **Page 4** What is the main idea of this page? (Although they are small, when ants work together they can be as strong as a large animal.)
- **Page 4** What is another word that means almost the same as *venom?* (poison)
- **Pages 4–7** How are fire ants and army ants able to kill large animals and even people? (Their bites have venom, or poison, in them. By attacking in a swarm and biting the victim many times, these types of ants can kill much larger prey.)
- **Page 6** What are larvae? (Larvae are young, underdeveloped ants.)
- **Pages 8–9** What happens if several queens hatch in a colony? (All but one queen leave the nest and fly off to begin their own colonies.)
- **Page 9** What causes ants to grow up to do different jobs? (The type of food an ant is fed determines the kind of job the ant will do.)
- **Pages 12–13** What sentence states the main idea of pages 12 and 13? (Honey ants are probably the strangest producers of all.)
- **Page 15** What is one job of the housekeeper ants ? (They take away dead ants and dirt from the nest.)
- **Page 16** According to the author, what has allowed ants to survive for millions of years? (They use cooperation and work hard.)
- **Page 16** How is information in this book organized? (Most of the information is organized by giving a main idea about ants or about a specific kind of ant, and then giving interesting details about the main idea.)

Ongoing Assessment

Reading Strategies

If... a student has trouble recalling characteristics of different types of ants,	**Then...** have the student use the Five-Column Chart on page 153 to record details as he or she reads.
If... a student has trouble explaining how the text is organized,	**Then...** use **Model Your Thinking** below.

Model Your Thinking

Comprehension Skill: Text Structure

Text structure is the way a piece of writing is organized. Fiction tells made-up stories and is usually organized in chronological, or time, order. Nonfiction tells about real people, events, or information. It can be organized in different ways: chronological order, main idea and supporting details, or as relationships, such as cause and effect. I know this book is nonfiction because it gives factual information about ants. As I read, I see the book is organized by main ideas and descriptive supporting details. For example, on page 4, the author says that "when [ants] work together, they can be as strong as a large animal." She supports this main idea by giving details about how colonies of fire ants and army ants use their venom to kill large prey. Identifying the text structure helps me figure out the best way to read the book. I read nonfiction texts slowly and carefully to make sure I understand all the information.

After Reading

Revisiting the Text

Comprehension Assign pairs a section of the book to reread. Have them use the Main Idea organizer on page 142 to record the section's main ideas and supporting details. Then have pairs create Amazing Fact Cards about ants.

134B

Apple Cider Days

by Robert R. O'Brien
Leveled Reader 134B
Genre: Informational Article
Level: Easy/Average

Summary

Readers spend a year with apple growers. The book takes them from icy January through blossoms of spring to apple cider days of fall. It describes how growers tend an orchard and produce cider.

Leveled Reader Practice

After students have read *Apple Cider Days,* use Leveled Reader practice page 181 to assess their understanding of the Leveled Reader and the target comprehension skill. Additional after reading activities are provided on page 65.

At a Glance

Links to the Student Edition

Comprehension Skill: Text Structure

Selection Vocabulary: *condition, nectar, producers, react, storage*

Program Theme: Learning and Working
Unit Theme: A Job Well Done

Apple growers work hard not only during growing season but all year round.

Before Reading

Motivating the Reader

Build Background About Apples

Use Web 3 to record students' ideas about apples. Use each web strand as a category, and have students list related details in the strand's circles. Categories include physical attributes of apples, how they grow, how they are used, types of apples, and so on. Students can draw pictures and write captions about what is good about apples.

Preview and Predict

Have students scan the cover, text, and illustrations to get an idea of what the book is about. Ask them if the book is fiction or nonfiction and how they know. Encourage them to use the title and picture clues to make predictions about what information is in the book and how it is organized. Students can set their own purposes for reading, such as reading to learn how to tend an apple orchard or how to make apple cider.

Point out selection vocabulary and any unfamiliar words, such as *fertilizer, nutrients,* and *harvest,* that might be important to understanding the book.

During Reading

Guiding Comprehension

Use the following questions to support students as they read.

- **Pages 2–3** What time of year do these pages tell about? (They tell about mid-winter from January to March.) What happens in the orchard during this time? (Farmers use chainsaws and shears to prune the apple trees.)
- **Page 3** What are suckers? Why do growers remove them from trees? (Suckers are small branches. They take water and food from the apples.)
- **Pages 3–4** What does it mean to prune an apple tree? Use context clues and pictures to help you explain. (It means to cut away parts of an apple tree to help it grow better.)
- **Page 5** What happens in April and early May? (Growers spread fertilizer and weed killer.)
- **Page 6** Why is late May a tricky time? (It is when the apple trees blossom, but snow and frost may still come and damage the blossoms.)
- **Pages 7–8** Why do apple producers kill some buds in each cluster? (They direct the branch's nutrients to one bud to grow one big apple; otherwise you would have five small apples.)
- **Pages 9–11** What is a blemish? (It is some type of flaw, such as a mark or a bruise on an apple.) Why do you think blemished apples are okay for cider? (Apples get mashed in the grinder, so blemishes on the outside skins don't matter.)
- **Page 12** Why are cider containers made of stainless steel? (It won't react with cider to change the taste.)
- **Page 14** What happens after the cider is pressed from the crushed apples? (It is stored in a refrigerator tank until it is poured into jugs to be sold.)
- **Page 16** How is information in this book organized? (It is organized in chronological order to show what happens in each season.)

Ongoing Assessment

Reading Strategies

If... a student doesn't understand on page 6 how bees help apple growers,	**Then...** explain that when bees spread pollen it helps turn the blossoms into apples.
If... a student has trouble explaining how the text is organized,	**Then...** use **Model Your Thinking** below.

Model Your Thinking

Comprehension Skill: Text Structure

Text structure is the way a piece of writing is organized. Fiction texts are about made-up people and events. They usually are organized in chronological, or time order. Nonfiction texts are about real people, events, or information. They may be organized to show cause and effect, problem and solution, comparison and contrast, or chronological order. Since this book tells about real apple orchards, I know it is nonfiction. As I read, I notice the names of months and seasons. I see words that show time, like *first* and *then.* This book is organized according to chronological order. Identifying the text structure helps me figure out how to read the book. I read slowly and carefully to learn what happens in each month.

After Reading

Revisiting the Text

Comprehension Students can use the Time Line on page 143 to show the book's chronological text structure. Write the seasons or months on the short lines below the time line. Have pairs or groups fill in on the slanted line the events that occur during this time period. Invite volunteers to imagine they are apple growers and have them use their time lines to tell what they see and do over the course of a year.

135A

Sheepdogs on Guard

by Susan McCloskey
Leveled Reader 135A
Genre: Informational Article
Level: Easy

Summary

Guard dogs are regular partners for many sheep ranchers. This book highlights the best breeds for the job, desirable traits, and proper training. It describes the dog's importance to the rancher and its fierce loyalty to the flock.

Leveled Reader Practice

After students have read *Sheepdogs on Guard,* use Leveled Reader practice page 182 to assess their understanding of the Leveled Reader and the target comprehension skill. Additional after reading activities are provided on page 67.

At a Glance

Links to the Student Edition

Comprehension Skill: Summarizing

Selection Vocabulary: *instinct, confusion, chaos*

Program Theme: Learning and Working
Unit Theme: A Job Well Done

Since ancient times, people have relied on animals to help them with their work.

Before Reading

Motivating the Reader

Build Background About Dogs

Show students pictures or videotapes of different dog breeds. Invite students to share what they know about the traits of each type of dog or about dogs in general. Write *Working Dogs* in the center of a word web on the chalkboard. Have students list different ways dogs and humans work together.

Preview and Predict

Have students scan the cover, text, and illustrations to get an idea of what the book is about. Ask students to use the pictures of the various sheepdogs to predict what traits are needed to be a good sheepdog. Suggest students read to find out if their predictions are correct.

Point out selection vocabulary and any unfamiliar words, such as *predators, dispositions, herders, guardians,* and *substantially,* that might be important to understanding the book. Model the pronunciations of the dog breeds shown.

During Reading

Guiding Comprehension

Use the following questions to support students as they read.

- **Page 2** How do sheep ranchers earn money? (by selling sheep for meat or selling their sheep's wool)
- **Pages 2–3** What problems do sheep ranchers have? (They have trouble protecting their sheep from predators.)
- **Page 3** What are the problems with using poison or traps against predators? (Poisons and traps can kill harmless animals.)
- **Page 4** When did sheep ranchers in the United States begin using sheepdogs to protect their sheep? (in the 1980s)
- **Page 7** What are three ways that different breeds of sheepdogs are alike? (They all have an instinct to guard, they are all big dogs that look somewhat alike, and they are gentle and calm.)
- **Page 7** What does *dispositions* mean? Use the next sentence to help you figure out the meaning. (It means "ways of acting toward others.")
- **Page 8** What does it mean that a guard dog is loyal to sheep? (They will protect and guard the sheep. They won't hurt them.)
- **Page 10** What does a sheepdog do if a predator approaches? (It tries to scare the predator off, tries to confuse it into backing away, or attacks the predator.)
- **Page 13** Why are young pups placed with sheep? (The pup thinks it is part of the flock and learns to be loyal to the sheep. The sheep see that the pup is a friend.)
- **Page 14** Why does an American sheepdog have a tougher job than a European sheepdog? (It must guard more land, work alone, watch for porcupines, and avoid traps.)
- **Page 16** What is the main idea of the book? (Using sheepdogs to guard sheep is a good solution to a difficult problem.)

Ongoing Assessment

Reading Strategies

If... a student does not understand predator, prey, and guardian,	**Then...** help the student use these terms to classify the different animals in the book.
If... a student has difficulty summarizing the book's main ideas,	**Then...** use **Model Your Thinking** below.

Model Your Thinking

Comprehension Skill: Summarizing

A summary tells the main ideas of a text or the plot of a story in just a few sentences. A good summary focuses on the most important information. It doesn't include unnecessary details or unimportant ideas. In a summary of this book, I would include these main ideas: *There is a long history of dogs being used as guards. Sheepdog breeds have many traits in common. The most important traits are an instinct to guard and loyalty. Ranchers and farmers who train and use dogs to guard their sheep will cut their losses to predators.* Summarizing information helps me be sure I've understood it and it helps me remember it.

After Reading

Revisiting the Text

Comprehension Write *Sheepdogs* in the center of Web 1 on page 132. Have students identify main ideas they would include in a summary of the book and record them on the web's outer lines. Then have them review the completed webs to make sure they include only the most important ideas. If appropriate, suggest combining some details under a more general statement.

135B

The Mystery of the Silver Stump

by Alice Mead
Leveled Reader 135B
Genre: Animal Fantasy
Level: Easy/Average

Summary

Life is good for the creatures at Umbagog Pond. Then two humans arrive, bringing a strange silver thing. Chaos breaks out as Turtle, Raccoon, and the others argue over the mysterious silver stump. They each think it is something different, but good. Each one wants it for himself or herself. They soon learn they've made a big mistake—the mysterious stump contains only rotting garbage. It is a garbage can!

Leveled Reader Practice

After students have read *The Mystery of the Silver Stump*, use Leveled Reader practice page 183 to assess their understanding of the Leveled Reader and the target comprehension skill. Additional after reading activities are provided on page 69.

At a Glance

Links to the Student Edition

Comprehension Skill: Summarizing

Selection Vocabulary: *sensible, raid, civil, unexpected*

Program Theme: Learning and Working
Unit Theme: A Job Well Done

The new and unknown can create suspicion and problems. When the good of the group is ignored, the problems multiply.

Before Reading

Motivating the Reader

Build Background About Animal Characters

Show pictures of a well-known fictitious animal character and its real-life counterpart. Have students tell how the fantasy character is similar to and different from the real-life animal. For example, a fantasy bear may talk, but a real bear growls. Both bears like honey. Have pairs of students use the Venn Diagram on page 147 to compare and contrast other pairs of fantasy and real-life animals.

Preview and Predict

Have students scan the cover, text, and illustrations. Encourage them to use word and picture clues to make predictions about the characters and events in the book. Point to the title and ask:

> When you see the word *mystery*, what story features do you expect? (a puzzle, clues, and a solution)

Suggest students read to find out what the mystery of the silver stump is and how the mystery is solved.

Point out selection vocabulary and any unfamiliar words, such as *obvious, rare, heron,* and *loon,* that might be important to understanding the book.

During Reading

Guiding Comprehension

Use the following questions to support students as they read.

- **Page 2** **Where does this story take place?** (at Umbagog Pond) **What is the pond like?** (It is quiet, safe, and peaceful. The animals all watch out for one another.)
- **Pages 2–3** **What types of creatures are the two strangers? How do you know?** (Descriptions of them as tall, living in a cabin, and paddling a log (canoe) suggest they are humans. The illustration shows human figures.)
- **Pages 3–4** **What do the animals think the silver thing is?** (Each animal thinks it is something different, but all think it is something good.) **How does the appearance of the silver stump affect the animals?** (They each want to have it. They begin arguing about it with one another.)
- **Page 5** **What feature of the stump changes daily?** (Its smell changes.) **What do you think the stump is? Why?** (Students may be able to use story clues to predict that it is a garbage can.)
- **Page 7** **Why does Turtle think the stump is his cousin?** (because the stump has a hard outer shell like a turtle) Repeat this question for the Chipmunk and the Raccoon to help students understand that each character thinks the stump is similar to something they are familiar with—a turtle shell, a nut, and an egg.
- **Page 9** **Why do the animals guard the stump?** (They think it is valuable, and they're afraid someone may steal it.)
- **Page 13** **How do the animals feel about what Raccoon did? How do you know?** (They're angry. They boo and hiss at Raccoon.)
- **Pages 15–16** **What does the silver stump turn out to be?** (a garbage can full of trash) **What happens to life at the pond once the mystery of the silver stump is solved?** (Life returns to the way it used to be.)

Ongoing Assessment

Reading Strategies

If... a student has difficulty reading and understanding how the relationships among the animals change,	**Then...** have the student focus on the dialogue and words describing how it is said, such as *snapped.*
If... a student predicts that the silver stump is a garbage can early in the story,	**Then...** praise the student for identifying important clues.
If... a student has difficulty summarizing,	**Then...** use **Model Your Thinking** below.

Model Your Thinking

Comprehension Skill: Summarizing

Summarizing means telling the main ideas of a text or what happens in a story in just a few sentences. A good summary of a fiction story focuses on the most important events, such as the problem, how the characters deal with it, and how it is solved. It doesn't include unnecessary details, repeated actions or thoughts, or unimportant ideas. A summary of this book might be: *The animals at the pond are curious about the secret contents of a mysterious silver object. Their curiosity turns to greed, and soon the animals are all fighting over the stump. They decide the only way to solve the problem is to open up the stump. The silver stump turns out to be a worthless garbage can. Life at the pond returns to normal.*

After Reading

Revisiting the Text

Comprehension Have small groups reread the book and use the Story Sequence organizer on page 139 to record important story elements. Invite each group to use its organizer to act out their favorite part of the story.

136A When in Rome

by Jeffrey B. Fuerst
Leveled Reader 136A
Genre: Time Fantasy
Level: Easy

Summary

When the narrator is suddenly sent back in time to see how the Romans ate, he learns first-hand that good table manners mean different things to different people.

Leveled Reader Practice

After students have read *When in Rome,* use Leveled Reader practice page 184 to assess their understanding of the Leveled Reader and the target comprehension skill. Additional after reading activities are provided on page 71.

At a Glance

Links to the Student Edition

Comprehension Skill: Compare and Contrast

Selection Vocabulary: *winced, records, dismayed*

Program Theme: Traditions
Unit Theme: Time and Time Again

While many traditions stay the same over long periods of time, some traditions have certainly changed, such as the Roman custom of burping to say "Thanks for the good meal."

Before Reading

Motivating the Reader

Build Background About Table Manners

Ask students to describe the ways different foods are eaten. List ideas on the chalkboard. Then have students use the Four-Column Chart on page 152. They complete the top row with tools used for eating such as spoon, fork, fingers, and chopsticks. Then students write the types of foods that are eaten with each tool. Encourage students to think about what kinds of table manners are appropriate in different circumstances.

Preview and Predict

Have students scan the cover, text, and illustrations to get an idea of what the book is about. Read the first paragraph aloud and point out the pronoun *I,* which indicates someone is telling a story. Encourage students to use picture and word clues to make predictions about where and when the story take place and what happens to the narrator. Suggest students read to find out about food customs in ancient Rome.

Point out selection vocabulary and any unfamiliar words, such as *barbarian, etiquette, custom,* and *time machine,* that might be important to understanding the book. You might also wish to point out unfamiliar vernacular, such as *my kind of place, wackiest, cracked up, bust a gut, P-tooey,* and *doggie bag.*

During Reading

Guiding Comprehension

Use the following questions to support students as they read.

- **Page 3** **What is Uncle Kronos's latest invention? What does he do with this invention?** (It's a remote-controlled time machine. He sends the narrator back in time to ancient Rome.)
- **Page 4** **What is another word that means the same as *dismayed*?** (annoyed, alarmed, upset)
- **Page 5** **Why does the host think the narrator is the leader of the barbarians?** (He dresses differently and is wearing a nobleman's purple stripe.)
- **Page 5** **If you lived in Rome at this time, where would you sit to eat?** (on a stool in front of the adults)
- **Page 6** **What is a dining couch? What do we use today instead of dining couches?** (It's a place where people lie down and eat. Today, most people use chairs.)
- **Page 7** **Why does the Freckle Lady say the narrator eats like a barbarian?** (She thinks he is a barbarian because he uses all five fingers of his left hand to eat instead of using only three fingers of the right hand.)
- **Page 9** **Why did the ancient Romans congratulate someone who sneezed?** (They thought it got rid of sickness.)
- **Page 10** **What behavior of the ancient Romans does the boy find rude?** (pointing)
- **Page 12** **How did Romans clean their fingers while eating?** (They wiped them on bread or on a large serviette.) **How do we keep our fingers clean while eating today?** (We use a napkin to wipe them clean.)
- **Page 16** **Why do you think the narrator's uncle sent him back in time to ancient Rome?** (The uncle wanted to teach the narrator about the importance of good table manners when eating.)

Ongoing Assessment

Reading Strategies

If... a student does not understand the humor in the book,	**Then...** have him or her contrast the Roman custom with today's modern ways of behaving at the dinner table.
If... a student has trouble with the book's use of vernacular,	**Then...** partner that student with a more proficient reader.
If... a student has difficulty comparing and contrasting characters or events in the book,	**Then...** use **Model Your Thinking** below.

Model Your Thinking

Comprehension Skill: Compare and Contrast

When you compare, you tell how two or more things are alike. When you contrast, you tell how they are different. In this book, I can compare and contrast what I know about table manners today with those in Rome long ago. Each time the boy does something to upset the party guests, I learn something new about the table manners of the ancient Romans. In this book, we learn about the Roman's custom of washing hands. I wash my hands before and after eating, but I don't wash my feet and I don't wash between each course of food.

After Reading

Revisiting the Text

Comprehension Ask students to reread the book, noticing all the eating customs that are unfamiliar to the boy. Have them use the T-Chart on page 150 to list the customs of the Romans on the left side. Then have them write about modern table manners on the right side. Students can use their charts to compare and contrast table manners in ancient Rome to their own customs. Invite volunteers to act out the differences in table manners.

136B

From the High Hills

The Hmong of Laos

by Anne Sibley O'Brien
Leveled Reader 136B
Genre: Informational Article
Level: Easy/Average

Summary

This books describes the Hmong living in the mountains of Laos. The traditions and beliefs of these people helped them survive the hardships of refugee life and the challenges of resettlement in new and strange countries.

Leveled Reader Practice

After students have read *From the High Hills: The Hmong of Laos,* use Leveled Reader practice page 185 to assess their understanding of the Leveled Reader and the target comprehension skill. Additional after reading activities are provided on page 73.

At a Glance

Links to the Student Edition

Comprehension Skill: Compare and Contrast

Selection Vocabulary: *impression, insult, sprouts*

Program Theme: Traditions
Unit Theme: Time and Time Again

People displaced from their countries bring their traditions with them to enrich their new homes.

Before Reading

Motivating the Reader

Build Background About Immigrants

Explain that large groups of people are sometimes forced to leave their homes because of war or famine. Use Web 2 on page 133. Have students write the words *moving to a new country* in the center of the web. Then have them complete the web by describing some challenges faced by people in a new and strange country. Have students share their ideas and webs. Invite any students whose families have faced sudden relocation to share their experiences.

Preview and Predict

Have students scan the cover, text, and illustrations to get an idea of what the book is about. Have students locate Laos on one of the maps. Explain that the Hmong are a group of people from this area. Ask students to use the illustrations to predict some things they will learn about the Hmong as they read the book. To help students set a purpose for reading, have them think of a few questions about the Hmong. Then suggest they read to look for the answers to their questions.

Point out selection vocabulary and any unfamiliar words, such as *headman, ritual,* and *refugee,* that might be important to understanding the book.

During Reading

Guiding Comprehension

Use the following questions to support students as they read.

- **Page 2 What kind of work did the Hmong do in their villages?** (They built their own houses, raised animals, and grew crops. They built a system of bamboo pipes to carry water from streams to the villages and fields.)
- **Page 3 Why didn't many people know that the Hmong existed?** (The Hmong kept mostly to themselves high up in the hills, so not many people got to meet them.)
- **Page 6 Why did the Hmong move from China to Laos?** (The Hmong were considered outcasts by some Chinese. They were forced to keep moving to stay safe from those who wanted to get rid of them. Laos was a safe place for them for many years.)
- **Pages 8–9 What dangers did the Hmong face when they escaped to Thailand?** (There were soldiers in the forests. They didn't have enough supplies. They had to cross the Mekong River, even though many couldn't swim.)
- **Page 11 How did the Hmong try to hold on to their way of life in the refugee camps?** (They planted vegetable gardens, and the women sewed flower cloths.)
- **Page 13 How was the role of the headman in the refugee camp like the role of a headman in the village?** (In both situations, the headman made decisions for the group, was respected for his leadership, and helped the group retain their traditions.)
- **Page 15 What new experiences did the Hmong have when they moved to a new country?** (They had to fly in an airplane. They had to learn to use new things such as washing machines. They had to learn new languages, adapt to new cultures, and find new ways to make a living.)

Ongoing Assessment

Reading Strategies

If... a student doesn't understand that the word *Hmong* refers to a group of people,	**Then...** give examples of other words, such as *Americans,* that describe an entire group of people.
If... a student has difficulty comparing and contrasting,	**Then...** use **Model Your Thinking** below.

Model Your Thinking

Comprehension Skill: Compare and Contrast

When you compare, you tell how things are alike. When you contrast, you tell how they are different. This book tells all about the lives of the Hmong. You can better understand them by comparing and contrasting what you have learned about them. You can compare and contrast their lives before and after the Vietnam War or their lives in Laos to their lives in their new countries. For example, on page 15, the author points out many of the new experiences the Hmong had when they moved to a new host country, such as using cars, washing machines, and electric stoves. The Hmong also learned new languages and cultures. At the same time, the Hmong also made sure to bring their own traditions like the flower cloths with them.

After Reading

Revisiting the Text

Comprehension Have pairs reread the book looking for comparisons between the Hmong's traditional way of life and their lifestyle today in the United States. Students can use the Venn Diagram on page 147 to record their comparisons and contrasts. Students can also compare and contrast the traditions of the Hmong to students' traditions or compare life in the village to life in the refugee camps.

137A

Alone in the Arctic

by Diane Hoyt-Goldsmith
Leveled Reader 137A
Genre: Realistic Story
Level: Easy

Summary

George and his family are Inupiat who live in the wilderness near Nome, Alaska. George thinks he will make a short and simple trip to a neighbor nearby, but a slip on the ice and a sudden storm put him in great danger. Lost and injured in the blizzard, George saves himself by remembering what his grandfather did in a similar situation.

Leveled Reader Practice

After students have read *Alone in the Arctic,* use Leveled Reader practice page 186 to assess their understanding of the Leveled Reader and the target comprehension skill. Additional after reading activities are provided on page 75.

At a Glance

Links to the Student Edition

Comprehension Skill: Main Idea and Supporting Details

Selection Vocabulary: *injuries, obstacles, overtakes, wilderness*

Program Theme: Traditions
Unit Theme: Time and Time Again
Strategies for survival in extreme situations are often passed on in stories from one generation to the next.

Before Reading

Motivating the Reader

Build Background About Snowstorms

Ask students to imagine they are lost in a snow storm. Discuss the types of things and actions that could help them survive. Have students use Web 2 on page 133. Have them write *surviving a snow storm* in the center oval and add their survival ideas in the outer ovals. Invite students to share and discuss their webs.

Preview and Predict

Have students scan the cover, text, and illustrations to get an idea of what the book is about. Point out the rock structure that appears on pages 10, 11, and 12. Ask students to make predictions about why the boy is building this structure. Encourage students to use the illustrations to predict the sequence of events in the story. They can record their predictions in the Story Prediction organizer on page 131 and then read to check whether their predictions are accurate.

Point out selection vocabulary and any unfamiliar words, such as *parka, muktuk, slab, snowbank, crust,* and *harpoon,* that might be important to understanding the book. List selection vocabulary and these words in the top box of students' Story Prediction organizers to help them make accurate predictions.

During Reading

Guiding Comprehension

Use the following questions to support students as they read.

- **Pages 4–5** **Why is George walking in the wilderness alone?** (He is on his way back from delivering medicine to Elly. George's dad thought George was now old enough to make this short trip on his own.)
- **Pages 4–5** **What preparations does George make for his return trip?** (He has a warm parka and some food.)
- **Page 5** **What is *muktuk*? What context clues help you figure this out?** (*Muktuk* is a snack of raw whale blubber. *Muktuk* is defined in the two sentences following the word.)
- **Page 6** **Do you think it was smart of George to decide to take the shortcut across the creek? Give reasons for and against his decision.** (It might make the trip shorter, but crossing the creek might be dangerous.)
- **Page 7** **How does George get across the creek?** (He uses a slab of ice as a raft and then guides the raft with an old tent pole.)
- **Pages 10–11** **Why is George building a tower with rocks?** (The tower will help his family find him in the snow.) **How did George know to build this tower?** (He remembered a story his grandfather had told him about getting lost and building a tower of rocks so the family could find him.)
- **Page 13** **What does this picture help show?** (It shows the hole George dug in the snow.)
- **Page 13** **What do George's actions tell you about him?** (They show he is smart and brave. He stays calm and remembers what his grandfather has taught him about survival.)
- **Page 16** **Why does George's father give him the seal?** (He gives it to George because he is proud of him.)

Ongoing Assessment

Reading Strategies

If... a student does not understand the phrase *fear overtakes* on page 13,	**Then...** point out that fear is compared to a person or an animal. When you are afraid, you may feel that you have been chased and captured by the emotion fear.
If... a student has difficulty identifying the book's main idea and supporting details,	**Then...** use **Model Your Thinking** below.

Model Your Thinking

Comprehension Skill: Main Idea and Supporting Details

To find the main idea of a fiction story, ask yourself what the story is all about. Then look for details in the story that support your answer. This book tells all about George's struggle to survive a snow storm in the wilderness. The pictures on pages 8, 11, and 13 show me some of the things George does to survive. Other story details, such as the description of the storm on page 10 and George's feelings of fear and loneliness on page 12, also support the main idea.

After Reading

Revisiting the Text

Comprehension Have pairs reread the book and complete the Main Idea organizer on page 142. Above the top box, write the question: *What is the book all about?* Have pairs work together to write the main idea in the top box. Then they should use the bottom three boxes to write words or draw pictures of details from the book that support their answer. Have pairs exchange organizers and compare them.

137B

A Very Cool Festival

by Sheri Reda
Leveled Reader 137B
Genre: Informational Article
Level: Easy/Average

Summary

The residents of Sapporo, Japan, have found a "cool" way to turn the cold and snowy days of winter into a time of festival. Every February, the intricate snow sculptures of the Sapporo Snow Festival draw visitors and snow sculptors from all over the world.

Leveled Reader Practice

After students have read *A Very Cool Festival,* use Leveled Reader practice page 187 to assess their understanding of the Leveled Reader and the target comprehension skill. Additional after reading activities are provided on page 77.

At a Glance

Links to the Student Edition

Comprehension Skill: Main Idea and Supporting Details

Selection Vocabulary: *announcer, cargo, delays, skids*

Program Theme: Traditions
Unit Theme: Time and Time Again

Sometimes traditions are created almost by accident. A successful event is repeated the next year and the year after that. With the passing years, the event becomes a local tradition.

Before Reading

Motivating the Reader

Build Background About Sculpture

Explain that a sculpture is a three-dimensional or solid work of art. Sculptures can be made of stone, metal, sand, and even snow. If students have built snowmen or other snow sculptures, have them share their experiences. If not, have them talk about sand sculptures or any other type of sculpture they have made or seen. Encourage students to speculate on reasons that people go to museums and other places to see sculptures.

Preview and Predict

Have students scan the cover, text, and illustrations to get an idea of what the book is about. Explain that the structures in the illustrations are made of snow. Ask how the word *cool* in the title can have more than one meaning. Then have students make predictions about what kind of festival the book will tell about and why this festival is described as a cool festival. Suggest students read to find out how these snow sculptures are created.

Point out selection vocabulary and any unfamiliar words, such as *festival, sculpture,* and *contestant,* that might be important to understanding the book.

During Reading

Guiding Comprehension

Use the following questions to support students as they read.

- **Page 2** **Why do so many people come to the town of Sapporo, Japan, in February?** (They go to a large outdoor festival.)
- **Page 4** **Why do you think the snow sculptures attracted so much attention?** (They were unusually large; they were a surprise to people passing by.)
- **Page 6** **How did the making of snow sculptures turn into a festival?** (Each year, the sculptures got larger and became more famous. People started coming from all over to see them, so the town decided to create a special yearly festival to celebrate this event.)
- **Page 7** **What new event took place at the festival in 1974?** (The town added an international sculpture contest to the festival.)
- **Pages 8–9** **What kinds of special clothing do people wear during the snow festival?** (long underwear, heavy jackets, hats, gloves, snow chains on shoes, body warmers)
- **Page 9** **What is the first step sculptors take to begin working on their sculptures?** (They have to get a cargo of snow down from the mountains.) **Why do you think people must bring extra snow into town for the sculptures?** (There are so many sculptures and sculptors now that there is not enough snow in town for all of them.)
- **Pages 9–13** **What information do these pages give?** (They describe the steps for making a snow sculpture.)
- **Page 15** **What is an abstract snow sculpture?** (It is one that doesn't look like a real object. It has interesting shapes instead.)
- **Page 16** **Do you think the author did a good job of explaining why this festival is a "cool" event? Why or why not?** (Answers will vary, but students should support their judgments with evidence from the text.)

Ongoing Assessment

Reading Strategies

If... a student has difficulty following the steps in making a snow sculpture,	**Then...** have the student make notes using the Steps in a Process organizer on page 148.
If... a student has difficulty identifying the book's main idea and supporting details,	**Then...** use **Model Your Thinking** below.

Model Your Thinking

Comprehension Skill: Main Idea and Supporting Details

The main idea of a book is the most important idea about the book's topic—what it is all about. Supporting details are smaller pieces of information that tell more about the main idea. In this book, the topic is the Sapporo Snow Festival. On page 16, the author says that the festival is a "cool" event—meaning it is something fun and interesting to see. I think this is the main idea of the book. To make sure, I check whether this idea covers all the important supporting details. Pages 2–7 tell where the festival is held, how it began, and describe some of the snow sculptures. Pages 8–12 tell how the snow sculptures are made. All these details support the main idea that the festival is a fun and interesting event.

After Reading

Revisiting the Text

Comprehension Have small groups reread the book and use the Main Idea organizer on page 142 to identify its main idea and important supporting details. Then have each group use its organizer to help them write a travel brochure about the festival.

138A

Soccer Bash

by Susan Blackaby
Leveled Reader 138A
Genre: Realistic Story
Level: Easy

Summary

Corky isn't at all sure that she wants the new girl Billie at her tenth birthday party, although her friend Becky tries to convince her to give Billie a chance. An accident during a soccer game provides a chance for Corky to get to know Billie better. Corky decides to invite Billie, and her party is a great success. Corky not only gets an interesting present, she also makes a new friend.

Leveled Reader Practice

After students have read *Soccer Bash,* use Leveled Reader practice page 188 to assess their understanding of the Leveled Reader and the target comprehension skill. Additional after reading activities are provided on page 79.

At a Glance

Links to the Student Edition

Comprehension Skill: Predicting

Selection Vocabulary: *lodge, bruised, pouch*

Program Theme: Traditions
Unit Theme: Time and Time Again

Sometimes it can be difficult to allow a new person to join an old traditional gathering.

Before Reading

Motivating the Reader

Build Background About Friendship

Invite students to share experiences of how they have made friends. Encourage them to tell about a friend they made that they weren't sure they would like when they first met that person. Then ask small groups to role-play situations about meeting someone new and becoming friends.

Preview and Predict

Have students scan the cover, text, and illustrations to get an idea of what the book is about. Have students use the Story Prediction organizer on page 130 to predict what problem they think the book will show. Suggest they read to find out if their predictions are accurate. They can complete their organizers after they read the book.

Point out selection vocabulary and any unfamiliar words that might be important to understanding the book. Discuss the two possible meanings for the word *bash*. You might also wish to have a volunteer describe the basic rules for soccer.

During Reading

Guiding Comprehension

Use the following questions to support students as they read.

- **Page 3** **What is Corky's problem?** (She doesn't want to invite the new girl Billie to her party, but her mom says she has to invite Billie.)
- **Pages 2–3** **How does Corky feel? How do you know?** (She is upset about having to invite Billie to the party. She yanks and punches at her shoelaces. She sighs. The picture shows her frowning.)
- **Pages 4–5** **How does Corky intend to solve her problem?** (She decides not to go to her own party.) **Do you think this is a good solution to the problem? Why or why not?** (Most students will likely say that Corky should try to get to know Billie better and that missing the party is hurtful to everyone, including Corky herself.)
- **Pages 8–9** **What happens next?** (Billie kicks the ball and it hits Corky in the face.) **What do you think will happen next?** (Possible answers: Corky and Billie will get into a fight. Corky may see how sorry Billie is and begin to like her.)
- **Page 11** **How does Billie feel about hitting Corky with the ball? How do you know?** (She feels miserable. She apologizes to Corky. Her usual smile disappears. She starts to cry.)
- **Pages 11–12** **Why does Corky change her mind about having Billie at her party?** (She realizes that Billie wants to be friends. She feels sorry that Billie is so upset.)
- **Page 12** **How do you think the story will end?** (Billie will go to Corky's party, and everyone will have a great time.)
- **Page 16** **How does Corky feel about Billie now?** (She likes her and is glad Billie came to her party.)

Ongoing Assessment

Reading Strategies

If... a student is confused by the transition to the lodge on pages 6 and 7,	**Then...** have the student restate the phrase "her mind was in the mountains" in his or her own words.
If... a student has difficulty making accurate predictions,	**Then...** use **Model Your Thinking** below.

Model Your Thinking

Comprehension Skill: Predicting

To predict means to tell what you think will happen next. To make a good prediction, I think about what I've already read and what I know from my own experiences. Then I continue reading to see if my prediction is correct, or I change my prediction based on new information. For example, when Billie kicks a ball into Corky's face, I predicted that Corky would be even more angry with Billie and might tell her not to come to the party. I know that Corky is already upset about having to invite Billie. I also know that a person can lose his or her temper over a situation like this. As I read page 11, I discover that Corky is surprised by how upset Billie is about the accident. I change my prediction because I now think Corky and Billie will be able to work out their problems.

After Reading

Revisiting the Text

Comprehension Have students reread the book and draw a picture of the story's problem in the Story Prediction organizers they started before reading. Discuss students' initial predictions, whether their predictions changed, and how the problem is resolved.

138B

Night Journey

by Lynn Cullen
Leveled Reader 138B
Genre: Realistic Story
Level: Easy/Average

Summary

Nurse midwives can never be certain of when their help will be needed at a birth. Most of them carry pagers, and they often work at night. In this book, a nurse-midwife narrator describes her thoughts and feelings as she drives to the hospital one night to help a mother give birth. She reflects on the role of midwives in the past and compares her own journey to a baby's journey into life.

Leveled Reader Practice

After students have read *Night Journey*, use Leveled Reader practice page 189 to assess their understanding of the Leveled Reader and the target comprehension skill. Additional after reading activities are provided on page 81.

At a Glance

Links to the Student Edition

Comprehension Skill: Predicting

Selection Vocabulary: *possession, reckless*

Program Theme: Traditions
Unit Theme: Time and Time Again

All professions, including that of being a midwife, have their own history and traditions.

Before Reading

Motivating the Reader

Build Background About Midwives

Explain to students that a *midwife* is a person who helps when a baby is born. Have students use Web 1 on page 132 to write some of the things a midwife might do or experience while working. Students might include such descriptions as: has unpredictable hours, experiences the joy of a new life, worries that something might go wrong. Encourage students to think about whether they would like to be a midwife as they read the book.

Preview and Predict

Have students scan the cover, text, and illustrations to get an idea of what the book is about. Draw their attention to the book's title and ask them to make predictions about who is making a night journey and why. Have students use the T-Chart on page 150. They can record their predictions on the left side of the chart and what actually happens on the right side. Encourage students to make, record, and check additional predictions as they read.

Point out selection vocabulary and any unfamiliar terms, such as *midwife, expectant mother,* and *certified,* that might be important to understanding the book.

During Reading

Guiding Comprehension

Use the following questions to support students as they read.

- **Page 3** **Who do you think is telling this story? How do you know?** (Answers may vary. The first sentence should help them predict that it is someone who helps deliver babies.) **When does this story take place?** (late at night)
- **Page 4** **Who is the narrator and where is she going?** (She is a midwife on her way to help deliver a baby.)
- **Page 4** **Why does the midwife say a pager is a very valued possession?** (A pager is an important tool for a midwife. It tells her when a baby is on the way. Expectant mothers can page the midwife if they have worries or if a problem occurs.)
- **Page 4** **What can you predict will happen in the book based on what you've read so far?** (A baby will be born.)
- **Pages 6–7** **What is the narrator describing on these pages?** (She is describing how people went to get a midwife in the past, before phones and pagers existed. A person might ride a horse or run barefoot through the streets to get a midwife.)
- **Page 8** **How are modern midwives different from midwives in the past? How are they the same?** (Different: Modern midwives are specifically trained and are certified to do their jobs. Before, midwives learned by experience. Same: Midwives do their job because they love to help deliver babies.)
- **Page 15** **What does a midwife do besides help deliver babies?** (She teaches a mother how to care for her unborn baby and herself.)
- **Page 15** **The word *journey* appears twice on this page. Is the same journey described each time? Explain.** (No. The first journey is a baby's passage into life; the second is the narrator's drive in her car.)

Ongoing Assessment

Reading Strategies

If... a student has difficulty understanding the term *expectant mother* on page 4,	**Then...** help the student identify the base word *expect* to figure out that it means "a mother who is expecting a baby."
If... a student has difficulty making accurate predictions,	**Then...** use **Model Your Thinking** below.

Model Your Thinking

Comprehension Skill: Predicting

Making a prediction means telling what you think will happen next in a story. Good readers make predictions using what they have read and what they already know. As they continue reading, they check to see if their predictions are correct or they revise their predictions based on new information. After reading page 3, I know that the narrator is driving at night and that she has something to do with babies being born. I predict that the narrator is someone who helps deliver babies, since I don't think a woman having a baby would be driving herself to the hospital. As I continue reading, I check to see if my prediction is correct. The text on page 4 tells me that the narrator is a certified nurse midwife.

After Reading

Revisiting the Text

Comprehension Have students return to the T-Charts they made before they began reading. If students did not complete the right side of the charts while reading, have them review the book and complete this side now. Discuss the predictions students made and whether they revised any of them.

139A

The Boy and the Eagle

A Pima Folk Tale

retold by Christopher Keane
Leveled Reader 139A
Genre: Folk Tale
Level: Easy

Summary

Kelihi is a Pima boy who longs for adventure. Disobeying his father, Kelihi climbs a mountain to find an eagle's nest. He is injured in a fall and dreams of a giant eagle who carries him home. When Kelihi awakes healed and near his home, he realizes it was not a dream after all. From his experiences, Kelihi learns the importance of respect and obedience.

Leveled Reader Practice

After students have read *The Boy and the Eagle: A Pima Folk Tale,* use Leveled Reader practice page 190 to assess their understanding of the Leveled Reader and the target comprehension skill. Additional after reading activities are provided on page 83.

At a Glance

Links to the Student Edition

Comprehension Skill: Context Clues

Selection Vocabulary: *responsible, overcame, ankle*

Program Theme: Traditions
Unit Theme: Time and Time Again

Traditional folk tales often tell of the great powers of animals. In this folk tale, a young boy is rescued by a giant eagle, who teaches him an important lesson.

Before Reading

Motivating the Reader

Build Background About Folk Tales

Ask students to share what they know about animals in folk tales. Write their responses on the chalkboard. If necessary, remind students that in many folk tales animals can talk and do surprising things. They often represent human qualities and can teach humans important lessons. Have volunteers describe similar examples from folk tales they've read or heard. Ask students to think about what role an eagle might have in a folk tale.

Preview and Predict

Have students scan the cover, text, and illustrations to get an idea of what the book is about. Draw students' attention to the boy and the eagle on the cover and ask them to predict what will happen in the book. Suggest students set their own purpose for reading, such as finding out why the boy is riding the eagle.

Point out selection vocabulary and any unfamiliar words, such as *gourd, mesquite, crevices,* and *eaglet,* that might be important to understanding the book.

During Reading

Guiding Comprehension

Use the following questions to support students as they read.

- **Page 2** **What do you know about the main character so far?** (He is a Pima boy named Kelihi whose family are farmers; he is restless and wants adventure.)
- **Page 4** **Why doesn't Kelihi's father want Kelihi to look for an eagle's nest?** (The mountain climb is difficult, and he thinks Kelihi is too young.)
- **Pages 4–5** **What does Kelihi decide to do?** (He decides to disobey his father, and he goes to climb the mountain.) **Do you think this is a good decision? Why or why not?** (Possible answer: No. He shouldn't disobey his father, and he could get hurt while climbing.)
- **Page 5** **What is a *ramada*? Point to it in the picture.** (It is an open structure where people can sleep. Students should point to the open structure on the left.)
- **Page 6** **Why does Kelihi sing a song of victory?** (He sings to celebrate reaching the top, especially since the climb was so difficult.)
- **Page 7** **What are *crevices*?** (They are cracks in the rock.) **How can Kelihi use crevices to climb?** (He can put his feet or hands in crevices to push or pull himself up.)
- **Page 9** **What causes Kelihi to fall?** (He is startled when the eaglet snaps at him, and he falls backward off the ledge.)
- **Page 11** **How does Kelihi feel about his adventure now?** (He is sorry he disobeyed his father's wishes.)
- **Pages 12–13** **What happens in Kelihi's dream?** (He speaks to a giant eagle and promises never to touch the eaglets again. The eagle gives Kelihi a ride off the mountain.)
- **Page 14** **Why is Kelihi surprised when he wakes up?** (He is back near his home and realizes his dream was real.)

Ongoing Assessment

Reading Strategies

If... the student is confused that the dream is real,	**Then...** remind the student that animals can often do fantastic things in folk tales.
If... a student can explain the meanings of unfamiliar words,	**Then...** praise the student and ask how he or she figured out these meanings.
If... a student has trouble using context clues to figure out the meaning of unfamiliar words,	**Then...** use **Model Your Thinking** below.

Model Your Thinking

Comprehension Skill: Context Clues

When I read a word I don't know, I use context clues—the words and sentences around the unfamiliar word or a nearby picture—to figure out what the word means. Sometimes the context will give a definition, an example, a word with nearly the same meaning, or a word with the opposite meaning. For example, on page 5, I can figure out the meaning of *ramada* because it is defined in the words that follow it: "an open structure close to the house." I look at the picture and can see the family sleeping in the ramada. The definition and the illustration help me figure out what this word means.

After Reading

Revisiting the Text

Comprehension Use the Vocabulary Chart on page 149. Write the selection vocabulary words and other key words in the first column. Have pairs locate the words in the book and use context clues to write a definition and sentence for each word. Allow students to verify definitions in dictionaries, if needed. Invite students to share their words, definitions, and sentences.

139B

Olympics

by Stacey Sparks
Leveled Reader 139B
Genre: Informational Article
Level: Easy/Average

Summary

This book explains the history of the Olympics from its beginnings in 776 B.C. through its revival in 1896 to present day. It details interesting events that occurred during these contests, such as the Roman emperor Nero's victory in every event he entered. It also describes the courage and achievements of selected athletes.

Leveled Reader Practice

After students have read *Olympics,* use Leveled Reader practice page 191 to assess their understanding of the Leveled Reader and the target comprehension skill. Additional after reading activities are provided on page 85.

At a Glance

Links to the Student Edition

Comprehension Skill: Context Clues

Selection Vocabulary: *athlete, confident, relay, sprint*

Program Theme: Traditions
Unit Theme: Time and Time Again

The Olympics is an athletic tradition that dates back to 776 B.C.

Before Reading

Motivating the Reader

Build Background About the Olympics

Conduct a class discussion about the Olympics to help students remember what they've seen while watching these events. If possible, show videotaped footage or photographs of different Olympic events. Have students use Web 2 on page 133. Have them write *Olympic Events* in the center and record details about four different events they have seen or know about in the outer circles. Invite students to share their webs.

Preview and Predict

Have students scan the cover, text, and photographs. Draw their attention to specific dates and the photographs and have them predict what time period this book will cover. Have students use the K-W-L Chart on page 135. They can list what they already know about the Olympics in the first column and record questions they predict the book will answer in the second column. Suggest students read to look for the answers to their questions. Students can complete their charts when they have finished reading.

Point out selection vocabulary and any unfamiliar words, such as *chariot, stadium,* and *marathon,* that might be important to understanding the book.

During Reading

Guiding Comprehension

Use the following questions to support students as they read.

- **Page 2** When were the first Olympic games held? (776 B.C.)
- **Page 4** When were women allowed to participate in the Olympics? (They were allowed to enter the 128th Olympics, about 500 years after the first Olympics were held.)
- **Page 5** What does the author mean when she says the Olympics reached its lowest point in A.D. 67? (That year, the Olympics were not a real competition because athletes were afraid to compete against the emperor. Nero won every event he entered.)
- **Page 6** Why did the baron believe the Olympics might help make wars less likely? (He thought international competition would help people from different countries understand one another better and thus be less likely to go to war.)
- **Pages 8–9** What was special about Spiridon Louis's marathon victory? (Many didn't even finish the race. He was a Greek, and the Greeks organized the first Olympics. He refused to take gifts for his victory.)
- **Pages 10–11** What do you think of the British official's actions? (Students will likely say that what he did was dishonest.)
- **Page 14** Use clues in the text to describe what happens in a relay race. (It is a race of four runners. A stick is passed from one runner to the next.)
- **Page 14** Why were Wilma Rudolph's Olympic victories particularly impressive? (She had a paralyzed leg when she was a child. She helped her team win the relay race even though her teammate dropped the stick.)
- **Page 16** How do you think the author feels about Olympic athletes? (She admires and respects Olympic athletes for their skill, talent, and determination.)

Reading Strategies

If... a student doesn't understand the use of B.C. and A.D.,	**Then...** draw a simple time line to help explain these dates.
If... a student has trouble using context clues to define words,	**Then...** use **Model Your Thinking** below.

Model the Skill

Comprehension Skill: Context Clues

When I come across an unfamiliar word while reading, I use context clues—the words or sentences near the unfamiliar word—to try to figure out the word's meaning. I look to see if the context includes a definition, an example, a synonym, or an antonym that is a clue to the word's meaning. For example, on page 4, I read the word *barred*. The next two sentences help me figure out that *barred* means the opposite of *allowed*. To check my understanding, I restate the sentence using my own definition, "not allowed," to see if it makes sense in the sentence. "At first, women, slaves, and foreigners were not allowed to compete." If I'm still not sure of the word's meaning, I can use a dictionary to check it.

After Reading

Revisiting the Text

Comprehension Have pairs choose five unfamiliar words from the book and write each word and its corresponding page number on an index card. Then have them review the text and and use context clues to write a definition for each word on another set of cards. Pairs can mix and exchange cards, challenging one another to match the cards. Students can use a dictionary to verify definitions as needed.

140A

Gifts

by Jim Fremont
Leveled Reader 140A
Genre: Realistic Story
Level: Easy

Summary

In this first-person narrative, a young girl describes fishing with her friend Michael on the day he is moving away. The narrator and Michael exchange special gifts as remembrances of their times together and as promises to stay in touch.

Leveled Reader Practice

After students have read *Gifts,* use Leveled Reader practice page 192 to assess their understanding of the Leveled Reader and the target comprehension skill. Additional after reading activities are provided on page 87.

At a Glance

Links to the Student Edition

Comprehension Skill: Author's Purpose

Selection Vocabulary: *reel, sheath, squished*

Program Theme: Traditions
Unit Theme: Time and Time Again

Important friendships often include sharing a special tradition, such as fishing.

Before Reading

Motivating the Reader

Build Background About Fly Fishing

Invite students to describe a special activity that they enjoy doing with a friend or family member. Ask how having someone share in the activity makes it special. Then explain that they will be reading a book about fly fishing. Bring pictures or show a videotape of fly fishing. Ask volunteers to identify the equipment used and steps for catching and releasing a fish. Ask students why fly fishing might be a good activity for two friends to share.

Preview and Predict

Have students scan the cover, text, and illustrations to get an idea of what the book is about. Ask students to make predictions about the relationship between the two characters and what the characters will do. Suggest students read to find out if their predictions are accurate. Remind them to check and revise their predictions as they read new information.

Point out selection vocabulary and any unfamiliar words, such as *poncho, whiz, rhythmic,* and *casting,* that might be important to understanding the book.

During Reading

Guiding Comprehension

Use the following questions to support students as they read.

- **Page 3** What does the narrator mean when she says, "The day matched my mood perfectly"? (It is not a nice day outside, so it means the narrator isn't in a good mood.) Why do you think the narrator feels this way? (Answers will vary, but students may conclude from the phone conversation that there is a problem between the two friends.)
- **Pages 4–5** Why were people surprised that Michael and the narrator became friends? (They had different interests.)
- **Pages 8–9** Why do you think Michael taught the narrator to think like a fish, a midge, or a grasshopper? (Thinking like a fish helps her figure out where a fish might be hiding. Thinking like the bugs helps her cast her fly so it fools the fish into thinking it's a real bug.)
- **Page 10** What is different about this fishing trip? (It is the last time the two will fish together before Michael has to move away.) What clues did the author give to hint about this event? (The two had nothing much to say on the phone. The narrator said her mood matched the rainy day.)
- **Page 12** What gifts do you think the narrator and Michael may have for each other? (Students may use clues about the characters to predict that Michael's gift will be related to fishing and the narrator's gift will be related to sports or a computer.)
- **Page 16** What is special about the gifts each person gave the other? (The gifts are reminders of the person, since they are related to activities each person likes. The computer will help the two friends stay in touch.)
- **Page 16** Why do you think the author wrote this book? (Possible answer: to entertain readers by telling an interesting story)

Ongoing Assessment

Reading Strategies

If... a student is confused by the two uses of *reel* on page 6,	**Then...** have the student tell how the word is used in each sentence, first as a verb and then as a noun.
If... a student has difficulty explaining the author's purpose,	**Then...** use **Model Your Thinking** below.

Model Your Thinking

Comprehension Skill: Author's Purpose

An author's purpose is the reason or reasons he or she has for writing something. Some of the reasons authors have for writing are to persuade, to inform, to entertain, and to express a mood or feeling. As I read the first two pages, I sense that there is something wrong between Michael and the narrator. I wonder why she says her mood matches the rainy day. I'm eager to read more. Because the author is presenting interesting characters who have an unusual friendship, I would say that the author's purpose is to entertain. Identifying an author's purpose helps me adjust how quickly or slowly I read. I read an entertaining book more quickly than I read a nonfiction book full of facts and detailed information.

After Reading

Revisiting the Text

Comprehension Use Web 1 on page 132. Have pairs write the author's purpose or purposes in the center of the web. Have them list details that support their choices at the ends of the web's spokes. Each pair can then write a short book review in which they describe key events, explain why they think the author wrote the book, and tell what they liked or didn't like about the book.

140B

The Great Auto Race of 1908

by Kana Riley
Leveled Reader 140B
Genre: Informational Article
Level: Easy/Average

Summary

The race is on to be the first automobile to travel around the world from New York to Paris. In 1908, cars were scarce and paved roads even scarcer. This book follows the travels of the American Thomas Flyer car and details the many difficulties its crew encountered before winning this unusual race.

Leveled Reader Practice

After students have read *The Great Auto Race of 1908,* use Leveled Reader practice page 193 to assess their understanding of the Leveled Reader and the target comprehension skill. Additional after reading activities are provided on page 89.

At a Glance

Links to the Student Edition

Comprehension Skill: Author's Purpose

Selection Vocabulary: *traditions, souvenirs, recall*

Program Theme: Traditions
Unit Theme: Time and Time Again

Racing to see who is fastest has a long tradition. In 1908, six cars and crews faced great obstacles in a race to be the first to drive around the world.

Before Reading

Motivating the Reader

Build Background About Map Reading

Use a globe to point out New York and Paris to students. Then have them find these two locations on a flat world map. Have students trace the route that will be described in the book—New York City, Albany, Buffalo, Wyoming, Idaho, San Francisco, Alaska, Seattle, across the Pacific Ocean to Russia, and on to Paris. Encourage students to imagine what they would see if they traveled this route.

Preview and Predict

Have students scan the cover, text, and illustrations to get an idea of what the book is about. To prepare students for reading, ask:

> Look at these photographs of cars. When do you think these photographs were taken? How are these cars like and unlike cars you see on the roads today?

Ask students to predict what types of adventures might happen in a long car race involving cars like those pictured. Suggest they read to find out more about the 1908 race.

Point out selection vocabulary and any unfamiliar words, such as *goggles, mechanic, contestant, spark plug,* and *penalty,* that might be important to understanding the book.

During Reading

Guiding Comprehension

Use the following questions to support students as they read.

- **Page 2** Why do you think it took so long to drive across the United States in 1908? (Cars were slower, and roads were not paved.)
- **Page 3** Who sponsored the race? (a Paris newspaper and a New York City newspaper) Why do you think two newspapers would sponsor such a race? (The race would make for interesting news. It would help them sell newspapers.)
- **Page 4** Why do you think car makers from around the world would enter the race? (Possible answer: to show people what their cars could do, to get publicity for their cars)
- **Page 5** What is another word that means almost the same as *throng?* (crowd) How do you think people felt about this race? How do you know? (People were excited about the race. Thousands of people came to watch.)
- **Pages 6–7** What problems did the Thomas Flyer crew have on the way to Albany? (The car kept getting stuck in the mud. They had to shovel a path through snow drifts. They hit a farmer's sleigh.)
- **Page 12** Did the cars drive the entire race route? (No. The cars sailed on boats from Seattle to Russia.)
- **Page 14** Why was the American car considered the winner when it came in four days after the Germans? (because the Germans had thirty days added to their travel time for using a train in Idaho)
- **Page 16** Why do you think President Roosevelt admired the drivers of the automobile race? (because they overcame great obstacles to finish and win the race)
- **Page 16** Why do you think the author wrote this book? (to inform readers about an interesting event in history)

Ongoing Assessment

Reading Strategies

If... a student cannot understand the consequences of the penalty against the Germans,	**Then...** have the student add thirty days to the Germans' finishing date and compare it to the Americans' date.
If... a student can explain why four cars might have dropped out of the race,	**Then...** praise the student for using details to draw logical conclusions.
If... a student has difficulty explaining why the author may have written the book,	**Then...** use **Model Your Thinking** below.

Model Your Thinking

Think ALOUD

Comprehension Skill: Author's Purpose

An author's purpose is the reason or reasons an author writes, such as to persuade, to inform, to entertain, or to express a mood or feeling. Since this book gives many interesting facts and details about a real race, I believe one reason the author had for writing this book was to inform readers about a special event in history. Identifying the author's purpose helps me decide how quickly or slowly I should read the text. With nonfiction books, I usually read more slowly to make sure I understand all of the information given. By the end of this book, I had learned a lot about the great 1908 car race.

After Reading

Revisiting the Text

Comprehension Use Web 1 on page 132 and write *To Inform* in the center. Have pairs reread the book and list things they learned about the race at the ends of the spokes. Discuss any other purposes they think the author may have had for writing this book. Then mount a world map on the bulletin board and help students use string and push pins to show the route of the car race.

141A

How I Settled the West

by Sharon Fear
Leveled Reader 141A
Genre: Tall Tale
Level: Easy

Summary

The narrator in this tall tale is determined to get the West settled once and for all. She packs her six children into a covered wagon, and the adventures begin. With the help of a singing coyote, some generous sleepy bears, and a herd of buffalo, she has their new farm all settled by the time her sailor husband joins the family.

Leveled Reader Practice

After students have read *How I Settled the West,* use Leveled Reader practice page 194 to assess their understanding of the Leveled Reader and the target comprehension skill. Additional after reading activities are provided on page 91.

At a Glance

Links to the Student Edition

Comprehension Skill: Setting

Selection Vocabulary: *stockings, splattered, parlor*

Program Theme: Journeys in Time and Space
Unit Theme: Traveling On

A determined woman sets out to settle the West. She succeeds by using her great strength and cleverness.

Before Reading

Motivating the Reader

Build Background About Pioneers

Use a map and historic photographs to initiate a discussion about the travels of pioneers who left their homes in the East to settle the western part of the United States. Have students share what they know about the experiences of these settlers. Describe some of the challenges these early pioneers faced. Then start a round robin story about the travels of an imaginary pioneer family. Each student can continue the story by describing different adventures of this family.

Preview and Predict

Have students scan the cover, text, and illustrations. Read aloud the first page with a great deal of expression. Then ask:

> Who is telling this story? What can you tell about the narrator so far? What kind of story do you think this will be? Do you think it will be realistic, funny, or sad?

If needed, explain that this book is a tall tale. Encourage students to use what they know about tall tales to make predictions about what kinds of characters and events will be in the book. Suggest they read to find out how the narrator settles the West.

Point out selection vocabulary and any unfamiliar words, such as *docked, shipshape, coyote, civil,* and *stampede,* that might be important to understanding the book.

During Reading

Guiding Comprehension

Use the following questions to support students as they read.

- **Page 2** **When does this story take place?** (It takes place long ago before the western part of the United States was settled.)
- **Page 2** **What goal does the narrator have? Is this goal something most people could do?** (She plans on settling the West. No one person could settle the West alone.)
- **Page 4** **What does *run down* mean?** (It means "to chase and catch.")
- **Page 4** **What unlikely events are described on this page?** (The mother chases and catches a rabbit, the daughter catches fish with her bare hands, and a coyote sings with the family.)
- **Page 6** **What is another word that means almost the same as *civil*?** (nice, polite)
- **Page 7** **Why does the robber say, "By thunder!"?** (He is surprised when the narrator lifts the wagon by herself.) **Why does the robber leave?** (He realizes how strong the narrator is and runs away scared.)
- **Page 8** **Why do you think this place is named Paradise?** (It is a good place to live with good land, water, and big trees.)
- **Page 9** **What is unusual about the events described on this page?** (The family builds a house, a barn, and a corral in just one day.)
- **Pages 10–12** **What problem does the family have?** (The family is freezing.) **How does the narrator solve it?** (She talks several bears out of their fur coats.) Repeat these questions for plowing the land.
- **Page 15** **Who do you think is shouting?** (Students should use story clues to predict that it is the narrator's husband.)
- **Page 16** **What words would you use to describe the narrator?** (Possible answers: smart, incredibly strong, fearless, loving)

Ongoing Assessment

Reading Strategies

If... a student is confused by the word *docked* on page 2,	**Then...** point out that the husband is a sailor and that a dock is a place where boats land. Encourage the student to look for other nautical words as he or she reads the book.
If... a student has trouble identifying the setting,	**Then...** use **Model Your Thinking** below.

Model Your Thinking

Comprehension Skill: Setting

The setting is the time and place in which a story happens. Sometimes the author tells exactly when and where the story takes place. Other times you have to figure this out using story details. For example, on page 2, the narrator talks about "settling the West," so I know the story takes place more than 100 years ago. Pages 8–12 describe Paradise, Texas, and the family farm in winter and in spring. Good readers also look to see how the setting affects story events. For example, the narrator's adventures happen *because* the story takes place in the wild West. It would be a very different story if it took place in another time or place.

After Reading

Revisiting the Text

Comprehension Write on the chalkboard: *On the Trail; Paradise, Texas (Winter); Paradise, Texas (Spring).* Have pairs choose one of these settings and use Web 2 on page 133 to record story details about it. Then have each pair draw a picture of an adventure the family has in the setting. Have pairs present their pictures.

141B

Molly McGill's Great Ride

by Dan Elish
Leveled Reader 141B
Genre: Time Fantasy
Level: Easy/Average

Summary

Molly McGill uses her singing talents to time travel ten years back in time and change the results of a mayoral election in which her father was defeated. Returning to the present, Molly finds her father is the current mayor, her family is living in the mayor's mansion, and her father's lying opponent is now busy stringing yo-yos.

Leveled Reader Practice

After students have read *Molly McGill's Great Ride,* use Leveled Reader practice page 195 to assess their understanding of the Leveled Reader and the target comprehension skill. Additional after reading activities are provided on page 93.

At a Glance

Links to the Student Edition

Comprehension Skill: Setting

Selection Vocabulary: *pavement, trolley, headlines, banners*

Program Theme: Journeys in Time and Space
Unit Theme: Traveling On

A young girl's trip to the past drastically changes her family's present.

Before Reading

Motivating the Reader

Build Background About Time Travel

Encourage students to share stories they know about characters who travel in time. Ask them to describe what sorts of things happen when someone time travels. If needed, point out that in some stories visits to the past can change what happens in the present or future. Ask students to suppose they could time travel to any place in the past or future. Have them use the Five-Column Chart on page 153 to describe the date and place to which they would travel, why they would go there, and what they would see and do. Invite students to share their charts.

Preview and Predict

Have students scan the cover, text, and illustrations to get an idea of what the book is about. Ask them to use word and picture clues to predict what Molly's great ride will be and how it will take place. Students can then read to find out if their predictions are accurate.

Point out selection vocabulary and any unfamiliar words, such as *complimented, unpleasant, funneling, mansion, horseshoes,* and *swooned,* that might be important to understanding the book.

During Reading

Guiding Comprehension

Use the following questions to support students as they read.

- **Page 2** **Where does this story take place?** (Mintville) **What is special about Mintville?** (It is the peppermint capital of the world.)
- **Page 5** **What is special about the trolley?** (If you sing very beautifully, the trolley will take you to the past.)
- **Page 6** **What does the expression "worked his fingers to the bone" mean?** (It means "worked very hard.")
- **Page 6** **What jobs do Molly's parents have?** (Her father strings yo-yos, and her mother fills pens with blue ink.) **Why does Molly say these jobs are unpleasant?** (The hours are long, and the work is probably boring.)
- **Page 8** **Why do you think the date is circled?** (Answers may vary, but students should recognize it is a hint that time travel in the trolley is possible.)
- **Page 10** **What does Molly learn from reading the banners?** (She finds out her dad ran for mayor ten years ago.)
- **Pages 10–11** **Who is Hamilton Gross? What is he like?** (He is the current mayor of Mintville. He is a bad mayor who misuses money and doesn't work hard.)
- **Page 12** **How might Mr. Gross's lie affect Molly's father?** (Because peppermint is the main industry of the town, people may not vote for someone who hates peppermint.)
- **Pages 14–15** **What happens when Molly sings?** (People stop and listen. Men cry. Women swoon. Mr. Gross confesses his lie and urges people to vote for Molly's father.)
- **Page 16** **What changes did Molly's trip to the past cause?** (Her father is now mayor. Her family lives in the mayor's mansion. Mr. Gross and his friends string yo-yos.)

Ongoing Assessment

Reading Strategies

If... a student doesn't understand the significance of the outcome of the election,	**Then...** have the student tell what happens if Mr. McGill loses and what happens if he wins.
If... a student has difficulty understanding the setting of the story,	**Then...** use **Model Your Thinking** below.

Model Your Thinking

Comprehension Skill: Setting

The setting is the time and place in which a story happens. Sometimes the author tells exactly when and where the story takes place. Other times you need to figure this out using story details. For example, on page 2, the author tells readers that the story takes place in Mintville. I can use the descriptive details and the illustrations to picture this busy town. The time in which the story takes place changes since Molly travels back in time. Once I read page 16, I realize Molly's trip to the past has now changed the present. The setting of this story is very important, so noting details about the time and place of this story helps me better understand what happens.

After Reading

Revisiting the Text

Comprehension Use the T-Chart on page 150. Have pairs label the columns of the chart: *Before Molly's Trip* and *After Molly's Trip.* Have pairs reread the story and record details about life in Mintville before and after Molly's trip. Have each pair create a set of "before" and "after" drawings with captions that tell how characters' lives changed because of Molly's trip.

142A
A Thousand Miles to Freedom

The Escape of Ellen and William Craft

by Veronica Freeman Ellis
Leveled Reader 142A
Genre: Narrative Nonfiction
Level: Easy

Summary
William and Ellen Craft, slaves on a plantation in Georgia, devised an unusual plan to escape north to freedom. Because of Ellen's pale complexion, she was able to disguise herself as a young white man and pretend to be William's master. By train and steamship, the couple made their way north to freedom, surviving several frightening close calls in the process. The Crafts later immigrated to England until the Civil War ended. They eventually returned to Georgia, this time as plantation owners.

Leveled Reader Practice
After students have read *A Thousand Miles to Freedom*, use Leveled Reader practice page 196 to assess their understanding of the Leveled Reader and the target comprehension skill. Additional after reading activities are provided on page 95.

At a Glance

Links to the Student Edition

Comprehension Skill: Paraphrasing

Selection Vocabulary: *plantation, slavery, runaway*

Program Theme: Journeys in Time and Space
Unit Theme: Traveling On

A dangerous trip north from Macon, Georgia, to Philadelphia, Pennsylvania, brings freedom to two runaway slaves.

Before Reading

Motivating the Reader

Build Background About Slavery

Invite students to share what they know about the practice of slavery in the United States. If necessary, remind them that before the Civil War (1861–1864) slavery was legal in many southern states, but not legal in northern states. Display a large map of the United States. At the time the events in the book take place, slavery was legal in Texas, Delaware, Maryland, Virginia, Kentucky, Missouri, and all the states south of the Virginia-Kentucky-Missouri borders. Have students use push pins to identify these states on the map. Encourage students to refer to this map as they read about Ellen and William Craft's journey to freedom.

Preview and Predict

Have students scan the cover, text, and illustrations. Ask students whether they think this book will tell about real people and events or imaginary characters. Encourage students to tell what picture or word clues they used to make this decision. Then have them predict what the book will be about. Students can set their own purpose for reading, such as finding out who the two people pictured on the cover are.

Point out selection vocabulary and any unfamiliar words, such as *disguise, docked, steamer,* and *conductor,* that might be important to understanding the book.

During Reading

Guiding Comprehension

Use the following questions to support students as they read.

- **Pages 2–3** *Who is the young white man?* (Ellen Craft, a slave with pale skin who is disguised as a man)
- **Page 3** *Do you think Ellen's disguise will work? Why or why not?* (Accept any reasonably supported answers.)
- **Page 4** *Why did Ellen's heart race?* (She is afraid that Mr. Cray will recognize her voice.)
- **Page 7** *What does this map show?* (It shows the route the Crafts took to Philadelphia. It shows how they traveled, by train and boat.)
- **Pages 8–9** *What problem do the Crafts have in Charleston?* (The chief customs officer wanted Ellen to sign her and William's names in a book. Ellen can't write.) *How is the problem solved?* (Ellen has bandaged her right hand so she has an excuse not to write. An army officer says Mr. Johnson (Ellen) is his friend, and the captain signs for Ellen.) Ask similar questions for the incidents in Wilmington and Baltimore.
- **Page 13** *How do you think Ellen sounded when she spoke to the man in the ticket office?* (confident, angry)
- **Page 14** *How long did it take Ellen and William to get from Macon to Philadelphia?* (five days)
- **Pages 15–16** *How are these two pages different from the previous pages?* (The text is set differently. Students should also recognize that these pages provide mostly statements of fact that summarize the Crafts' lives, unlike the previous pages, which tell a narrative account of their five-day journey.)
- **Page 16** *Why did the Crafts move to England?* (Because of the Fugitive Slave Law, the Crafts could still be captured and returned to their owners.)

Ongoing Assessment

Reading Strategies

If... a student has difficulty understanding the events on pages 8 and 9,	**Then...** help the student list all the characters and tell whether each one is or isn't helping the Crafts.
If... a student understands why the Crafts moved to England,	**Then...** praise the student for drawing logical conclusions about the Fugitive Slave Law.
If... a student struggles to explain events in his or her own words,	**Then...** use **Model Your Thinking** below.

Model Your Thinking

Comprehension Skill: Paraphrasing

Paraphrasing means explaining something in your own words. When I paraphrase, I make sure I have used my own words and that I have included all of the author's ideas. I also make sure I haven't changed the meaning of what the author has written or added my own opinions. For example, I can paraphrase the first paragraph on page 3 like this: "Because Ellen looked white, her husband decided she could disguise herself as a young white man and he could pretend to be her servant. They could then escape north to freedom."

After Reading

Revisiting the Text

Comprehension Assign students key passages or paragraphs from the book to paraphrase. Students can use the T-Chart on page 150, copying the text in the left column and writing a paraphrase of it in the right column. Have students retell the story by having each student read aloud his or her paraphrase in chronological order.

142B

Nelson Mandela

by Veronica Freeman Ellis
Leveled Reader 142B
Genre: Biography
Level: Easy/Average

Summary

Black South African leader Nelson Mandela has spent most of his life fighting to end apartheid in South Africa. He spent twenty-seven years in prison for his political demonstrations against the South African government. After many years of public demands to free Mandela, President F. W. de Klerk released Mandela in 1990. Soon after, Mandela was elected president of South Africa. This election was the first time black South Africans were able to vote.

Leveled Reader Practice

After students have read *Nelson Mandela*, use Leveled Reader practice page 197 to assess their understanding of the Leveled Reader and the target comprehension skill. Additional after reading activities are provided on page 97.

At a Glance

Links to the Student Edition

Comprehension Skill: Paraphrasing

Selection Vocabulary: *quickened, vow, liberty, unconscious*

Program Theme: Journeys in Time and Space
Unit Theme: Traveling On

Nelson Mandela helped lead black South Africans on a journey of change from the oppression of apartheid to the freedom of citizens with protected civil rights.

Before Reading

Motivating the Reader

Build Background About South Africa

Use a globe or world map to point out the location of South Africa. Define *apartheid* for students as a set of laws used to segregate black South Africans from the white minority. Discuss what students already know about the struggle for freedom in South Africa. Encourage them to compare and contrast the fight to end apartheid in South Africa to the fight for civil rights for African Americans in the United States.

Preview and Predict

Have students scan the cover, text, and photographs to get an idea of what the book is about. Encourage them to use what they know about biographies to make predictions about whom this book will be about and what sorts of information it will give about that person. Have students prepare to read by writing a few questions of inquiry they think the book will help them answer about Nelson Mandela, apartheid, or South Africa. Suggest students look for answers to their questions as they read.

Point out selection vocabulary and any unfamiliar terms, such as *apartheid, passes, protesters,* and *political prisoners,* that might be important to understanding the book. Show students how to use the pronunciation guides to help them pronounce words.

During Reading

Guiding Comprehension

Use the following questions to support students as they read.

- **Pages 2–3** **What event do these pages describe?** (They describe the release of Nelson Mandela from a South African prison.)
- **Page 3** **How do you think the author feels about Nelson Mandela? How do you know?** (The author admires Mandela and believes him to be a very important person. She compares Mandela to a king and says he "walked with dignity." She says his release is something the world will remember forever.)
- **Page 5** **How did Nelson Mandela learn to be a leader?** (He went to school and learned about African history. He watched his cousin, a chief, deal with people.)
- **Page 7** **What were some of the effects of apartheid?** (Blacks had to live in blacks-only towns and get passes to travel to other areas. They couldn't own land or vote.)
- **Page 8** **How did Nelson Mandela try to get the apartheid laws changed?** (As president of the ANC, he spoke out against the laws. He opened a law office to help Africans.)
- **Page 9** **What was does the word *tried* mean in this sentence?** (It means "to be put on trial.")
- **Page 10** **What happened as the result of the fight with police in Sharpeville?** (The ANC was banned. Mandela and others went to prison for helping the protesters.)
- **Pages 13–14** **What actions led to Nelson Mandela's release from prison?** (Possible answers include the continued work of Mandela's supporters, pressure from the U.S. and other countries, and President F. W. de Klerk's work to end apartheid.)
- **Pages 14–15** **What happened in 1994?** (Mandela was elected president of South Africa.) **What was special about this election?** (It was the first time blacks could vote.)

Ongoing Assessment

Reading Strategies

If... a student doesn't understand what political prisoners are,	**Then...** ask the student to think about why Mandela was arrested.
If... a student has trouble explaining events in his or her own words,	**Then...** use **Model Your Thinking** below.

Model Your Thinking

Comprehension Skill: Paraphrasing

Paraphrasing means explaining something in your own words. I think about what the author is trying to say and then I restate the author's ideas in my own words. For example, I could paraphrase the second paragraph on page 3 like this: "After being held prisoner for twenty-seven years, Nelson Mandela proudly walked through the prison gates." When I paraphrase, I make sure I use my own words. I include all of the author's ideas, without changing them or adding my own opinions. If I had left out the fact that he had been in prison for twenty-seven years or if I had said Mandela was imprisoned unfairly, then I would not be giving an accurate paraphrase of what the author wrote. Paraphrasing an author's ideas helps me check that I understand what I've read.

After Reading

Revisiting the Text

Comprehension Use the Time Line on page 143. Have pairs reread the book and find five passages with dates that tell about important events in Nelson Mandela's life. Have them write the dates below the horizontal line and write a paraphrase of each passage on the diagonal lines. Invite pairs to read their paraphrases aloud so students get a sense of how information can be restated in different ways.

143A Riding the Bullet

by Darrell H. Y. Lum
Leveled Reader 143A
Genre: Narrative Nonfiction
Level: Easy

Summary

Kenji convinces his sister and grandmother to ride the bullet train from Tokyo to Hiroshima. The bullet train is one of the world's fastest passenger trains, traveling up to 300 kilometers (about 162 miles) an hour. While his grandmother enjoys the more leisurely rides of slower trains and his sister likes the idea of flying, Kenji loves whizzing through tunnels and watching the world speed past.

Leveled Reader Practice

After students have read *Riding the Bullet*, use Leveled Reader practice page 198 to assess their understanding of the Leveled Reader and the target comprehension skill. Additional after reading activities are provided on page 99.

At a Glance

Links to the Student Edition

Comprehension Skill: Visualizing

Selection Vocabulary: *excursions, thrill*

Program Theme: Journeys in Time and Space
Unit Theme: Traveling On

Making a special trip with family members can create memories that last a lifetime.

Before Reading

Motivating the Reader

Build Background About Transportation

Ask students to name different ways to travel, such as by horse, bicycle, car, plane, train, or boat. Take a vote on a favorite way to travel and record the results on the chalkboard. Have small groups select one mode of travel. Give them copies of the Three-Column Chart on page 151. They can list sensory details in the first column that tell what a person might see, hear, feel, or smell using this mode of transportation. In the next two columns, they can list advantages and disadvantages of the method of travel. Give each group two minutes to convince other groups that their way of traveling is the best. Once everyone is finished, take a second vote and compare the results.

Preview and Predict

Have students scan the cover, text, and illustrations to get an idea of what the book is about. Encourage students to use picture and word clues to predict what the title *Riding the Bullet* means, where the events take place, and what the train riders will experience. Then have students read to find out more about Japan's bullet trains.

Point out selection vocabulary and any unfamiliar terms, such as *speed display, whoosh, cafeteria,* and *double-decked,* that might be important to understanding the book.

During Reading

Guiding Comprehension

Use the following questions to support students as they read.

- **Page 2** What is another word that means almost the same as *excursion?* (trip) What kind of excursion are Kenji and his family taking? (They are taking a bullet train from Tokyo to Hiroshima.)
- **Page 3** Why do you think the train is called a bullet train? (It travels at very high speeds.)
- **Page 3** Use context clues to figure out the meaning of *speed display.* (It is something that shows how fast the train is going.)
- **Pages 4–5** What does this map show? (routes for the bullet train in Japan) In which direction will Kenji's family be traveling? (west)
- **Page 4** Do Kenji's sister and grandmother want to take the bullet train? Explain. (His sister wants to go by airplane because it is faster. His grandmother wants to take a slow train so she can shop at stops on the route.)
- **Page 5** What convinces them to take the bullet train? (An airplane ride is too expensive. Kenji tells his grandmother she will be able to see Mount Fuji from the train. He promises to buy his sister peanuts and a rice ball.)
- **Pages 6–7** Which fact do you find the most interesting? Why? (Answers will vary.)
- **Page 8** Which paragraph on this page helps you picture what a bullet train looks like? (the first paragraph)
- **Page 14** How does Kenji's view change as the train leaves the city? (Instead of factories and office buildings, he sees farms, rice fields, bright sunlight, and clean air.)
- **Pages 15–16** Why does Kenji get excited near the end of the book? (His train passes another bullet train going in the opposite direction.)

Ongoing Assessment

Reading Strategies

If... a student confuses kilometers and miles,	**Then...** remind the student to check the units of measure carefully and tell him or her there are about 1.6 kilometers in 1 mile.
If... a student has difficulty visualizing,	**Then...** use **Model Your Thinking** below.

Model Your Thinking

Comprehension Skill: Visualizing

Visualizing means creating pictures in your mind as you read. To help me visualize, I combine what I already know with descriptive details in the book. I know what it is like to travel in a train, but I've never ridden in a bullet train. As I read, I look for words the author uses to describe the train. Sometimes an author will use imagery—words that give strong mental pictures. For example, "swooping in like a seabird" (page 9) helps me picture how fast the train can move. Authors also use sensory details—words that describe how something looks, sounds, smells, tastes, or feels. "Hissing whoosh" on page 9 helps me experience the sound and feel of the train stopping. If I have trouble visualizing, I reread the passage or read more slowly to make a better picture in my mind.

After Reading

Revisiting the Text

Comprehension Have students reread the book and use Web 1 on page 132 to record the descriptive details about the bullet train. Then have pairs create a magazine ad for the bullet train, using words and pictures to convince people to ride the train.

143B

Pound Pals

by Jeffrey B. Fuerst
Leveled Reader 143B
Genre: Animal Fantasy
Level: Easy/Average

Summary

Muggsy and Mitzi are two dogs from a city dog pound. Adopted by different owners and thrown into very different environments, Muggsy and Mitzi exchange letters describing their adventures in their new homes.

Leveled Reader Practice

After students have read *Pound Pals,* use Leveled Reader practice page 199 to assess their understanding of the Leveled Reader and the target comprehension skill. Additional after reading activities are provided on page 101.

At a Glance

Links to the Student Edition

Comprehension Skill: Visualizing

Selection Vocabulary: *clinging, feelers, gale*

Program Theme: Journeys in Time and Space
Unit Theme: Traveling On

Moving from a familiar neighborhood to a new and very different home can be as trying for a dog as it is for a person.

Before Reading

Motivating the Reader

Build Background About Point of View

Ask students to think of a favorite animal and make secret notes about this animal, such as what it looks like, how it moves, things it likes to do, things it likes to eat, and so on. Then ask students to imagine what this animal might say if it could talk. Invite them to pretend to be this animal and act out, with dialogue, an event that would likely happen in this animal's daily life. Challenge other students to guess what animal is being performed.

Preview and Predict

Have students scan the cover, text, and illustrations. Ask them to describe the two main characters (two dogs, Muggsy and Mitzi) and the structure of the book (an exchange of letters). Point out the different parts of a letter (greeting, body, close, signature, postscript) and the two decorative stationery borders to help students identify who is writing and who is receiving the letters. Encourage students to use word and picture clues to make predictions about what each character will write about. Suggest students read to find out more about Muggsy and Mitzi.

Point out selection vocabulary. Since this book contains several instances of idiomatic language and clever word play, you may also wish to preview these phrases before students begin reading.

During Reading

Guiding Comprehension

Use the following questions to support students as they read.

- **Page 3** How is Mitzi's new life different from how she lived before? (She now lives in the country, not the city. She has only one friend. She now has to get up early for a job.)
- **Pages 4–6** What happens to Muggsy? (He gets adopted by a fancy lady.) Are the lady and Muggsy alike or different? How do you know? (Students should use story details to conclude the two are very different.)
- **Page 9** What do you think will happen next? (Predictions may vary, but students should recognize that the fox tricked Mitzi into leaving so he could get into the henhouse.)
- **Page 11** What joke does Muggsy make? (He writes "ruff" instead of "rough." "Ruff" is a sound for a dog bark.)
- **Pages 11–12** Why do you think Muggsy says he wants to leave his new home? (He isn't used to being treated so well. He is embarrassed to be called silly names and dressed up in outfits.)
- **Page 14** What can you conclude from Muggsy's postscript? (He doesn't hate being dressed up as much as he pretends.)
- **Page 16** Why does Mitzi decide she likes country life? (The night sounds in the woods are so beautiful they make Mitzi smile.)
- **Page 19** Why does Muggsy decide his city life isn't so horrible? (He realizes he no longer has to worry about having food or a bed.)
- **Pages 21–22** How does Mitzi outfox the fox? (She gets fleas to jump on the fox. She makes the fox promise never to return before she tells the fleas to leave.)
- **Page 24** What clues tell you that Muggsy has accepted his new life? (He likes dog shows now. He wants people to think he is cute. He calls himself Russell.)

Ongoing Assessment

Reading Strategies

If... a student has trouble following what happens to each dog,	**Then...** have the student summarize events using a separate Plot/Story Sequence organizer (page 137) for each dog.
If... a student has difficulty visualizing characters and events,	**Then...** use **Model Your Thinking** below.

Model Your Thinking

Comprehension Skill: Visualizing

When I create pictures in my mind as I read, I am visualizing. Good readers visualize by combining what they already know with descriptive details in the book. Authors often describe things using imagery—words that give them strong mental pictures. They also use sensory details—words that describe how something looks, sounds, smells, tastes, or feels. For example, on page 3, I try to visualize Mitzi's new home. First I think about what I know about dogs and farms. Then I use the details about Gus, Flo, rabbits, the hen house, and sunrise to picture Mitzi working on this specific farm. If I have trouble visualizing, I reread or I read slowly to get a better picture.

After Reading

Revisiting the Text

Comprehension Assign pairs different letters to reread. Have pairs use the Five-Column Chart on page 153 to record sensory details that help them visualize what happens in the letter. Pairs can then illustrate what they visualize and write a summary of each letter. Have students present their drawings and summaries, either in letter order or by focusing on one character at a time.

144A

To Your Good Health

A Russian Tale

retold by Jan M. Mike
Leveled Reader 144A
Genre: Folk Tale
Level: Easy

Summary

Pavel is working in his shoe shop when Larissa, the czar's daughter, enters. It is love at first sight for this pair. Larissa returns to the shop each day to buy more and more items so that she can continue to see Pavel. The easily angered czar won't allow Pavel and Larissa to get married until Pavel—with Larissa's help—has survived three challenges and resisted a bribe of an enormous treasure.

Leveled Reader Practice

After students have read *To Your Good Health,* use Leveled Reader practice page 200 to assess their understanding of the Leveled Reader and the target comprehension skill. Additional after reading activities are provided on page 103.

At a Glance

Links to the Student Edition

Comprehension Skill: Context Clues

Selection Vocabulary: *superiors, disobey, issue, permission*

Program Theme: Journeys in Time and Space
Unit Theme: Traveling On

This folk tale tells of a time long ago when a young shoemaker must pass several dangerous tests to win the hand of the czar's daughter.

Before Reading

Motivating the Reader

Build Background About Folk Tales

Many folk tales include plots in which two characters, one poor and the other wealthy, fall in love. Before they can marry, the couple must first overcome several obstacles. Ask students to share examples of folk tales that contain these story elements. Have small groups use the Plot/Story Sequence organizer on page 137 to outline the typical events in such a tale. Invite groups to act out some of these tales. Each group can select a narrator to tell the story, while the other group members act it out.

Preview and Predict

Have students scan the cover, text, and illustrations to get an idea of what the book is about. Discuss the kind of story this book is. Encourage students to use what they know about folk tales to predict the kinds of events that are likely to occur in this book. Students can set their own purposes for reading, such as reading to find out what the title means or what happens to Pavel.

Point out selection vocabulary and any unfamiliar terms, such as *apprentice, czar, dancing slippers, decreed, high minister,* and *wild boar,* that might be important to understanding the book.

During Reading

Guiding Comprehension

Use the following questions to support students as they read.

- **Pages 2–3** **Do you think Pavel and Larissa are ordinary? Why or why not?** (Encourage well-supported answers.)
- **Page 5** **Why does Larissa own so many shoes, purses, belts, and gloves?** (Buying these items gives her a reason to see Pavel.)
- **Page 6** **What other word means almost the same as *decreed*?** (commanded, ordered)
- **Page 6** **What happens when the czar sneezes?** (Bells ring out. By law, everyone must shout, "To your good health!")
- **Page 9** **Why is Pavel acting the way he is?** (He wants to gain the czar's attention.)
- **Page 10** **Why does the czar throw Pavel into a bear cage?** (Pavel won't say "to your good health." The czar gets angry when Pavel asks permission to marry Larissa.)
- **Pages 11–13** **How does Pavel survive the bear cage?** (The bear won't attack if Pavel stares at it. Larissa and Pavel sing to the bear.) Ask similar questions about the boars and rats.
- **Page 14** **How many boars are in the pen?** (ten) **Is this number important?** (Yes. Pavel said he wasn't afraid of dying ten deaths.)
- **Pages 18–19** **How many rats do you think are in the rat pit? Why?** (one hundred; Pavel said he wasn't afraid of dying a hundred deaths.)
- **Page 22** **Why do you think the czar decides to offer Pavel treasure?** (He thinks Pavel only wants to marry Larissa because she is wealthy.)
- **Page 23** **Why does the czar change his mind about the marriage?** (He realizes how much in love the two really are.)

Ongoing Assessment

Reading Strategies

If... a student recognizes the significance of the number of boars and rats,	**Then...** praise the student for drawing logical conclusions.
If... a student cannot figure out the meaning of unfamiliar words,	**Then...** use **Model Your Thinking** below.

Model Your Thinking

Comprehension Skill: Context Clues

Good readers use context clues to figure out the meanings of unfamiliar words. Context clues may come just before and after the unfamiliar word or be in another part of the story or article. Context clues include synonyms, antonyms, definitions, explanations, or examples. On page 3, I can figure out what czar means because it is defined within the sentence. A czar is a Russian king. As I continue to read, the words king and respect help me figure out that superiors means "people who have a higher rank or more power than another person." To check my understanding, I reread the sentence and replace the unfamiliar word with my definition. If I'm still not sure what a word means, I can verify it by using a dictionary.

After Reading

Revisiting the Text

Comprehension Have pairs select five unfamiliar words and list them in the first column of the Vocabulary Chart on page 149. Have pairs use the book's context clues to figure out what each word means. In the chart's second column, students can write definitions and sentences for each word. Have pairs read their words, definitions, and sentences. Work together to revise definitions as needed.

144B

Passing Through Ellis Island

by Frank Brooks
Leveled Reader 144B
Genre: Informational Article
Level: Easy/Average

Summary

More than seventeen million immigrants passed through Ellis Island. This book describes the experiences many immigrants had when they arrived in the United States around 1907. After surviving a long sea voyage in crowded conditions, immigrants had to make their way through the health tests on Ellis Island before they could gain entry into the country. Today, Ellis Island is a museum with exhibits that tell the stories of these brave immigrants.

Leveled Reader Practice

After students have read *Passing Through Ellis Island,* use Leveled Reader practice page 201 to assess their understanding of the Leveled Reader and the target comprehension skill. Additional after reading activities are provided on page 105.

At a Glance

Links to the Student Edition

Comprehension Skill: Context Clues

Selection Vocabulary: *cable, translated, agreement, representatives*

Program Theme: Journeys in Time and Space
Unit Theme: Traveling On

Although immigrants faced many hardships on their journey to the United States, they also saw it as an opportunity to start a new life.

Before Reading

Motivating the Reader

Build Background About Immigration

Invite students to share stories about how their families came to live where they do today. Discuss important journeys that ancestors may have made, such as immigration to or relocation within the United States. Use a world map and have students use colored pins or yarn to trace these journeys. If some students have immigrated recently, have them share their experiences. Discuss how methods of travel and traveling conditions for immigrants have changed. Use the T-Chart on page 150 to compare immigration as it was a hundred years ago with immigration today.

Preview and Predict

Have students scan the cover, text, and illustrations. Students can complete the first two columns of the K-W-L Chart on page 135. Have them list what they already know about immigration and Ellis Island in the first column. In the second column, have them write questions about Ellis Island that they predict the book will help them answer. Students can complete the chart as they read or when they have finished reading.

Point out selection vocabulary and any unfamiliar words, such as *immigrant, immigration, administer,* and *baggage,* that might be important to understanding the book.

During Reading

Guiding Comprehension

Use the following questions to support students as they read.

- **Page 2** **What are immigrants?** (They are people who move from their homelands to another country.) **What happened at Ellis Island?** (Immigrants had to pass tests there in order to be able to stay in the United States.)
- **Pages 3–4** **Where is steerage?** (It is in the bottom of the ship, near the ship's engines.) **Why do you think third-class tickets were the cheapest?** (People had to stay in an area; they had poor food and little fresh air.) Ask similar questions about second- and first-class tickets.
- **Page 8** **Why was climbing the stairs a test?** (Doctors watched to see if people coughed, stopped, limped, or blinked while climbing.)
- **Page 11** **What happened to those who did not pass the health tests?** (They were either sent to a hospital or sent back home.)
- **Page 12** **Why were the doctors so worried about diseases?** (They wanted to prevent U.S. citizens from catching diseases from immigrants. They wanted to make sure immigrants were healthy enough to work.)
- **Page 14** **Why do you think inspectors asked people about their plans for earning money or whether they had family to meet them?** (They wanted to make sure that the immigrants had a way to take care of themselves or had family to take care of them.)
- **Page 20** **What helped immigrants make an easier adjustment to their new life?** (They moved into neighborhoods where people spoke the same language, ate the same food, and had the same customs as themselves.)
- **Page 24** **How can you learn more about what life was like for an ancestor who passed through Ellis Island?** (Ask relatives, use a telephone and computer to do research, or visit the museum at Ellis Island.)

Ongoing Assessment

Reading Strategies

If... a student cannot understand why checking for disease was important,	**Then...** ask the student to tell what might happen if someone with a disease entered the United States.
If... a student has difficulty understanding how the immigrants felt,	**Then...** ask the student to imagine going through the same process in a country where the student couldn't understand or speak the language.
If... a student cannot figure out the meanings of unfamiliar words,	**Then...** use **Model Your Thinking** below.

Model Your Thinking

Comprehension Skill: Context Clues

Context clues are the words that help you figure out the meanings of unfamiliar words. They may come just before or after an unfamiliar word or be in a different part of the story or article. Context clues include synonyms, antonyms, definitions, explanations, and examples. For instance, on page 4, the word *pitched* is used to describe the ship's movement. The synonym *rocked* helps me understand what *pitched* means. To check my understanding, I reread the sentence and replace the unfamiliar word with my definition. If the sentence makes sense, my definition is probably good. If I'm not sure, I can check a dictionary.

After Reading

Revisiting the Text

Comprehension Write the selection vocabulary and other key words from the book on the board. Help students use context clues to write a definition for each word. Then have small groups use these words to write interesting facts about Ellis Island.

145A

Papa Lincoln

by David Neufeld
Leveled Reader 145A
Genre: Historical Fiction
Level: Easy

Summary

This work of historical fiction focuses on the relationship between President Lincoln and his ten-year-old son, Tad, during the time just before Lincoln's Gettysburg Address. While Tad worries about the danger to his father's life, he also realizes that his father has an important job to do.

Leveled Reader Practice

After students have read *Papa Lincoln,* use Leveled Reader practice page 202 to assess their understanding of the Leveled Reader and the target comprehension skill. Additional after reading activities are provided on page 107.

At a Glance

Links to the Student Edition

Comprehension Skill: Paraphrasing

Selection Vocabulary: *fate, lingers, magnified, tread*

Program Theme: Journeys in Time and Space
Unit Theme: Traveling On

Readers are transported back to 1863 to see what life is like for President Lincoln and his son during the Civil War.

Before Reading

Motivating the Reader

Build Background About Abraham Lincoln

Provide small groups with simple reference materials that describe Abraham Lincoln's life. Have groups use the Time Line on page 143 to list five important dates and events in Lincoln's life. Invite students to share their time lines and work together to combine them into one large time line. Discuss reasons for the Civil War and why President Lincoln was assassinated.

Preview and Predict

Have students scan the cover, text, and illustrations. Read aloud the Forward on page 2. Explain that historical fiction often includes real-life settings and people. Authors use what they know about a specific time, place, and group of people to imagine what these people may have said or done. Encourage students to make predictions about what Tad's life at the White House might have been like and what events the book might describe. Suggest students read to find out what Tad and his father did together.

Point out selection vocabulary and any unfamiliar words, such as *monument, engineering, tutor,* and *carriage,* that might be important to understanding the book.

During Reading

Guiding Comprehension

Use the following questions to support students as they read.

- **Page 2** **What information is given in the Forward?** (the time and place of the story's setting, the names of two main characters)
- **Page 3** **What caused the hole in Lincoln's hat?** (a bullet) **Why would people want Lincoln dead?** (Some people strongly disagreed with Lincoln's ideas about how to run the country.)
- **Pages 6–7** **How would you describe Lincoln based on the actions described here?** (Lincoln was a kind and caring man who didn't think he was more important than others.)
- **Page 12** **Restate Lincoln's response to Tad's question in your own words.** (Although they are not officers now, African Americans are capable of being officers, and someday they will be officers.)
- **Page 14** **What does *magnified* mean in this sentence?** (It mean "exaggerated.")
- **Page 15** **Why would the giant have more brains in his stomach than in his head if he ate the small man?** (The small man is saying that he has more brains than the giant. If the giant ate him, then the giant would have the small man's brains in his stomach.)
- **Pages 17–18** **What do Tad's and Lincoln's reactions tell you about Walt Whitman's poetry?** (His poetry must be well-written and very descriptive since both Tad and Lincoln can easily visualize Whitman's words.)
- **Page 19** **Why do you think the author includes this mention of a play at the Ford Theater?** (It foreshadows Lincoln's assassination at the theater two years later.)
- **Page 23** **What is Tad doing on this page?** (He is acting out the speech his father will be making about the Battle of Gettysburg.)
- **Page 24** **How would you feel if you were Tad? Why?** (Answers will vary.)

Ongoing Assessment

Reading Strategies

If...	Then...
If... a student is confused by the use of *can* on page 12,	**Then...** discuss the difference between being able to do something and being allowed to do something.
If... a student does not understand the tone or significance of the book's ending,	**Then...** point out that Lincoln will soon be assassinated.
If... a student has difficulty paraphrasing,	**Then...** use **Model Your Thinking** below.

Model Your Thinking

Comprehension Skill: Paraphrasing

Paraphrasing is explaining something in your own words. When I paraphrase, I think about what the author is trying to say. I make sure I don't change the author's meaning or add my own opinions. For example, I could paraphrase the last two sentences on page 2 as: "Tad was President Lincoln's son. He lived in the White House and spent a lot of time with his father." This paraphrase states the same ideas in my own words. If I had left out the fact that Tad is Lincoln's son or if I said that Tad loved living in the White House, then I would not be giving an accurate paraphrase. Paraphrasing helps me check my understanding of what I have read.

After Reading

Revisiting the Text

Comprehension Have pairs select a paragraph or short passage from the book. Have them use the T-Chart on page 150. They can copy the paragraph or passage in the left column and write a paraphrase of it in the right column. Pairs can draw pictures to go with their paraphrases.

145B Elena's Ride

by Susan Blackaby
Leveled Reader 145B
Genre: Realistic Story
Level: Easy/Average

Summary

Elena is spending the summer at her uncle's ranch in Texas, which has been in the family for many years. While Elena is learning to get used to many things on the ranch, she has trouble overcoming her fear of horses. However, when her cousin Pepe falls down an old mine shaft, Elena doesn't hesitate to ride his horse down the mountain to get help. Her fearless ride helps her realize that ranch life is in her blood after all.

Leveled Reader Practice

After students have read *Elena's Ride,* use Leveled Reader practice page 203 to assess their understanding of the Leveled Reader and the target comprehension skill. Additional after reading activities are provided on page 109.

At a Glance

Links to the Student Edition

Comprehension Skill: Paraphrasing

Selection Vocabulary: *steed, fearless, glimmer, somber*

Program Theme: Journeys in Time and Space
Unit Theme: Traveling On

A courageous horseback ride to get help for her cousin helps Elena learn more about herself and how she is connected to her family's roots.

Before Reading

Motivating the Reader

Build Background About Riding Horses

Invite any students who have ridden horses to describe their experiences. If possible, show pictures of people riding horses. Have students use Web 3 on page 134 to record five categories of terms associated with riding. They might use one branch of the web for characteristics of a horse, one for a rider's clothing, one for action words such as *gallop* and *trot,* one for equipment such as *saddle* and *reins,* and one for reasons that people ride horses.

Preview and Predict

Have students scan the cover, text, and illustrations to get an idea of what the book is about. Have them use picture and word clues to describe the story's setting and its characters. Encourage students to make predictions about what will happen in the story. Suggest students read to find out what kind of ride Elena will take and why she takes it. Direct students' attention to the notes on pages 3 and 12, and remind them to read these notes.

Point out selection vocabulary and any unfamiliar words, such as *seam, tree line, lathered, stirrup, pommel, gallop,* and *tack,* that might be important to understanding the book.

During Reading

Guiding Comprehension

Use the following questions to support students as they read.

- **Pages 2–4** Where does this story take place? (on Tío Diego's ranch in Texas)
- **Page 4** Why is Elena staying on the ranch? (Her mom is going to school and her dad is starting a new job as a pilot.)
- **Page 6** Restate the last sentence of this first paragraph in your own words. (Elena's family has lived on this land for three generations.)
- **Page 7** What problem does Elena have? (She is afraid of her uncle's horses.)
- **Page 9** Why does Tía Marta say that the land and horses are in Elena's blood? (Elena's aunt thinks Elena should have inherited an interest in the land and horses since her family has been ranching this land for many years.)
- **Page 14** Why does Elena suggest that Pepe might be renaming his horse "Tumbleweed"? (She thinks the horse is too near the edge of the cliff and might tumble.)
- **Page 17** What do you think will happen next? (Students are likely to predict that Pepe will get into some type of accident.)
- **Pages 18–19** What happens to Pepe? (There is a cave-in, and he gets stuck.)
- **Pages 20–21** What is surprising about Elena's actions on these pages? (Elena races down the mountain on a horse, even though she is afraid of riding.)
- **Page 23** Do you think Elena was scared about riding the horse? Why or why not? (No. Elena forgot her fear of horses because she was worried about Pepe.)
- **Page 24** How has Elena's attitude toward the horses changed? (She is less fearful of them. She realizes that horses are in her blood.)

Ongoing Assessment

Reading Strategies

If... a student stumbles over the use of *Tío* and *Tía*,	**Then...** model their pronunciation and explain that they are Spanish terms for *Uncle* and *Aunt*.
If... a student is confused by the sudden shift back to the present at the top of page 8,	**Then...** have the student reread page 3 to recall that Elena was writing a note to her mother.
If... a student has difficulty paraphrasing,	**Then...** use **Model Your Thinking** below.

Model Your Thinking

Comprehension Skill: Paraphrasing

When you explain something in your own words, you are paraphrasing. A good paraphrase includes only the author's ideas. When I paraphrase, I think about what the author is trying to say. I restate these ideas in my own words without changing them or adding my own opinions. For example, I could paraphrase the first sentence of the book as: "Elena made her bed just as the sun was beginning to rise." If I had left out the detail about the time of day or if I had added that it was a beautiful sunrise, then I would not be giving an accurate paraphrase of the author's ideas. Paraphrasing sentences or paragraphs in my own words helps me make sure I've understood what I've read.

After Reading

Revisiting the Text

Comprehension Have students work with a partner. One student selects a sentence or paragraph from the book and reads it aloud. The other student then paraphrases it. Students switch roles and repeat. Encourage pairs to discuss the accuracy of their paraphrases. Listen to make sure students are not summarizing.

146A

The Great Bake-off

by Steven Otfinoski
Leveled Reader 146A
Genre: Play
Level: Easy

Summary

A group of school children need to raise money for a class trip. They've already tried a car wash and a backyard circus, but neither worked out well. Now they decide to have a bake sale and make the items themselves. Their inexperience results in a burned cake, a blob of bread, and peanut butter dog biscuits instead of cookies. However, the dog biscuits give them a new idea. They hold a school pet fair that is a grand success.

Leveled Reader Practice

After students have read *The Great Bake-off,* use Leveled Reader practice page 204 to assess their understanding of the Leveled Reader and the target comprehension skill. Additional after reading activities are provided on page 111.

At a Glance

Links to the Student Edition

Comprehension Skill: Theme

Selection Vocabulary: *fragrance, pastries, pleasures, inspects*

Program Theme: Creativity
Unit Theme: Think of It!

When you have a group of creative people working together to solve a problem, chances are that someone will have a great idea that saves the day.

Before Reading

Motivating the Reader

Build Background About Cooking

Invite students to share their cooking experiences, especially times when things did not go as well as expected. Brainstorm a list of "Do" and "Don't" tips for beginning cooks. Then distribute copies of a simple recipe for a typical bake sale item, and have students examine the recipe. Discuss what steps you would follow to make the item and what students would do to double or triple the recipe.

Preview and Predict

Have students scan the cover, text, and illustrations to get an idea of what the book is about. Prepare students for reading by discussing the characteristics of a play. Encourage students to make predictions about what will happen in the play. Then suggest students read to find out what a great bake-off is.

Point out selection vocabulary and any unfamiliar cooking-related vocabulary, such as *yeast, shortening, recipe, cookie sheet,* and *pot holder,* that might be important to understanding the book. You might also wish to preview some of the puns that Luís is fond of making.

During Reading

Guiding Comprehension

Use the following questions to support students as they read.

- **Page 3** What problem are the children trying to solve? (how to raise money for a class trip)
- **Page 5** Why does Shawn laugh? (Luís has made a pun or word-play joke since Jenna's dad works at the Kitty Boutique.) Ask similar questions for other puns in the play.
- **Page 6** How do the children try to solve their problem? (They decide to have a bake sale and cook the food themselves.)
- **Page 6** Why are some words in parentheses? (They are stage directions that tell the actors how to say a line or what movements to make.)
- **Page 9** What does Jenna's dad mean when he says, "You can have too much of a good thing"? (If you use too much of an ingredient, you can ruin what you're making.)
- **Page 10** Do you think Jenna and Juanita have made a good decision? Why or why not? (No. 550 degrees is too hot. The cake will burn if the oven is too hot.)
- **Page 17** What happens to the cake? (It burns.) Why did this happen? (The girls set the oven at too high a temperature.)
- **Page 18** What caused the bread to become a blob? (Too much yeast made it rise too high.)
- **Page 22** How do the children finally solve their problem? (They hold a pet fair instead of a bake sale and sell their dog biscuits.)
- **Page 24** What lessons do you think the children have learned? (If you work together, you can find a way to solve problems. You need to follow directions carefully when cooking.)

Ongoing Assessment

Reading Strategies

If... a student has difficulty understanding the play's slang words and puns,	**Then...** have the student work with a partner to restate dialogue in their own words.
If... a student uses prior knowledge about cooking to make reasonable judgments,	**Then...** ask him or her to tell how he or she made these judgments.
If... a student has trouble identifying the play's theme,	**Then...** use **Model Your Thinking** below.

Model Your Thinking

Comprehension Skill: Theme

Theme is the underlying meaning or message of a story. It's a statement, lesson, or generalization that can stand on its own outside of the story. To identify a story's theme, I ask myself: "What did the characters learn? What can I learn from reading this play?" In this play, the characters' plan for a bake sale has awful results. One lesson they learn is to follow directions more carefully when cooking. However, when I read what Luís says on page 24 about things working out fine, I think there is a bigger lesson that they've learned. This theme can be stated as: Even terrible problems can sometimes be solved, especially if you work together.

After Reading

Revisiting the Text

Comprehension Work with students to complete the Story Elements organizer on page 144. Encourage them to state the play's theme in their own words. Have students write the theme as closing dialogue for the narrator. Assign roles and have students perform a Readers Theater of the play using this new dialogue.

146B

Clever Manka

retold by Sharon Fear
Leveled Reader 146B
Genre: Folk Tale
Level: Easy/Average

Summary

Manka is a kind-hearted peasant's daughter who helps others by finding clever answers to riddles and smart solutions to problems. Her talents are rewarded as she marries the judge and lives a life of privilege. However, when she interferes with one of the judge's rulings, he sends her back to live with her father. She asks if she may take her most beloved possession with her. Her husband agrees and is secretly pleased to discover that he is her most beloved possession. The two live happily ever after. Manka continues to help people with her wisdom, and everyone notices that the judge's rulings improve as well.

Leveled Reader Practice

After students have read *Clever Manka,* use Leveled Reader practice page 205 to assess their understanding of the Leveled Reader and the target comprehension skill. Additional after reading activities are provided on page 113.

At a Glance

Links to the Student Edition

Comprehension Skill: Theme

Selection Vocabulary: *trial, privilege, scowling*

Program Theme: Creativity
Unit Theme: Think of It!

Resolving disputes requires creative thinking to come up with judgments that will seem fair to all the people concerned.

Before Reading

Motivating the Reader

Build Background About Riddles

Give students an example of a riddle, such as: What is black and white and red all over? (a newspaper) Discuss how most riddles have tricky answers that require thinking in a different or creative way. For example, in the riddle above, the person solving the riddle must know that *red* and *read* are pronounced in the same way. Provide other examples of riddles and challenge students to solve them. Invite students to share some of their own. Discuss how the riddles can be solved. Create a class bulletin board to display students' favorite riddles.

Preview and Predict

Have students scan the cover, text, and illustrations to get an idea of what the book is about. Have them make predictions about the kinds of characters they will find in the book and what these characters are like. Tell students that the book will include riddles and challenging problems to solve. Encourage students to pause as they read to make predictions about answers and solutions. Then have them set their own purpose for reading, such as reading to find examples of how Manka shows she is clever.

Point out selection vocabulary and any unfamiliar terms, such as *olden times, uncommonly, dispute, objections, peasant, interfere,* and *downcast,* that might be important to understanding the book.

During Reading

Guiding Comprehension

Use the following questions to support students as they read.

- **Pages 2–3** **What problem do the men have?** (They can't agree who should own the cup.)
- **Page 4** **What do you think of the judge's method of solving the disagreement?** (Some may say since both men have an equal chance to answer the riddles, it is a fair method.)
- **Page 5** **What do you think the answers to the riddles are?** (Answers will vary.) Ask similar questions for other problems Manka solves.
- **Page 7** **What does the phrase *uncommonly clever* mean?** (wiser than the average person)
- **Page 9** **Why do you think the brothers were happy with Manka's decision?** (Since the second brother gets first choice, the first brother will work hard to divide the land in a way that benefits them both.)
- **Page 10** **How did the judge's father feel about the marriage?** (He felt that a peasant's daughter shouldn't marry a judge.)
- **Page 12** **Why does Manka drag one foot on the ground?** (She's dragging her foot so she is neither walking nor riding.)
- **Page 17** **Why do the man's words make the judge change his mind?** (He realizes that the foal was birthed by the mare, not the wagon, therefore the owner of the mare should be the owner of the foal.)
- **Page 21** **Why do you think Manka is having the judge carried to her father's house?** (The judge is Manka's most beloved possession.)
- **Page 24** **Why are the judge's opinions wiser?** (He is listening to Manka's ideas.)
- **Page 24** **What message do you think this story tells? How do you know?** (Accept reasonably supported answers.)

Ongoing Assessment

Reading Strategies

If... a student gets frustrated if he or she cannot solve the riddles or problems presented,	**Then...** point out how attempting to solve them helps the reader appreciate how clever Manka is.
If... a student has trouble identifying the book's theme,	**Then...** use **Model Your Thinking** below.

Model Your Thinking

Comprehension Skill: Theme

A story's theme is its underlying meaning or message. It may be a statement, lesson, or generalization that can stand on its own outside the story. To identify the theme, I ask myself: "What does the author want me to learn from reading this story?" As I read this folk tale, I note the clever thinking that Manka uses to solve difficult problems. Therefore, one possible theme might be: It takes clever thinking to solve challenging problems. I also think that the judge learned an important lesson. His work became better once he began to listen to Manka's ideas. Therefore, another important theme is: You can learn a lot by listening to others. A story may have more than one theme. Always be sure you can support your ideas with examples from the story.

After Reading

Revisiting the Text

Comprehension Have small groups use copies of Web 1 on page 132 to record the story's theme or themes. In the center of each web, they identify a theme of the story and list supporting evidence at the ends of the spokes. Then have each group design a poster about the theme.

147A The Assignment

by Lynn Cullen
Leveled Reader 147A
Genre: Realistic Story
Level: Easy

Summary

Tyler needs to get a good grade on his Oregon Trail report or his mother will make him drop soccer. Tyler groans when his pesky sister Nancy tags along with him to the library. However, he is surprised when Nancy shows him how to use the reference materials in the library. Together, they find a way to complete the assignment quickly. Tyler now can spend some of his weekend with his friends—thanks to a pesky sister who is also pretty smart.

Leveled Reader Practice

After students have read *The Assignment,* use Leveled Reader practice page 206 to assess their understanding of the Leveled Reader and the target comprehension skill. Additional after reading activities are provided on page 115.

At a Glance

Links to the Student Edition

Comprehension Skill: Steps in a Process

Selection Vocabulary: *clenched, cornmeal, essay, flyer, grease*

Program Theme: Creativity
Unit Theme: Think of It!

Homework assignments give students two ways to use creativity—thinking of ideas to complete the assignment and devising efficient ways to get the job done quickly.

Before Reading

Motivating the Reader

Build Background About Reference Sources

Write *The Oregon Trail* on the chalkboard and remind students that this was a route taken by pioneer families settling the West. Then ask for volunteers to describe the steps they would take to find information about the Oregon Trail in a library. Encourage students to consider both print and multimedia reference sources. Have other volunteers write these steps on the chalkboard, clarifying them as needed. If time allows, plan a trip to the school's media center. Encourage students to compare the steps they listed with the steps Tyler and Nancy follow in the book.

Preview and Predict

Have students scan the cover, text, and illustrations to get an idea of what the book is about. Encourage them to use picture and word clues to make predictions about who the characters are, what their relationship might be, and what they will do. Remind students to check and revise their predictions as they read the book.

Point out selection vocabulary and any unfamiliar words, such as *assignment, pioneer, appetite, advertising, settlers, pestering, authentic, terminal,* and *description,* that might be important to understanding the book.

During Reading

Guiding Comprehension

Use the following questions to support students as they read.

- **Page 2** How does Tyler feel about his sister Nancy? How do you know? (He thinks she is a pest. He shouts at her to go away and shuts his bedroom door so she can't come in.)
- **Page 6** What other word could you substitute for *pestering* that would make sense in this sentence? (bothering, bugging, nagging)
- **Page 6** Why do you think Nancy keeps interrupting Tyler? (She is bored or lonely. She wants Tyler to pay attention to her.)
- **Pages 8–9** What does Tyler do to try to find out what the pioneers ate while on the Oregon Trail? (He finds the chapter on The Oregon Trail and skims it looking for information about the foods pioneers ate.)
- **Page 14** What is the first thing Tyler does to use the computer terminal? (He uses a mouse to point and click on the picture marked "catalog.")
- **Pages 14–15** What kinds of information does the computer show? (which books the library has on the Oregon Trail, a short description of each book, where each book can be found)
- **Page 15** What kinds of books would be found in Juvenile Nonfiction? (nonfiction books written for young people)
- **Page 20** How does Tyler feel about the information he found? (He is upset because he can't find any mention of foods that he would be able to cook for his class.)
- **Page 23** In what ways has Nancy helped Tyler? (She talked their mother into driving them to the library. She helped Tyler find a book he can use and a food he could make.)
- **Page 24** How have Tyler's feelings for Nancy changed? (He realizes how smart she is. He is thankful for the help she gave him.)

Ongoing Assessment

Reading Strategies

If... a student has difficulty drawing reasonable conclusions about the characters,	**Then...** remind the student to think about what the characters think, say, and do.
If... a student cannot follow the steps used to find information,	**Then...** use **Model Your Thinking** below.

Model Your Thinking

Comprehension Skill: Steps in a Process

Steps in a process are the steps you follow to do or make something. Good readers look for clue words, such as *first*, *next*, or *finally*, to help them figure out the order of the steps. They can use their common sense to picture steps in their mind. For example, on pages 8–9, I read about how Tyler tries to figure out what the pioneers ate. I visualize the steps he follows to find this information: He gets his social studies textbook. He looks up the chapter on the Oregon Trail. He skims the paragraphs looking for information about food. He reads the passage that mentions food carefully. He decides that the textbook's information about buffalo meat isn't helpful. Thinking about these steps helps me understand the process of skimming a textbook for information. As I continue reading, I can outline the steps Tyler and Nancy follow to find a library book with more helpful information.

After Reading

Revisiting the Text

Comprehension Have students reread pages 13–23 and make a list summarizing the steps Tyler and Nancy follow to choose a food that Tyler can make for his assignment. Draw a flowchart on the chalkboard. Have students use their lists to direct you as you write each step. Clarify steps or the order of steps as needed.

147B

Beetles

by Alice Mead
Leveled Reader 147B
Genre: Informational Article
Level: Easy/Average

Summary

There are over 300,000 kinds of beetles. They come in many different shapes, sizes, and colors. They all have three body parts as well as hard and soft wings. The book describes the life cycles and habits of several kinds of beetles, including two of the most well known—fireflies and ladybugs.

Leveled Reader Practice

After students have read *Beetles,* use Leveled Reader practice page 207 to assess their understanding of the Leveled Reader and the target comprehension skill. Additional after reading activities are provided on page 117.

At a Glance

Links to the Student Edition

Comprehension Skill: Steps in a Process

Selection Vocabulary: *comparing, primitive*

Program Theme: Creativity
Unit Theme: Think of It!

Thinking about beetles can boggle the mind—there are more than 300,000 different kinds.

Before Reading

Motivating the Reader

Build Background About Beetles

Show colorful pictures of different types of beetles that students will likely recognize, such as the firefly or ladybug. Or, if possible, take a quick nature walk or bring live beetles into the classroom. (Be sure the insects have air and food and release them afterwards.) Ask students to describe what they know about beetles or what they have learned by watching them. Encourage students to tell the names of the different kinds of beetles they know about, what they look like, how they move, and where they can be found.

Preview and Predict

Have students scan the cover, text, and illustrations to get an idea of what the book is about. Ask students to make predictions about what kinds of information about beetles they will learn by reading this book. To help students set a purpose for reading, have them write a few questions of inquiry about beetles that they think the book will help them answer. Suggest they look for the answers to these questions as they read.

Point out selection vocabulary and any unfamiliar words, such as *arthropod, thorax, abdomen, scarab, larva, pupa, dormant, armored, scavengers, predator, entomologist,* and *preserved,* that might be important to understanding the book.

During Reading

Guiding Comprehension

Use the following questions to support students as they read.

- **Page 3** What makes beetles different from other arthropods? (Only beetles have both hard and soft wings.)
- **Page 4** Do you think you and a beetle see the world in the same way? Why or why not? (No. Humans have only one lens in each eye, but a beetle has many lenses.)
- **Pages 4–5** Point to the three main body parts on this illustration. (Students should point to the head, thorax, and abdomen.)
- **Page 6** What evidence does the author give to support the statement that the scarab beetle was important to ancient Egyptians? (They made valuable jewelry in the shape of scarab beetles that was used as charms.)
- **Page 9** When does a beetle look most like a worm? (when it is a larva)
- **Pages 11–12** How do fireflies use their ability to make light? (They use their flickers as signals so males and females can find each other at night.)
- **Page 15** At which stage is a firefly ready to fly? (at the adult stage)
- **Page 17** How are the new ladybugs different from the North American ladybugs? (The new ladybugs hide for the winter in the cracks in people's houses. The North American ladybugs hide in the bases of trees.)
- **Page 20** What are scavengers? (animals that eat dead animals)
- **Page 21** How can beetles damage trees? (Some beetles burrow into trees to lay eggs. When an egg hatches, the larva eats tunnels in to the wood.)
- **Pages 22–23** What do the beetles shown here have in common? (They all live in the water.)

Ongoing Assessment

Reading Strategies

If... a student has difficulty understanding the idea of a life cycle,	**Then...** draw a circle and mark the four stages on it. Show the student how the fourth stage, adult, leads into the first stage, egg.
If... a student has difficulty following the steps in a beetle's growth process,	**Then...** use **Model Your Thinking** below.

Model Your Thinking

Comprehension Skill: Steps in a Process

Steps in a process are the steps taken to make or do something. To identify the order of the steps in a process, good readers look for clue words, such as *first, next, then,* and *last.* They also use common sense to help them picture the steps in their minds. On page 9, I read that beetles grow in four steps. I notice there are clue words at the beginning of the next four paragraphs: *first, after, when,* and *finally.* Therefore, I know that each paragraph will describe a step in this growth process. As I read on, I use the illustration on page 8 and the descriptive details on page 9 to find out what happens in each of the four steps described: egg, larva, pupa, and adult. Identifying these steps helps me better understand the life cycle of beetles.

After Reading

Revisiting the Text

Comprehension Have pairs reread pages 8–9. Students can draw pictures and describe what happens during the four stages of growth in the first four boxes of the Steps in a Process organizer on page 148. Then assign pairs other pages to reread. Have them create fact cards describing other interesting facts about beetles.

148A

Winning Tubby

by Lynn Cullen
Leveled Reader 148A
Genre: Realistic Story
Level: Easy

Summary

Liz has a school contest she very much wants to win. If she writes the best essay, she will get to keep Tubby the class hamster over winter break. Taking the advice of her parents and brother, Liz writes the winning essay. However, she later decides to give Tubby to a lonely girl named Charlotte who doesn't have any pets. Charlotte's bright smile feels like a pretty good prize to Liz.

Leveled Reader Practice

After students have read *Winning Tubby,* use Leveled Reader practice page 208 to assess their understanding of the Leveled Reader and the target comprehension skill. Additional after reading activities are provided on page 119.

At a Glance

Links to the Student Edition

Comprehension Skill: Plot

Selection Vocabulary: *fascinated, seldom*

Program Theme: Creativity
Unit Theme: Think of It!

Family members are a good resource for creative ideas, especially when you're trying to write the world's best essay.

Before Reading

Motivating the Reader

Build Background About Writing

Ask students to imagine they have a friend who has to write a very important essay, but this friend is having a difficult time getting started. Invite students to share writing tips that they use to make themselves better writers. List students' tips on the chalkboard. If students have trouble thinking of tips, give them prompts by asking if they write in a special place, use special writing materials, create helpful graphic organizers, have a favorite get-started routine, and so on.

Preview and Predict

Have students scan the cover, text, and illustrations to get an idea of what the book is about. Encourage students to use word and picture clues to make predictions about the characters and what happens in the book. Suggest students read to find out who Tubby is and what the title *Winning Tubby* means.

Point out selection vocabulary and any unfamiliar words, such as *essay, yucky, hamster, miniature, host, pitiful,* and *heavy-hearted,* that might be important to understanding the book.

During Reading

Guiding Comprehension

Use the following questions to support students as they read.

- **Page 2** What problem does Liz have? (She has to write an important essay and is having trouble getting started.)
- **Page 3** Who is Ranger? (the family dog) What is one way Liz and Ranger are alike? (They both like to chew on things.)
- **Page 5** What advice does Liz's mom give her? (She tells Liz to imagine her essay is an argument. She should try to convince Mr. Quinn that she should get Tubby by showing that she knows how to take care of him.)
- **Page 6** What advice does Liz's dad give her? (He says she should also try to prove that she will make the hamster's life better.)
- **Page 8** What is another word that means almost the same as *miniature?* (small, tiny)
- **Page 11** What are two ways Liz promises she will make Tubby's life better? (She will get him into the best shape of his life. She will teach him new tricks.)
- **Page 15** What is Charlotte like? (She is a quiet girl who hardly ever talks.)
- **Page 16** Who do you think should get Tubby, Liz or Charlotte? Why? (Encourage well-supported answers.)
- **Page 19** What is a word that means almost the same as *heavy-hearted?* (sad)
- **Page 21** Why do you think Charlotte doesn't take Tubby immediately? (She is shy; she can't believe Liz is willing to give up Tubby.)
- **Page 23** How does Liz feel after giving Tubby to Charlotte? (She is a little sad not to get Tubby, but she feels good about making Charlotte happy.)
- **Page 24** Why does Liz say she and Ranger are "in this together"? (They both have to break the habit of chewing on things.)

Ongoing Assessment

Reading Strategies

If... a student can explain why Liz changes her mind about Tubby,	**Then...** praise the student for drawing sensible conclusions.
If... a student cannot identify important events in the story,	**Then...** use **Model Your Thinking** below.

Model Your Thinking

Comprehension Skill: Plot

The plot includes the important events in a story: the conflict, rising action, climax, and the resolution or outcome. The conflict is a problem or a goal that a main character has. For example, Liz's goal is to write the best essay so she can get to take Tubby home with her. The rising action includes those events related to the conflict, where the action builds up to the climax. In this book, the rising action includes Liz's talking with her family, writing the essay, and thinking about Charlotte. The climax is the turning point in the story, where the character directly confronts the conflict. I think the climax is when Liz decides to give Tubby to Charlotte. The resolution, or outcome, shows how the conflict is solved. Liz realizes that making someone else happy is a pretty good prize, and she sets a new goal—training Ranger not to chew anymore. Identifying the plot helps me understand the story better.

After Reading

Revisiting the Text

Comprehension Have pairs reread the book and use the Plot Structure organizer on page 138 to map out the story's plot. Then have pairs create a comic strip to show important story events in sequential order.

148B

A Marvelous Event

by Susan McCloskey
Leveled Reader 148B
Genre: Tall Tale
Level: Easy/Average

Summary

Don Roberto falls into a deep sleep and is believed to be dying. His wife invites family and friends to gather for a last visit. The visitors begin to tell stories of Don Roberto's remarkable talents. As unlikely as these stories seem to be, they must be true because the townspeople have a reputation for loving the truth and never lying. When one storyteller makes a small error, Don Roberto suddenly wakes up so he can correct her mistake.

Leveled Reader Practice

After students have read *A Marvelous Event,* use Leveled Reader practice page 209 to assess their understanding of the Leveled Reader and the target comprehension skill. Additional after reading activities are provided on page 121.

At a Glance

Links to the Student Edition

Comprehension Skill: Plot

Selection Vocabulary: *foolishness, generous, rascals*

Program Theme: Creativity
Unit Theme: Think of It!

Family members and friends show their creative storytelling talents as they recall events in Don Roberto's remarkable life.

Before Reading

Motivating the Reader

Build Background About Family History

Write the words *Family History* in the center of a web. Have students tell how they can learn about events that have happened in their families. Mention such ways as photographs, videotapes, letters, journals, and storytelling. Invite students to give examples of a story that is often told and retold when family and friends gather together.

Preview and Predict

Have students scan the cover, text, and illustrations to get an idea of what the book is about. Explain that this book is a tall tale. Have volunteers share what they know about the events in tall tales, such as characters performing impossible feats of strength. Encourage students to use word and picture clues to make predictions about what might happen in this book. Suggest that students read to find out which story event might be described as "a marvelous event."

Point out selection vocabulary and any unfamiliar words, such as *marvelous, residents, Andalucía, estate, ailments,* and *reputation,* that might be important to understanding the book.

During Reading

Guiding Comprehension

Use the following questions to support students as they read.

- **Page 3** **What problem does Don Roberto have?** (He is very sick.)
- **Page 3** **How does the narrator's uncle describe the people in Don Roberto's town?** (They love the truth and never lie.)
- **Page 4** **What does the word *complaints* mean in this sentence?** (sicknesses or illnesses) **What other word in this paragraph is a synonym for *complaints*?** (ailments)
- **Page 6** **Why does Don Roberto's wife invite Don Roberto's friends and relatives to the house?** (She wants his friends and relatives to see Don Roberto one last time before he dies.)
- **Page 8** **What story does Don Tomás tell?** (He says that Don Roberto's horse could run so fast it took three people to see him go past.) **Do you think this story is true? Why or why not?** (No. Horses can't run that fast.) Ask similar questions about the other stories told.
- **Page 13** **Does the acorn prove that Doña Estrella's story is true? Why or why not?** (No. The acorn does not prove that Don Roberto could do the things she claimed.) Ask similar questions about the other proof that the storytellers give to support their claims.
- **Page 13** **What do you think the other stories will be like?** (Students should recognize that the stories will tell about some amazing ability that Don Roberto has.)
- **Page 18** **Why do the crows peck at the painting?** (They think the painting is real fruit, and they want to eat it.)
- **Page 21** **What causes Don Roberto to wake up?** (He hears an untruth in Doña María's story that he must correct because people in their town love the truth.)

Ongoing Assessment

Reading Strategies

If... a student is confused by the use of *Don* and *Doña*,	**Then...** explain that these are common Spanish titles similar to *Mr.* and *Mrs.*
If... a student has difficulty identifying the story's plot,	**Then...** use **Model Your Thinking** below.

Model Your Thinking

Comprehension Skill: Plot

A plot includes the important events in a story. It usually has a conflict, rising action, a climax, and a resolution, or outcome. The conflict, or problem, in the story is Don Roberto's illness. The rising action includes those events related to this conflict that help move the story along. The stories that the friends and relatives tell are all part of the story's rising action. These stories are also examples of flashbacks. In a flashback, the action in the present is interrupted to talk about something that happened in the past. While the flashbacks interrupt the time order of events, they continue to move the plot toward the climax. The climax is the turning point of the story. In this story, it is when Don Roberto suddenly wakes up. The resolution, or outcome, of the conflict happens when the family urges Don Roberto to stay awake for more stories. Identifying the plot helps me understand the story better.

After Reading

Revisiting the Text

Comprehension Have students reread the book and use the Plot Structure organizer on page 138 to map out the story's plot. Then invite students to choose character roles, including a story narrator, and act out the story. Encourage them to use their own words for dialogue.

149A

How the Cat Got His Hat

The Story of Dr. Seuss

by Mark Spann
Leveled Reader 149A
Genre: Biography
Level: Easy

Summary

"Dr. Seuss" was the pen name of Ted Geisel, the illustrator and writer famous for his rhyming children's books. This biography describes the main events in Geisel's life and tells how some of his most famous books came to be written. For example, *Green Eggs and Ham* was the result of a challenge from a friend to write a book using only fifty words.

Leveled Reader Practice

After students have read *How the Cat Got His Hat: The Story of Dr. Seuss,* use Leveled Reader practice page 210 to assess their understanding of the Leveled Reader and the target comprehension skill. Additional after reading activities are provided on page 123.

At a Glance

Links to the Student Edition

Comprehension Skill: Making Judgments

Selection Vocabulary: *critical, survey, opinion, career*

Program Theme: Creativity
Unit Theme: Think of It!

How do famous writers get their ideas? Many of Dr. Seuss's books came from observing life. Others were specifically written using only the words beginning readers would understand.

Before Reading

Motivating the Reader

Build Background About Dr. Seuss

Bring several of Dr. Seuss's books to show students. Ask students to recall any experiences they had reading these books. List some of the common characteristics of his books, and discuss why they have remained so popular with children and critics over the years. Students can work in pairs using the Story Comparison organizer on page 140 to compare two of Dr. Seuss's books.

Preview and Predict

Have students scan the cover, text, and illustrations to get an idea of what the book is about. Encourage them to use what they know about biographies and their previewing scan to make predictions about what kinds of information they will find in the book. Have students complete the first two columns of the K-W-L Chart on page 135. Then suggest they read to look for the answers to the questions they wrote about Dr. Seuss. They can complete the third column after they have read the book.

Point out selection vocabulary and any unfamiliar words, such as *advertisement, illustration, publisher, manuscript, pen name, critic, cartoonist, critical,* and *illiteracy,* that might be important to understanding the book.

During Reading

Guiding Comprehension

Use the following questions to support students as they read.

- **Page 3** How did Ted Geisel feel about his job as a cartoonist? (He knew it was a good job that he was lucky to have, but he really wanted to write children's books instead.)
- **Page 3** What does the author mean by the phrase *spare time?* (This is time when Geisel wasn't working at his job.)
- **Page 5** Would you quit if you were Ted Geisel? Why or why not? (Encourage well-supported answers.)
- **Page 7** What is a pen name? (It is a name that an author uses that appears on the author's books. It is not the author's real name.)
- **Page 9** What childhood experience got Geisel interested in drawing pictures of odd-looking creatures? (His father was a zookeeper. Geisel would visit the zoo often and draw funny pictures of the animals.)
- **Pages 10–11** How did Geisel's wife Helen help him to succeed? (She encouraged him to become an artist. She read his work and gave him suggestions for revising it.)
- **Page 11** What are critical notes? Think about other words that look like *critical.* (These are notes that include criticisms, suggestions for how to make the writing better.)
- **Pages 17–19** Why did Geisel write a book using a list of 250 words? (He wanted to help children learn to read. The list contained words that new readers needed to learn to read.) Do you think it would be difficult to write a book using a list of words? Why or why not? (Encourage well-supported answers.)
- **Page 24** Why does the author say Dr. Seuss will be here forever? (If people can continue to read books by Dr. Seuss, it's as if Geisel is still alive.)

Ongoing Assessment

Reading Strategies

If... a student is confused by the text structure,	**Then...** point out that pages 2–8 focus on 1937. Pages 9–24 tell events from Geisel's birth to death.
If... a student has difficulty making judgments,	**Then...** use **Model Your Thinking** below.

Model Your Thinking

Comprehension Skill: Making Judgments

Making judgments means forming an opinion about someone or something. Characters make judgments about situations and other characters. Authors make judgments about the subject of their writing. Readers make judgments about characters, authors, and ideas. Good readers use their own experiences and values to make judgments about what they've read. They support their judgments with evidence from the text. For example, on page 3, I read that Ted Geisel kept his cartooning jobs while working on his children's books in his spare time. I think this was a smart way to work since jobs were so hard to get during the Great Depression. I know it can sometimes take a lot of time to make your dream come true. Geisel's actions show he was both practical and determined to succeed.

After Reading

Revisiting the Text

Comprehension Have students reread the book and use the T-Chart on page 150 to list judgments about Ted Geisel in one column and judgments about the author in the other column. Have students give evidence to support their judgments. Students can use these charts to help them write short book reviews of the biography.

149B

A Grand Opening

by Mike Dion
Leveled Reader 149B
Genre: Realistic Story
Level: Easy/Average

Summary

Tina is opening a new flower shop and her younger brother Jake wants to help. Tina gives Jake two problems to solve: getting rid of the old junk in the back room and helping spread the word about the shop's grand opening. Jake and his friends find a creative solution that solves both problems at once. While the grand opening is not as successful as Tina had hoped, she is pleased with her new business and impressed by her brother's abilities.

Leveled Reader Practice

After students have read *A Grand Opening,* use Leveled Reader practice page 211 to assess their understanding of the Leveled Reader and the target comprehension skill. Additional after reading activities are provided on page 125.

At a Glance

Links to the Student Edition

Comprehension Skill: Making Judgments

Selection Vocabulary: *efficient, maneuvered, resolved, shattered*

Program Theme: Creativity
Unit Theme: Think of It!

Anyone starting a small business needs creative—and inexpensive—ideas for promotion and advertising.

Before Reading

Motivating the Reader

Build Background About Advertising

Ask students to imagine that they are opening a new business. Have them name types of businesses they think they would like to own and vote to pick one business. Have students think of a name for the business and decide what products or services they will sell. Discuss different ways businesses advertise to attract customers to their stores, such as using radio, television, newspapers, magazines, billboards, flyers, and websites. Organize students into groups, and have each group create an advertisement appropriate for one of the methods of advertising listed above.

Preview and Predict

Have students scan the cover, text, and illustrations to get an idea of what the book is about. Draw their attention to the book title and discuss what a grand opening is. Encourage students to use word and picture clues to make predictions about who the characters are and what problems or challenges these characters may face. Suggest students read to find out whether Tina will have a successful grand opening of her flower shop.

Point out selection vocabulary and any unfamiliar words, such as *expensive, advertise, reopening, tarnished, banner, customers, downtown,* and *department store,* that might be important to understanding the book.

During Reading

Guiding Comprehension

Use the following questions to support students as they read.

- **Page 3** Why do you think the store is called Rosie's Flower Shop? (The person who started the shop is named Rose.)
- **Pages 5–7** Do you think Tina treats Jake fairly? (Some may say yes because she doesn't get very angry when he breaks the vase and she gives Jake other tasks to do. Others may say that she is too critical since she assumes he will do a poor job painting.)
- **Page 8** Why does Jake call his sister "Tina the Efficient"? (She is very organized and seems to have thought of everything.)
- **Page 9** Why would it help Tina's business to put a flower cart out front? (People passing by might notice the cart and go into the shop.)
- **Page 10** What does the word *draw* mean in this sentence? (It means "to attract or catch someone's attention.")
- **Page 11** What do the boys plan to do with the stuff in the back room? (They will use the cart to help them sell the old gardening tools and vases and advertise for the shop's opening.)
- **Page 15** Do you think the plan to use ribbons and silk flowers for signs is a good idea? Why or why not? (Yes. The ribbons and flowers are different from most signs, so they will get people's attention.)
- **Page 17** Why does Ben say the children are "little walking ads"? (People will see the ribbons that the children are waving around.)
- **Pages 18–19** What happens the day of the opening? (No one goes to the shop. Most people go to the opening of a new department store downtown instead.)
- **Page 23** How did the boys get people to come to the shop? (He and his friends rolled the cart downtown and got people to follow them back to the shop.)

Ongoing Assessment

Reading Strategies

If... a student can't understand how the flower cart and ribbons will help the shop's opening,	**Then...** ask the student to think about what makes him or her go into a new shop.
If... a student has difficulty making reasonable judgments,	**Then...** use **Model Your Thinking** below.

Model Your Thinking

Comprehension Skill: Making Judgments

Making judgments means forming an opinion about someone and something. Characters make judgments about situations and other characters. Authors make judgments about the subject of their writing. Readers make judgments about characters, authors, and ideas. They support their judgments with evidence from the text. For example, I think the boys have some good advertising ideas. I know that I would more likely read a sign written on bright yellow ribbon with a silk flower than a flyer or hand-written sign taped on a lamp post. I would also stop if I were walking by the flower cart. Making judgments helps me better understand what I've read.

After Reading

Revisiting the Text

Comprehension Use the T-Chart on page 150. Write *Characters* on one side and *Author* on the other side. Have pairs reread the book and record their judgments in their charts. Then have students write a short book review summarizing the story and telling what they liked and didn't like about it.

150A

Pablo Picasso

by Janet Buell
Leveled Reader 150A
Genre: Biography
Level: Easy

Summary

This biography of Pablo Picasso describes events from his childhood and the main stages of his career. Photographs of his artwork show the changes in style from his more traditional early work to the more well-known abstracts of his Blue Period, Rose Period, Cubist phase, and later sculptures.

Leveled Reader Practice

After students have read *Pablo Picasso,* use Leveled Reader practice page 212 to assess their understanding of the Leveled Reader and the target comprehension skill. Additional after reading activities are provided on page 127.

At a Glance

Links to the Student Edition

Comprehension Skill: Visualizing

Selection Vocabulary: *artistic, sculpture, represent, style*

Program Theme: Creativity
Unit Theme: Think of It!

By breaking many rules, Picasso created a new art style.

Before Reading

Motivating the Reader

Build Background About Art Styles

Show examples of different styles of art, both traditional and abstract. Initiate a discussion about abstract art by asking why an artist might choose to create art in which the art images do not look the same as real-life objects. Encourage students to think about how abstract art might help them see things in a new way. Ask students to imagine a series of human faces: a face in a mirror, a face in a fun house mirror, a face in a broken mirror, a face made up of parts from other peoples' faces, and so on. Have students draw pictures to show what they visualize.

Preview and Predict

Have students scan the cover, text, illustrations, and captions. Point out the photos showing the artist Picasso. Explain that the other illustrations are examples of this artist's paintings or sculptures. Encourage students to use what they know about biographies and their preview of the book to make predictions about the kinds of information they will learn about Pablo Picasso. Suggest they read to find out what Picasso's paintings are like.

Point out selection vocabulary and any unfamiliar words, such as *charcoal, techniques, galleries, art show, old masters, art form, ceramics, texture,* and *studio,* that might be important to understanding the book.

During Reading

Guiding Comprehension

Use the following questions to support students as they read.

- **Page 2** If you pushed against a boundary such as a fence, you would expand the inside space and make it bigger. What do you think it means "to push against the boundaries of art and beauty"? (It means to expand the ways art and beauty are shown. Picasso wanted to make room for new kinds of art and beauty.)
- **Page 6** Why do you think Picasso's father reacted to Picasso's drawing behind the sofa differently than Picasso's mother? (Because Picasso's father was an art teacher, he saw the talent that the drawing showed.)
- **Page 7** Do you think most teenagers could paint a self-portrait like this one? Why or why not? (No. Most teenagers would not have the talent or training to produce a similar portrait.)
- **Page 13** Why do you think this 1908 painting looks so different from the 1901 painting on page 11? (The earlier painting shows Picasso's work before he started to develop a style of his own.) Why is this painting an example of Picasso's "Blue Period?" (He used a lot of blue paint. It gives a feeling of sadness, of being blue.)
- **Page 14** Why do you think Picasso used pinks and earth tones during his "Rose Period"? (These colors expressed his happier mood.)
- **Page 16** Does the Cubist painting here look like what you visualized after reading the description on page 15? (Answers will vary.)
- **Pages 20–23** What other kinds of art forms did Picasso enjoy creating? (collages, sculptures, ceramics, prints)
- **Page 24** What does the author think of Picasso? How do you know? (She greatly admires Picasso's work. She uses the word *courage* several times to describe him.)

Ongoing Assessment

Reading Strategies

If... a student has difficulty understanding the changes in Picasso's style,	**Then...** have the student compare his earlier artwork, shown on pages 7, 9, and 11, with his later artwork.
If... a student has difficulty visualizing,	**Then...** use **Model Your Thinking** below.

Model Your Thinking

Comprehension Skill: Visualizing

Visualizing means creating pictures in your mind as you read. Authors help readers visualize by using imagery—words that help you make a strong mental picture, or image. They also may use sensory details—words that describe how something looks, sounds, smells, tastes, or feels. For example, on page 5, I try to visualize Picasso painting his sister's face and hair. First, I imagine an egg yolk. Then I try to imagine what it looks like and how it might feel to put that on someone's face. The words *circles, dabbed,* and *streaked* help me visualize Picasso's actions. If I have trouble visualizing, I reread a passage or I read more slowly to make a better picture in my mind.

After Reading

Revisiting the Text

Comprehension Use the Five-Column Chart on page 153. Across the top, write the heads *Early Work, Blue Period, Rose Period, Cubist Work,* and *Other Art Forms.* Have small groups reread the book and record details that help them visualize Picasso's artwork in each stage in his career. If possible, show students other examples of his artwork and have them use their charts to help them classify the artwork.

150B

Behind the Scenes

by Robert R. O'Brien
Leveled Reader 150B
Genre: Informational Article
Level: Easy/Average

Summary

Movies today are full of all kinds of special effects. This book gives a brief history of early films and then explains in simple terms how different special effects are created. Effects described include the use of miniatures, mattes, blue screen and stop-motion photography, telephoto lenses, computer-generated images, animatronics, and claymation.

Leveled Reader Practice

After students have read *Behind the Scenes,* use Leveled Reader practice page 213 to assess their understanding of the Leveled Reader and the target comprehension skill. Additional after reading activities are provided on page 129.

At a Glance

Links to the Student Edition

Comprehension Skill: Visualizing

Selection Vocabulary: *deceive, viewer, realistic*

Program Theme: Creativity
Unit Theme: Think of It!

What may look real in a movie is often just a special effect created to fool viewers.

Before Reading

Motivating the Reader

Build Background About Movies

Have students describe favorite movie scenes that use special effects. Show scenes from special effects movies from different time periods so students get a sense of how special effects have developed, or show documentaries that give behind-the-scenes examples of how movies are created. To help students understand that movies are made up of a series of still photographs, or frames, moving very fast (twenty-four frames per second), have a media librarian show students a piece of actual film or demonstrate the concept using a flipbook.

Preview and Predict

Have students scan the cover, text, and illustrations. Discuss the meaning of the book's title, and encourage students to make predictions about what information they will find in the book. Suggest they set their own purposes for reading, such as reading to find out how special effects are created.

Point out selection vocabulary and any unfamiliar words, such as *illusions, performers, techniques, miniatures, explosions, studio, location, photography, director,* and *computer-generated,* that might be important to understanding the book.

During Reading

Guiding Comprehension

Use the following questions to support students as they read.

- **Page 3** Judging from the last paragraph, what will the book be about? (how movies began; how special effects are used in movies)
- **Page 6** Why do you think some people reacted the way they did to early movies? (They had never seen movies before so they weren't sure what was or wasn't real.)
- **Page 9** Compare what the theater audience saw watching the movie *King Kong* with what actually happened. (The audience saw a giant ape climbing up a tall building; the filmmakers actually used an 18-inch tall ape doll and a small model building.)
- **Pages 12–13** What does the third image show? (It shows the combination of the two mattes so that it looks as if the girl and the dog were really inside a castle.)
- **Pages 13–15** What image replaces the blue screen that is behind the weather reporter? (a weather map)
- **Pages 16–17** What do these four illustrations show? (the steps to make a traveling matte)
- **Page 18** What special effect can a telephoto lens create? (It can make two things that are far apart look close together.)
- **Pages 19–20** What is a CGI? (It's a computer-generated image.) What helps make movement in a CGI look real? (The image is based on a scan of a real person moving.)
- **Page 21** How do animatronic creatures move? (Either they are programmed to move on their own or someone uses a remote control to make them move.)
- **Page 22** Why is stop-motion photography a slow process? (You have to keep moving the model and shooting a few frames until the action is done.)

Ongoing Assessment

Reading Strategies

If...	Then...
If... a student has difficulty summarizing information,	**Then...** have the student work with a partner and use the Main Idea organizer on page 142 to summarize passages or pages.
If... a student has difficulty visualizing,	**Then...** use **Model Your Thinking** below.

Model Your Thinking

Comprehension Skill: Visualizing

Visualizing means creating pictures in your mind as you read. To help readers visualize, authors may use imagery—words that give readers a strong mental picture, or image. They may also use sensory details—words that describe how something looks, sounds, smells, tastes, or feels. For example, to visualize how miniatures were used to make the movie *King Kong*, I first think about what I know about models. The words *giant ape, Empire State Building, ape dolls, eighteen inches*, and *miniature replica* help me visualize what the audience sees and how the effect was created. The dolls and the model building were used to create the image of a giant ape climbing the Empire State Building. If I have trouble visualizing, I can reread the passage or read more slowly to make a better picture in my mind.

After Reading

Revisiting the Text

Comprehension Assign small groups one of the special effects described in the book. Have groups use the T-Chart on page 150 to record details about the effect on one side and details about what a film audience would see on the other. Have each group then draw two pictures showing what they visualized.

Name ____

Book Title ____

Read the title and look at the pictures in the book.
What do you think a problem in the book might be?

I think a problem might be ____

____

____

After reading ______________,
draw a picture of one of the problems in the book.

Name ______________________________

Book Title ______________________________

Look at the book title above and the list of words and phrases below. Write sentences that predict who and what this book might be about.

Words and Phrases

Characters: ______________________________

____

Problem: ______________________________

____

____

____

Events: ______________________________

____

____

Outcome: ______________________________

____

____

Name ______________________________

Name ____________________

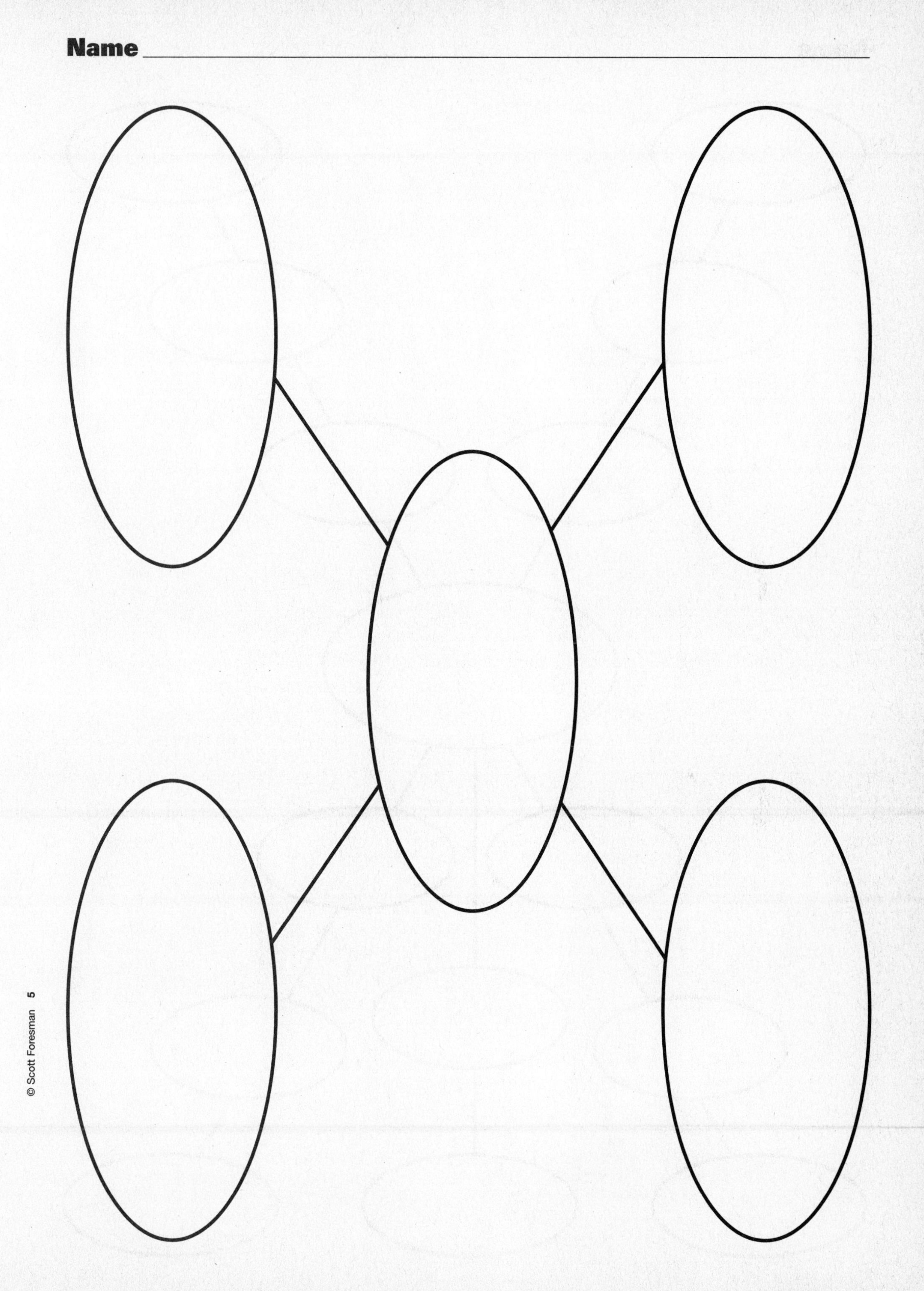

© Scott Foresman 5

Name ______________________________

Name ______________________________

Topic ______________________________

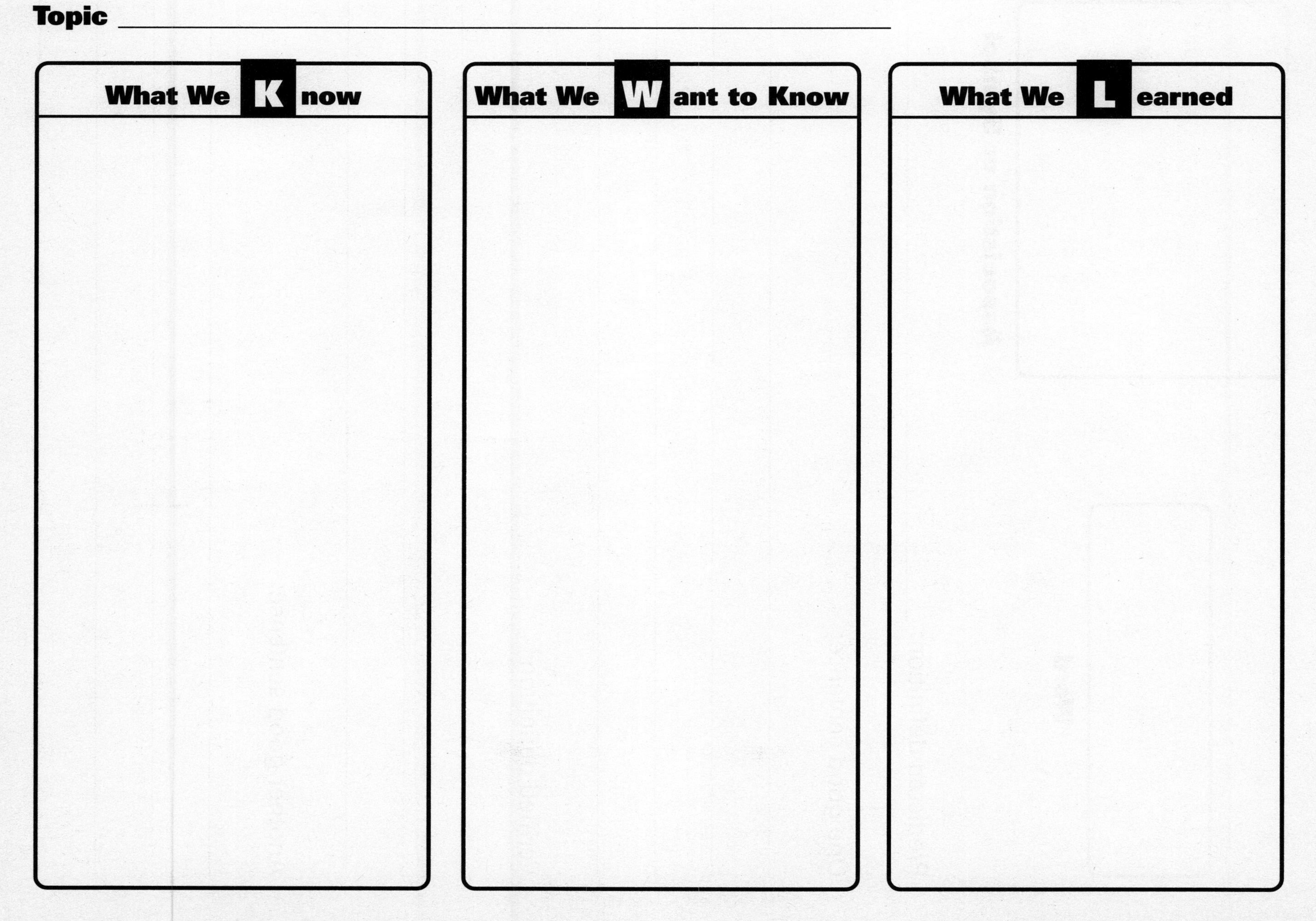

Name ______________________________

Word

Association or Symbol

Predicted definition: ______________________________

One good sentence:

____

____

____

____

Verified definition:

____

____

____

Another good sentence:

____

____

____

____

Name ______________________________

Book Title ______________________________

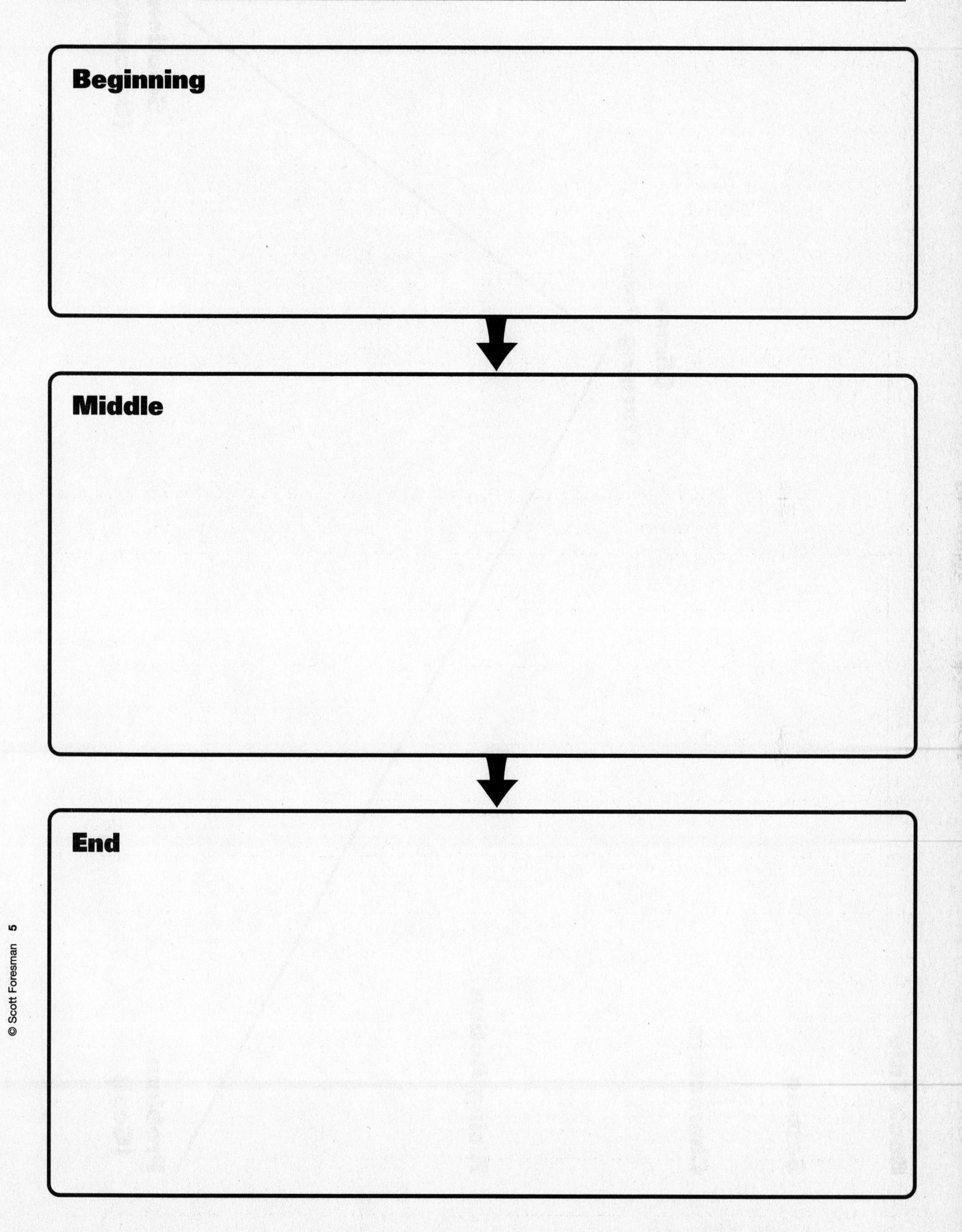

Name ______________________________

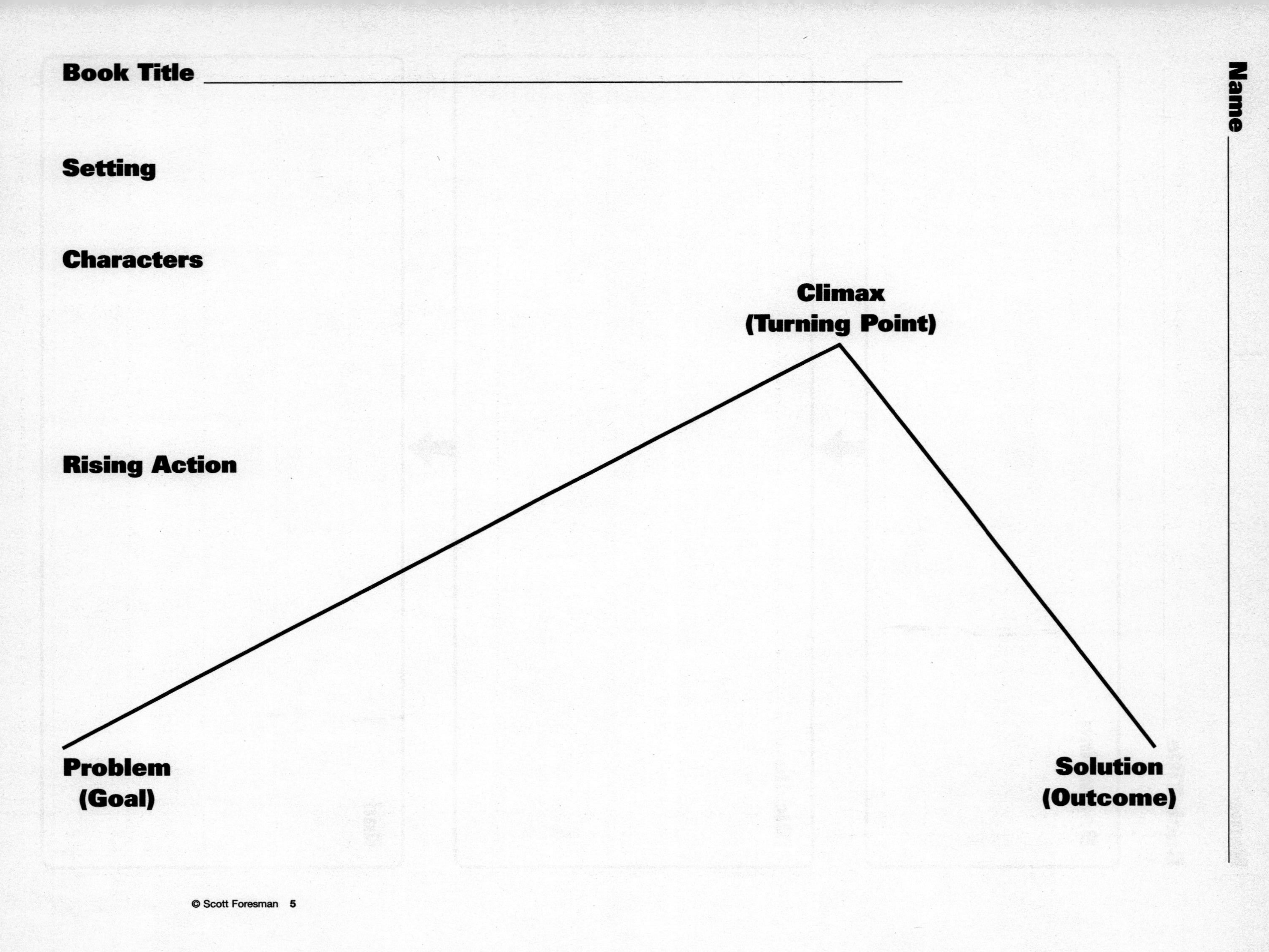

Book Title ______________________
Setting
Characters
Rising Action
Climax (Turning Point)
Problem (Goal)
Solution (Outcome)

Name ______________________________

Title

Characters

Problem

Events

____

____

____

____

____

____

____

Solution

Name ______________________________

Title A ______________________	Title B ______________________
Characters	**Characters**
Setting	**Setting**
Events	**Events**
Ending	**Ending**

Name ______________________________

Book Title ______________________________

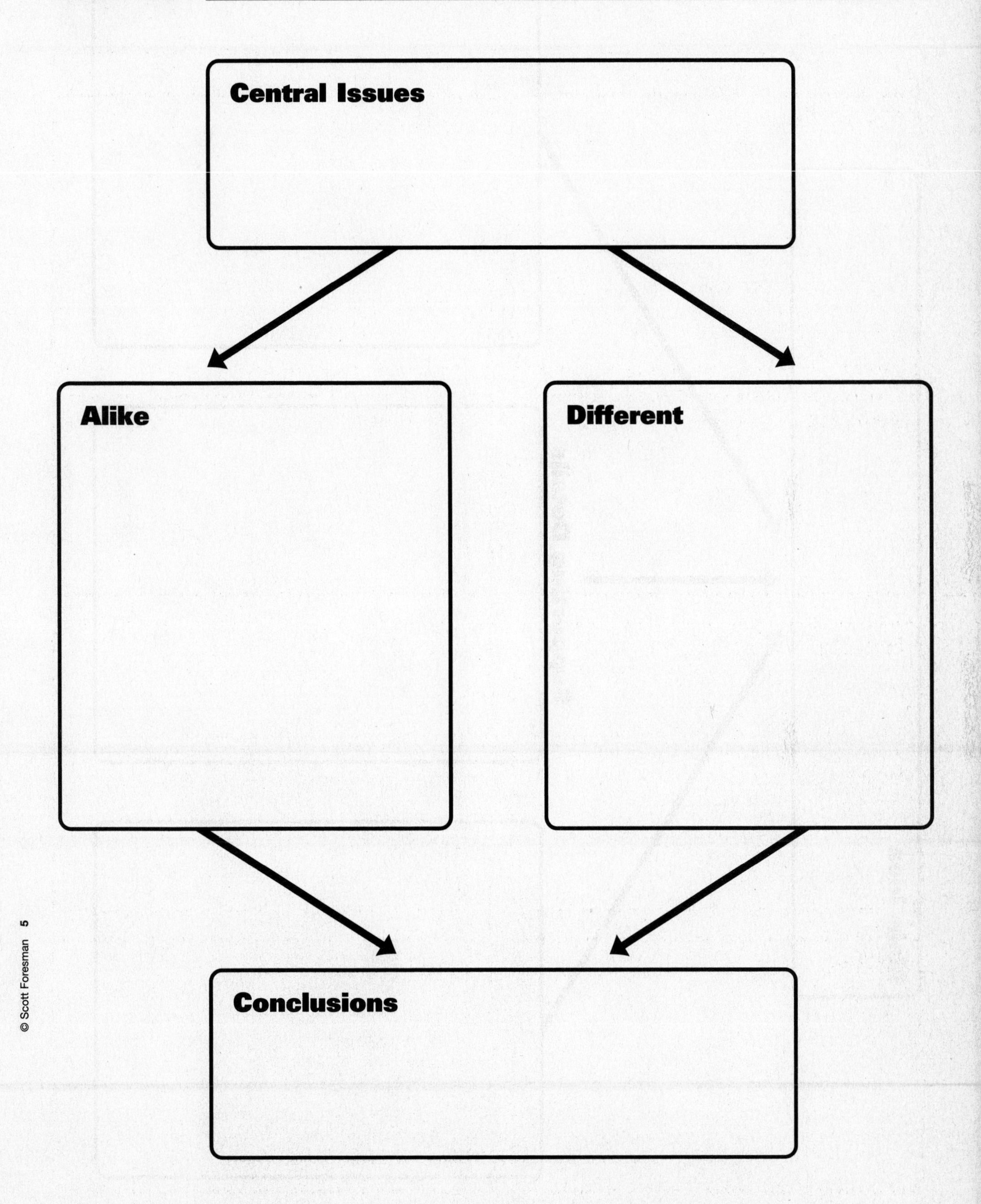

Name ____

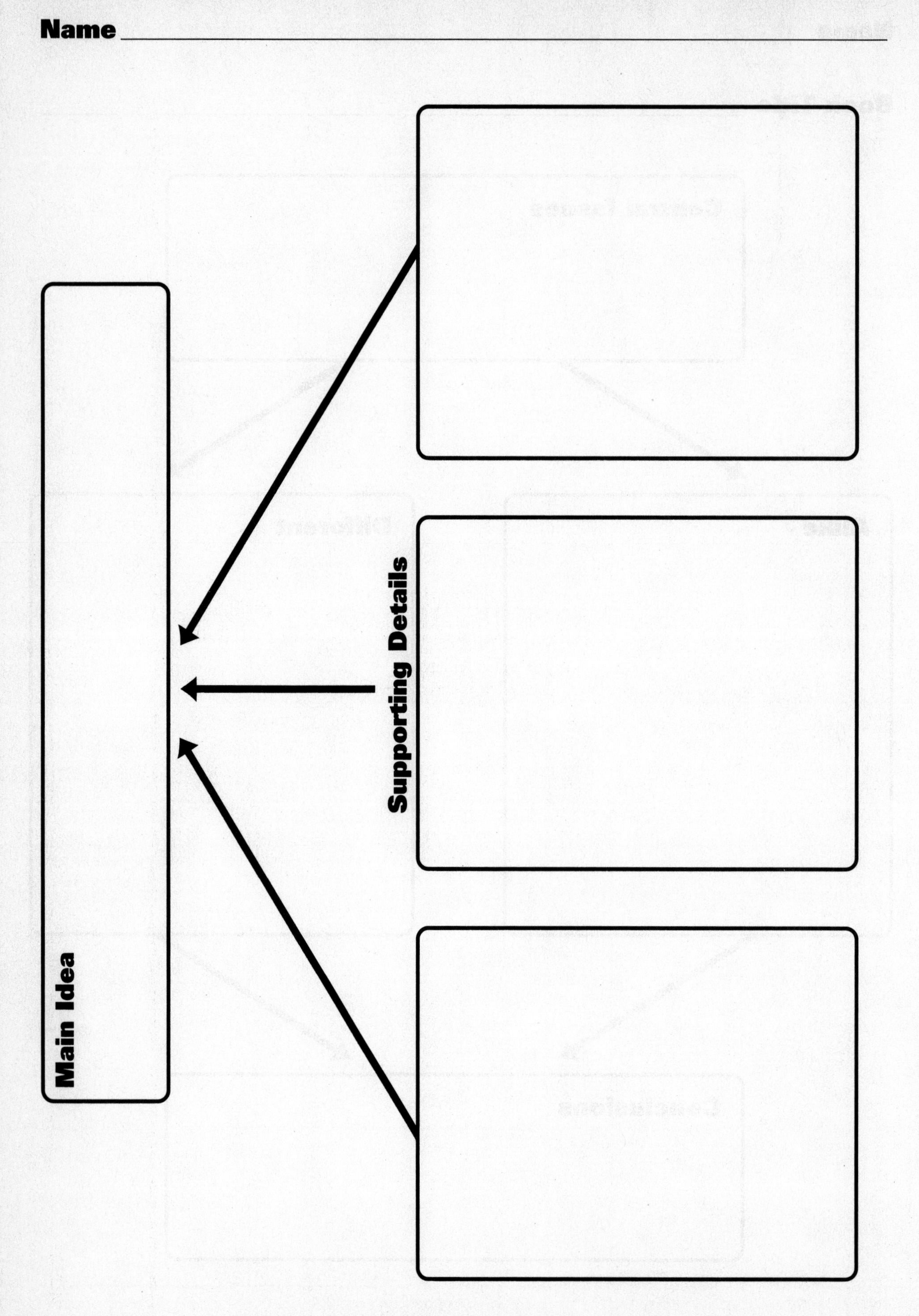

Name ______________________________

Name ______________________________

Book Title ______________________________

This story is about ______________________________

____

(name the characters)

This story takes place ______________________________

____

(where and when)

The action begins when ______________________________

____

____

Then, ______________________________

____

Next, ______________________________

____

After that, ______________________________

____

The story ends when ______________________________

____

____

Theme: ______________________________

Name ____________________

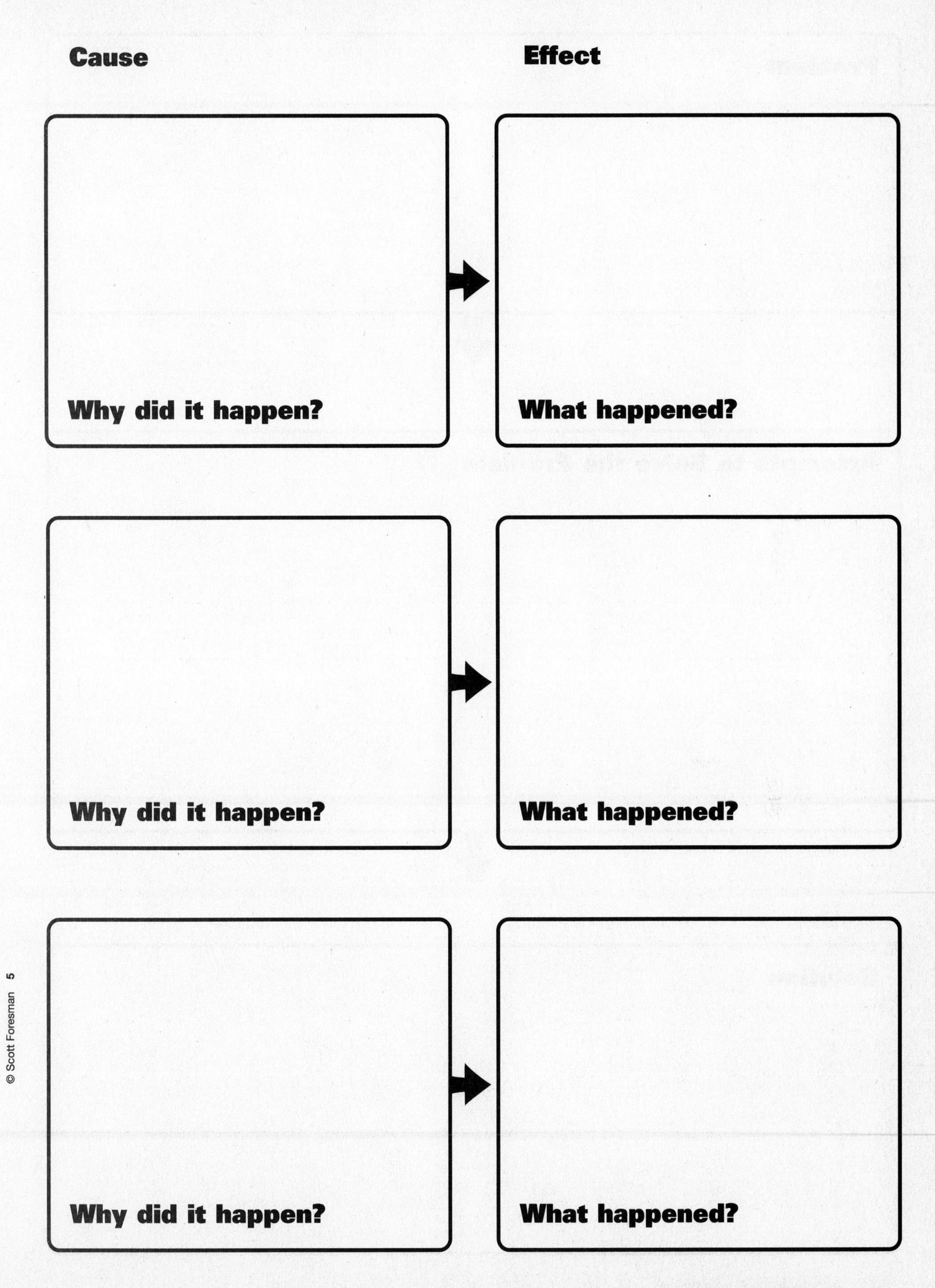

Cause
Effect
Why did it happen?
What happened?
Why did it happen?
What happened?
Why did it happen?
What happened?

Name ______________________________

Problem

Attempts to Solve the Problem

Solution

Name ______________________________

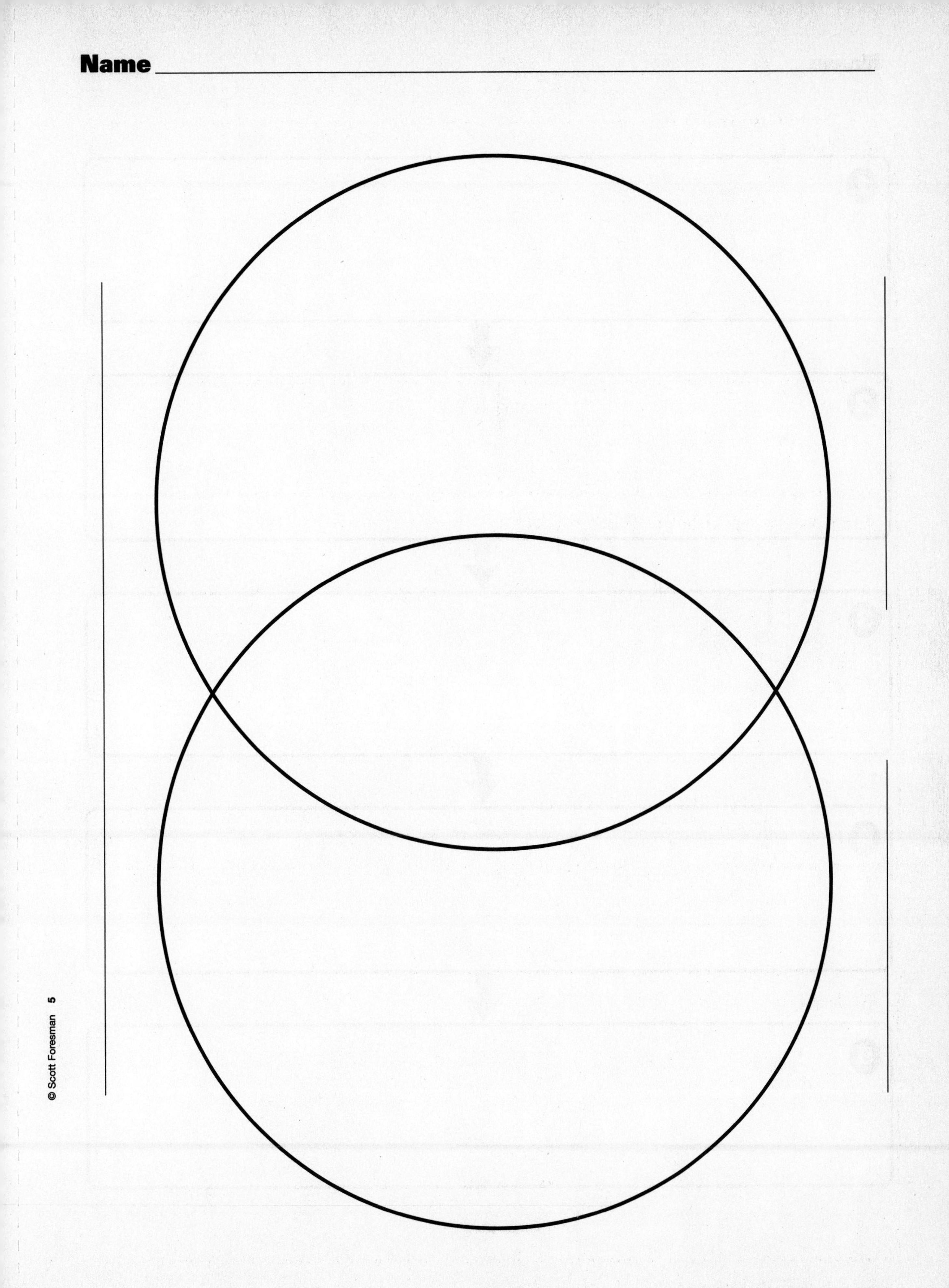

Name ____________________

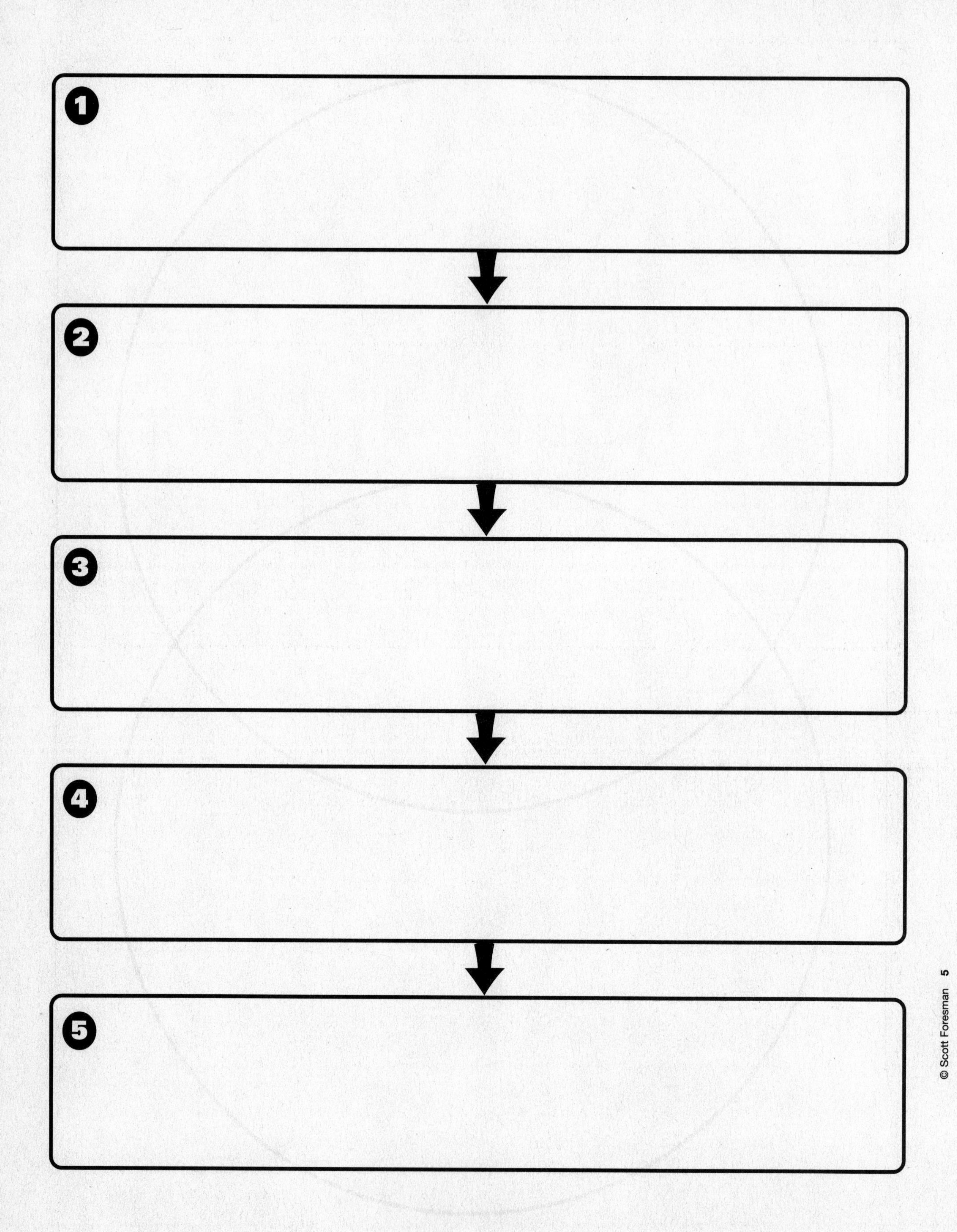

Name ___________________

Name ______________________________

Name ______________________________

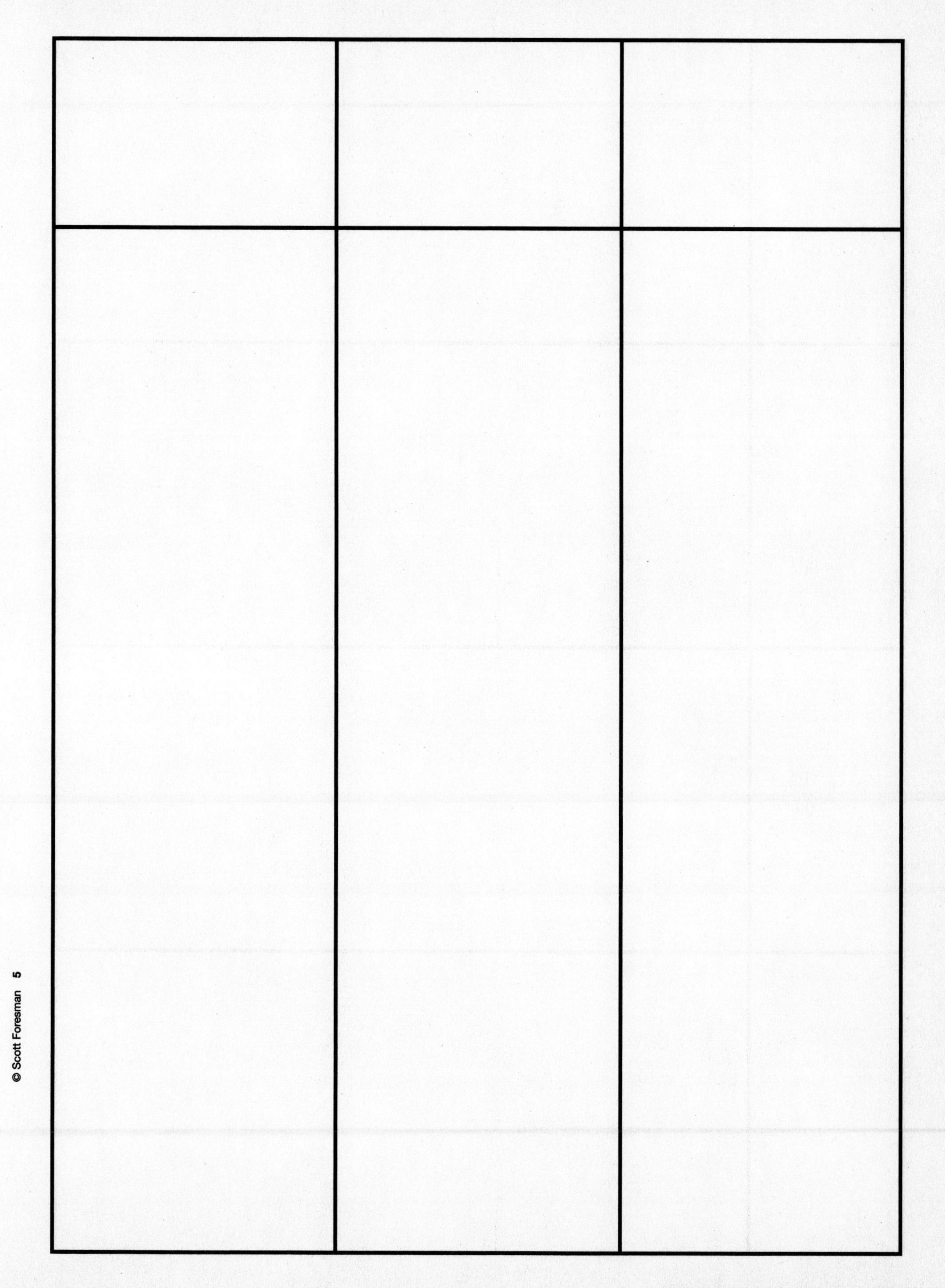

Name ______________________________

Name ____

Name ______________________________

Sequence

Read the story *Robo-Police* and then answer Numbers 1 through 5.

1. What problem do Juan and Carla notice in their school cafeteria?

   A. The robot is too big.
   B. It is always a mess.
   C. It is too crowded.
   D. The food is not good.

2. How do they decide to solve the problem?

   F. They ask Juan's father to help them.
   G. They ask Ms. Jones to help them.
   H. They do the job themselves.
   I. They create a robot police.

3. When Juan demonstrates the vacuum cleaner for Carla, what does he do FIRST?

   A. He turns on the vacuum cleaner.
   B. He presses the remote.
   C. He tips over a garbage can.
   D. He takes the robot to school.

4. What does Robo do just BEFORE Juan turns it off? Use details from the story to support your answer.

____

____

____

____

5. Why do Juan and Carla decide that Robo is NOT going to work out after all? Use details from the story to support your answer.

____

____

____

____

Name ____

 Sequence

Read the story *Rusty's Song* and then answer Numbers 1 through 5.

1 What special talent does Rusty have?

A. She can write.
B. She can sing.
C. She can dance.
D. She can talk.

2 What happens right AFTER the Old Cowboy sees the sign for the contest?

F. He decides to enter Rusty in the contest.
G. He and Rusty sleep under the stars.
H. He and Rusty run out of money.
I. He decides to go and watch the contest.

3 Why does the audience start to laugh and boo?

A. Rusty is singing the saddest song she knows.
B. Rusty wins first prize in the contest.
C. The Old Cowboy is trying to sing, but he cannot get a word out.
D. The Old Cowboy is singing very badly.

4 What happens AFTER Rusty starts to sing? Use details and examples from the story to support your answer.

____

____

____

____

5 How does Rusty feel about the Old Cowboy? Use details and examples from the story to explain your answer.

____

____

____

____

Name ______________________________

Character

Read the story *The Visitor From Space* and then answer Numbers 1 through 5.

1 Why is Carrie worried at the very beginning of the story?

A. She hears something in the shed.
B. She is afraid of the dark.
C. She has not been able to reach her dad.
D. She wants to go to Artemis with her dad.

2 Read this sentence about Carrie from the story.

Shivering in anticipation, she walked to the field.

This sentence shows that Carrie

F. is afraid to walk in the field.
G. is angry that her dad is not back.
H. is tired of looking for clues.
I. is nervous about what she may find.

3 Why is Carrie's dad on the planet Artemis?

A. He is studying the planet and hoping to find some signs of life.
B. He is looking for a puppy to bring home to Carrie.
C. He wants to meet ancient Egyptians who live on the planet.
D. He has friends he wants to visit there.

4 What is Carrie's dad like? Use details and examples from the story to explain your answer.

____

____

____

5 Why is Carrie's dad so interested in the puppy? Use details and examples from the story to explain your answer.

____

____

____

Name ____

Character

Read the story *Chiapas* and then answer Numbers 1 through 5.

1 At the beginning of the story, how does Carlos feel about going to Chiapas?

A. He thinks it will be scary.
B. He thinks it will be boring.
C. He is very excited
D. He is confused.

2 Where did Gabino take Carlos and Ino on the second day?

F. to a museum
G. to a park to swim
H. to San Cristobal
I. to get tamales

3 What are the old ruins of Palenque?

A. Egyptian pyramids
B. Mayan temples
C. shops and restaurants
D. old tunnels

4 How does Carlos's opinion of Chiapas change at the end of the story? Use details and examples from the story to support your answer.

____

____

____

____

5 Why did the author write this story? Use details and examples from the story to support your answer.

____

____

____

____

Name ____

Generalizing

Read the story *Lilah's Gift* and then answer Numbers 1 through 5.

 What is Lilah's problem?

A. She cannot hear.
B. She fell off the slide.
C. Her sister is mean.
D. She cannot keep Lolly.

2 What does Lilah see as she looks out the window at school?

F. A girl falls down, and a dog alerts the girl's mother.
G. A dog is sleeping next to a lady who is reading a book.
H. Her dog Lolly comes to the park and sits near the slide.
I. A dog pushes a girl and causes her to fall down.

3 Lilah learns that some special dogs can

A. help children when they fall and get hurt.
B. warn people that it is time to go inside.
C. alert hearing-impaired people of danger.
D. live at the Humane Shelter with other dogs.

4 How does Lilah's mother feel about Lilah's decision? Use details and examples from the story to explain your answer.

____

____

____

 According to the story, what kind of dogs do hearing dog trainers select? Use details and examples from the story to support your answer.

____

____

____

____

Name ______________________________

Generalizing

Read the story *The Lion and the Ant* and then answer Numbers 1 through 5.

1 What does Queen Ant tell her daughter to do at Lion's celebration?

A. tease Lion as much as possible
B. show Lion that ants can be important friends
C. play with Worm and stay away from Lion
D. crawl up on Lion's back and into his ear

2 Which statement BEST describes the way the other animals treat Ant?

F. A few of the other animals ignore Ant.
G. All of the other animals ignore Ant.
H. None of the other animals ignore Ant.
I. Most of the other animals ignore Ant.

3 How are Ant and Worm ALIKE?

A. They sometimes feel unimportant because they are small.
B. They are always sent on errands by their mothers.
C. They usually just want to sleep.
D. They never want to go back to their homes.

4 How does Ant help Lion? Use details and examples from the story to support your answer.

____

____

____

5 What lesson does Lion learn about size? Tell how he learns this lesson. Use details and examples from the story to support your answer.

____

____

____

Name ____________________

Cause and Effect

Read the book *Great Talents* and then answer Numbers 1 through 5.

1 Why have most people NOT heard of Josh Gibson?

A. because he was not a very good hitter
B. because he did not play many games
C. because most people do not know about the major leagues
D. because most people do not know about the Negro Leagues

2 What did African Americans do when they were cut from major league baseball teams?

F. They argued that they should be allowed to play.
G. They watched the games instead of playing.
H. They organized teams of their own.
I. They quit playing baseball.

3 Who was the FIRST African American to play in the major leagues?

A. Jackie Robinson
B. Satchel Paige
C. Willie Mays
D. Rube Foster

4 What happened AFTER Satchel Paige and his all-star team beat many major league teams? Use details from the book to support your answer.

____

____

____

5 What was the author's purpose in writing this book? Use details and examples from the book to explain your answer.

____

____

____

Name ______________________________

Cause and Effect

Read the story *What Are Friends For?* and then answer Numbers 1 through 5.

1 In the beginning of the story, why is Carol mad at Yumiko?

A. Yumiko has been mean to her.
B. Yumiko is very fast, and Carol is jealous.
C. Yumiko has been running extra laps without her.
D. Yumiko is not taking the race seriously enough.

2 Who has won the Dover Dash for the last two years?

F. Carol
G. Dave
H. Yumiko
I. Lisa

3 What happens when Yumiko falls?

A. Carol laughs at her.
B. Carol stops to help her.
C. Carol runs faster.
D. Lisa slows her pace.

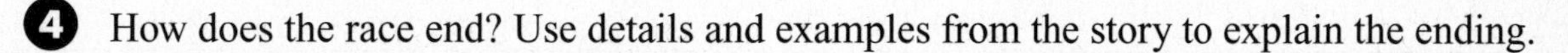

4 How does the race end? Use details and examples from the story to explain the ending.

____

____

____

____

5 Why does Carol want Yumiko to ride on the Fourth of July float with her? Use details from the story to explain your answer.

____

____

____

____

Name ____

Author's Purpose

Read the story *Aisha's New Look* and then answer Numbers 1 through 5.

1. Who is telling this story?

   A. Aisha's mother
   B. Aisha
   C. Danay
   D. a narrator

2. What problem does Aisha have?

   F. She wishes her eyes were big like Danay's eyes.
   G. She does not like her cousin Danay.
   H. She thinks she looks ugly in her new glasses.
   I. She cannot see with her new glasses.

3. Why does Danay look worried when she sees Aisha?

   A. She thinks Aisha's glasses are ugly.
   B. She does not want Aisha to come over.
   C. She is embarrassed to show her braces.
   D. She is worried about the little girl in the street.

4. Why does Aisha change her mind about her glasses? Use details from the story to support your answer.

____

____

____

____

____

5. What was the author's purpose in writing this story? Use details and examples from the story to support your answer.

____

____

____

____

Name ____________________

 Author's Purpose

Read the story *The Fifth Act Players* and then answer Numbers 1 through 5.

1 Who are the Fifth Act Players?

A. some fifth graders who have formed a drama club
B. a teacher and a group of his friends
C. a citizenship club led by Ms. Silver
D. a group of actors that includes Rita's dad

2 How do the students feel when Mr. Chin suggests that they write their own play?

F. bored
G. nervous
H. scared
I. excited

 **3** *The Fifth Act Players* is a

A. newspaper article.
B. play.
C. realistic story.
D. biography.

4 Do the students work well together while preparing their play? Use details and examples from the story to support your answer.

____

____

____

____

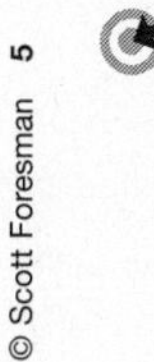

5 What was the author's purpose in writing this story? Use details and examples from the story to support your answer.

____

____

____

____

Name ____________________

Steps in a Process

Read the book *Turtles of the Sea* and then answer Numbers 1 through 5.

 How are sea turtles DIFFERENT from land turtles?

A. Their front legs are shaped like flippers.
B. Their backs have hard shells.
C. They are warm-blooded.
D. They are distant relatives of the dinosaur.

 What is one surprising ability that sea turtles have?

F. They can breathe underwater.
G. They can spend their entire life on land.
H. The female can watch over her eggs until they hatch.
I. They can go for a year without food.

 What is the FIRST thing the female sea turtle must do BEFORE she can lay eggs?

A. She must find twigs to make her nest.
B. She must cover herself with sand.
C. She must find a good place in the water to make her nest.
D. She must leave the water and make her nest on a beach.

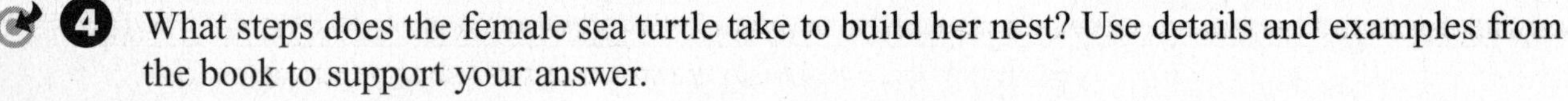 What steps does the female sea turtle take to build her nest? Use details and examples from the book to support your answer.

 Why are there fewer sea turtles today than there once were? Use details and examples from the book to explain your answer.

Name ______________________________

Steps in a Process

Read the story *The Big What-If* and then answer Numbers 1 through 5.

1 Why does Austin keep pouring sea water on the dolphin?

A. He and his friends are playing a game of "What-if."
B. He wants the dolphin to move.
C. He is afraid the dolphin is getting too hot.
D. He knows that dolphins need to stay wet.

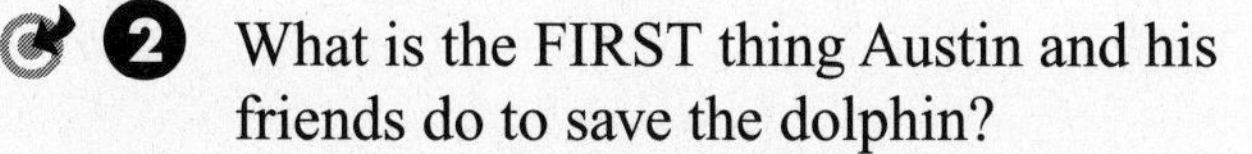

2 What is the FIRST thing Austin and his friends do to save the dolphin?

F. They talk to the dolphin.
G. They put more water on the dolphin.
H. They dig a canal for the dolphin.
I. They push the dolphin out to sea.

3 Why was Austin's mother so scared?

A. because she did not want Austin so close to the ocean
B. because she was afraid of the dolphin on the beach
C. because it was late, and Austin had not come home
D. because she did not like thunderstorms

4 What happens AFTER the boys turn the dolphin around? Use details from the story in your explanation.

____

____

____

____

5 What would be another good title for this story? Use details and examples from the story to explain your choice.

____

____

____

Name ______________________________

Graphic Sources

Read the story *Condor Morning* and then answer Numbers 1 through 5.

1. How did Aunt Connie get interested in condors?

   A. She wrote a report and discovered there were only 39 left.
   B. She began getting up early to watch them with her aunt.
   C. She worked with the ecology department at the zoo.
   D. She kept a journal with a list of all the birds she could identify.

2. Look at the journal on page 9. What did Aunt Connie see on July 14, 1972?

   F. a black-legged kittiwake
   G. a piping plover
   H. a common eider
   I. a common loon

3. Why did scientists capture all the condors?

   A. to set them free at the canyon
   B. to watch them and study their behaviors
   C. to protect them and give them a safe place to lay more eggs
   D. to keep them from hurting any of the other birds

4. What kind of information does Aunt Connie record in her journal? Name all the kinds of information she lists. Use details from the journal entry on page 9 to explain your answer.

____

____

____

5. When the condors are released, what does Aunt Connie do that surprises Jemma? Use details and examples from the story to support your answer.

____

____

____

____

Name ______________________________

Graphic Sources

Read the book *Disaster Super Heroes* and then answer Numbers 1 through 5.

1 Why was the Red Cross started?

A. to help wounded and sick soldiers during wars
B. to end all wars
C. to help people in Switzerland
D. to help people after a natural disaster

2 How did Clara Barton expand the role of the Red Cross in America?

F. She created the Biomedical Services to supply blood and organs.
G. She encouraged more than ten million people to volunteer.
H. She added disaster relief to its goals.
I. She started more than 175 Red Cross societies all over the world.

3 Look at page 6. How are the Swiss flag and the Red Cross flag DIFFERENT?

A. One has a cross in the middle, and one does not.
B. One is rectangular, and one is square.
C. One is white with a red cross. The other is red with a white cross.
D. One is much larger than the other.

4 Why does the author include many photographs in this book? Use information from the book to explain your answer.

____

____

____

5 What are some important things that the Red Cross does today? Use details from the book to support your answer.

____

____

____

____

Name ______________________________

Fact and Opinion

Read the book *One Hundred Houses* and then answer Numbers 1 through 5.

1. What does Habitat for Humanity do for people?

   A. It raises money to help people buy new homes.
   B. It finds homes for the homeless.
   C. It organizes a work force to help build homes for needy people.
   D. It goes to Houston each summer to build houses.

2. How is Habitat for Humanity DIFFERENT from other organizations?

   F. It only helps people in Texas.
   G. The people who donate their time come from many backgrounds.
   H. People who apply for a home must work to help build it.
   I. Volunteers must have a skill in order to participate.

3. Which of the following is a statement of fact?

   A. It is a thrilling moment for volunteers and homeowners alike.
   B. Every drop of sweat is worth it.
   C. Everyone takes pride in a job well done.
   D. Jimmy Carter has volunteered for the group since 1984.

4. Why is everyone so excited when a house is dedicated? Use details and examples from the book to support your answer.

____

____

5. What is the author's opinion of Habitat for Humanity? Use details and examples from the book to explain how you identified this opinion.

____

____

____

____

Name ______________________________

Fact and Opinion

Read the book *Fast and Forever* and then answer Numbers 1 through 5.

1 What is this book mostly about?

A. how far away the stars really are
B. how to use binoculars to study the stars
C. the Big Dipper and Orion
D. the Great Egyptian pyramids

2 How far can light travel in one second?

F. six trillion miles
G. 61 light years
H. around the Earth seven times
I. across the universe

3 Which of the following is a statement of fact that helps you understand the size of the universe?

A. The Big Dipper will make one of its regular light deliveries tonight.
B. The light from the North Star left before the Pilgrims came to America.
C. People throughout the ages have imagined pictures in the stars.
D. It is more fun to look up at space using binoculars.

4 What did ancient Egyptians probably think of astronomy? Use facts and details from the book to support your answer.

____

____

____

____

____

5 What is one way to find Sirius? List the steps given in this book.

____

____

____

____

Name ____

Author's Viewpoint

Read the book *The Trees* and then answer Numbers 1 through 5.

1 Why are sequoia trees so special?

A. Hale Tharp made his shelter out of one of them.
B. John Muir said they were special.
C. They provide shade for forest animals.
D. They are among the oldest living things on Earth.

2 Why did Chief Chappo and his people leave their land?

F. Hale Tharp told them to leave.
G. The settlers were taking their land, killing trees, and making them sick.
H. They wanted to fight Hale Tharp and the other white settlers.
I. A bearded stranger named John Muir came to visit.

3 How did John Muir help save the sequoias?

A. He asked Hale Tharp to stop cutting down the trees.
B. He often sat beneath the sequoias and thought about what to do.
C. He wrote essays and articles that convinced people to help save the trees.
D. He studied the plants and animals living in Yosemite.

4 Why did the author write this book? Use details and examples from the book to support your answer.

____

____

5 How does the author feel about saving the sequoias? Use details and examples from the book to support your answer.

____

____

____

____

Name ____

Author's Viewpoint

Read the book *A Walk Through a Salt Marsh* and then answer Numbers 1 through 5.

1 What is a salt marsh?

A. a place found along lakes
B. an area that is far from the ocean but filled with saltwater
C. an area near the coast that fills with saltwater during high tide
D. a place with few signs of life

2 How do salt marshes help people?

F. The water from the salt marsh can be used to make medicines.
G. People can live in salt marshes.
H. Monarch butterflies can stop and sip nectar on their long trip south.
I. During a hurricane, the marsh soaks up water like a sponge.

3 Which sentence from the book BEST helps you understand how the author feels about salt marshes?

A. Birds and ducks like to build their nests in the soft marsh grass.
B. A salt marsh may look like nothing but grass and mud.
C. Salt marshes are one of nature's most miraculous habitats.
D. Salt water enters a marsh through a stream or thin channel.

4 Would the author like to see more buildings and parking lots built in salt marshes? Use details and examples from the book to support your answer.

____

____

____

____

5 Describe what you might see if you visited a salt marsh. Use details and examples from the book in your description.

____

____

____

Name ____________________

Drawing Conclusions

Read the book *The California Gold Rush* and then answer Numbers 1 through 5.

1. How did James Marshall know he had found real gold?

   A. It passed three different tests that proved it was gold.
   B. It glittered when it was held in the sunlight.
   C. It broke when he hammered it with a flat rock.
   D. It was no bigger than a dime.

2. Why were the people who traveled to California for gold called "forty-niners"?

   F. They were all forty-nine years old.
   G. There were forty-nine of these people.
   H. The trip to California cost forty-nine dollars.
   I. They left for California in 1849.

3. Why did San Francisco's population go from 800 to 25,000 in just three years?

   A. Many people died from diseases and accidents.
   B. Many people struck it rich in San Francisco.
   C. People heard that the work in California was easy.
   D. People came to the area to find gold and then decided to stay.

4. What effects did the Gold Rush have on California? Use details and examples from the book to support your answer.

____

____

____

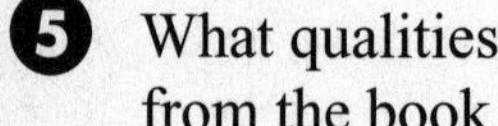

5. What qualities did a person need to have to join the Gold Rush? Use details and examples from the book to support your answer.

____

____

____

Name ______________________________

Drawing Conclusions

Read the story *Why the Spider Has a Tiny Waist* and then answer Numbers 1 through 5.

1 What is Anansi's problem at the beginning of the story?

A. The two elephants slap his hand away from the food.
B. The vine is squeezing his waist so he cannot go anywhere.
C. He wants to go to two feasts at the same time.
D. He only wants to go to the feast with the best food.

2 Which sentence BEST describes Anansi?

F. He is sneaky.
G. He is afraid.
H. He is funny.
I. He is curious.

3 Why does Anansi ask his friends to tie a long vine around his waist?

A. so that he can swing from the trees to the village
B. so that he can tie up the elephants at each feast
C. so that the elephants can tug on the vine and make his waist tiny
D. so that the elephant at each feast can tug on the vine when the food is ready

4 Why does Anansi tell the elephant from the eastern village that the animals from the western village say that his food is bad? Use details from the story to explain your answer.

____

____

____

____

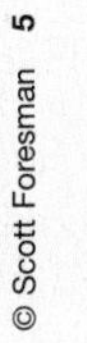

5 What lesson does this story teach? Use details and examples from the story to support your answer.

____

____

____

Name

 Character

Read the story *The Secret Fort* and then answer Numbers 1 through 5.

1 Why was Emily more comfortable in her old school than in her new school?

A. In her old school, many of the boys and girls were deaf.
B. In her old school, no one knew that she was deaf.
C. In her old school, the work was much easier.
D. In her old school, she had a deaf friend and a teacher who signed.

2 Emily thinks Lisa is lazy sometimes because Lisa

F. will not help her with the fort.
G. talks to her instead of signing.
H. will not let her have the computer.
I. messes up her fort.

 **3** Why is Emily angry when she sees the two girls near her fort?

A. She thinks they took all of her supplies.
B. She thinks the girls wrecked her fort.
C. She does not want to share the fort with anyone.
D. She knows the girls from school and does not like them.

 **4** Read page 8. What do Emily's actions tell the reader about her? Use details from the story to support your answer.

____

____

5 What is this story mostly about? Use details from the story to support your answer.

____

____

____

____

____

Name ______________________________

Character

Read the story *Grounding Grandma* and then answer Numbers 1 through 5.

1 Mr. and Mrs. Wingfield send Burt and Carol to Grandma Wingfield's so the children can

A. help Grandma with some work.
B. learn how to play basketball.
C. keep an eye on Grandma.
D. have some time off from school.

2 Which word BEST describes how Burt feels when he sees Grandma dunk the basketball?

F. joyful
G. mad
H. surprised
I. jealous

3 What secret is Grandma Wingfield trying to hide from everyone?

A. She knows how to fly.
B. She cannot remember very well.
C. She likes to work on her roof.
D. She fell off the ladder.

4 What kind of person is Grandma Wingfield? Use details and examples from the story to support your answer.

____

____

____

____

5 Will Burt be able to fly? Use details and examples from the story to support your prediction.

____

____

____

____

Name ____________________

Graphic Sources

Read the book *The Impossible Rescue* and then answer Numbers 1 through 5.

1. Why did the train heading for St. Paul crash into the train yard?

   A. The train's blower and generator were old and did not work properly.
   B. The brakes did not work, and some track switches were in the wrong position.
   C. The engineer was not paying attention to where he was going.
   D. Other trains were parked on the same tracks.

2. Look at the diagram on page 4. Where are the engineer's controls on a train?

   F. next to the engine
   G. in the middle near the generator
   H. at the back of the train
   I. at the front of the train

What happened to Richard Vitek when the train crashed?

A. He was rushed to a hospital.
B. He ran to help rescue the injured.
C. He was trapped under the wreckage.
D. He was hit by the train.

4. How do the pictures in the book help you understand what happened? Use details and examples from the book to support your answer.

____

____

____

Why did the author call this book *The Impossible Rescue?* Use details and examples from the book to explain your answer.

____

____

____

Name ______________________________

Graphic Sources

Read the book *These Old Shoes Remember* and then answer Numbers 1 through 5.

1 What does the map on page 2 show?

A. the coast of New England
B. the original 13 colonies
C. the western coast of America
D. the colonies where shoes were made

2 How did children in Colonial America help their families?

F. They worked on the farm and helped cook and clean.
G. They worked in the local blacksmith's shop.
H. They repaired broken equipment, such as axes, when necessary.
I. They helped rock the babies to sleep.

3 How did the children feel about the jobs they were expected to do?

A. They loved their jobs and usually asked if they could do more.
B. They were resentful because they really wanted to be in school.
C. They often complained because the jobs were so difficult.
D. They accepted them because they knew that everyone had to help.

4 Look at the picture on page 8. How were the homes of Colonial America DIFFERENT from the homes of today? Use information from the text and the picture in your answer.

____

____

____

____

5 Why did the author write this book? Use details and examples from the book to support your answer.

____

____

____

Name ____

Plot

Read the story *Head First* and then answer Numbers 1 through 5.

1 What problem does Cindy have at the beginning of the story?

A. She has to dive in the championship, and she is nervous.
B. She does not like the swimming instructor named Ellen.
C. She wants to learn the sidestroke and breaststroke like her brother.
D. She wants to learn to dive, but she is afraid to put her head underwater.

2 Why does Ellen say Cindy needs a good opponent if she wants to learn to dive?

F. because a good opponent will make her strive to do her best
G. because a good opponent will become her friend
H. because a good opponent will keep her from being nervous
I. because a good opponent will practice with her

3 How does Cindy become one of the divers in the meet?

A. She thinks she is ready and asks the coach to give her a chance.
B. Susan cannot make it, so the coach tells Cindy to take her place.
C. Her family is there and they want to see her dive.
D. She sees Laura dive and really wants to give it a try.

4 How does the story end? Use details from the story to explain the ending.

____

____

____

What lesson does this story teach? Use details and examples from the story to support your answer.

____

____

____

Name

Plot

Read the story *What Isn't Possible!* and then answer Numbers 1 through 5.

 What job do the brothers in this story have?

A. They work at a rich man's house.
B. They deliver newspapers.
C. They clean chimneys.
D. They are messenger boys.

2 What problem does Otis have at the beginning of the story?

F. He gets stuck in a chimney.
G. He drops a bracelet down a chimney.
H. He wants to get a bicycle but does not have the money to buy it.
I. He cannot fit down chimneys anymore because his shoulders are too big.

3 What does Otis find in one of the chimneys he is cleaning?

A. a small candle
B. a family of rats
C. a honeycomb with honey
D. a gold bracelet

4 Why does Mr. Pope take Otis to the carriage house? Use details from the story to support your answer.

____

____

____

____

5 How does Otis's life change in this story? Use details and examples from the story to explain your answer.

____

____

____

Name ______________________________

Text Structure

Read the book *Amazing Ants* and then answer Numbers 1 through 5.

1 This book is

A. science fiction.
B. a fantasy.
C. nonfiction.
D. a realistic story.

2 How is MOST of the information in this book organized?

F. The author gives main ideas and details to support those ideas.
G. The author tells a story in the order that the events occur.
H. The author describes a problem and offers numerous solutions to it.
I. The author identifies an effect and gives the causes for it.

3 Look at the diagram on page 2. Where is an ant's abdomen?

A. near its head
B. between its head and thorax
C. behind its hind legs
D. under its thorax

4 Describe the steps a queen ant follows to build a new colony. Use details and examples from the book to support your answer.

____

____

____

____

____

5 What is the main idea of this book? Use details from the book to explain your answer.

____

____

____

Name ______________________________

Text Structure

Read the book *Apple Cider Days* and then answer Numbers 1 through 5.

1 What is one reason that apple trees must be pruned?

A. to make sure that the nutrients go to the trees and not to the weeds
B. to make sure the small branches have room to grow
C. so that the deer will not be able to eat the apples off the trees
D. to let more light into the trees

2 In April and May, growers

F. spread the fertilizer.
G. prune the trees.
H. kill the buds that have not opened.
I. check the condition of the apples.

3 What is the FIRST step for making apple cider?

A. The mush is pressed so that juice squeezes out.
B. The apples are dumped into a grinder.
C. Cider makers fill a bin with apples.
D. Juice is extracted from the apples.

4 Why is it important to thin out the apple buds? Use details and examples from the book to explain your answer.

____

____

____

____

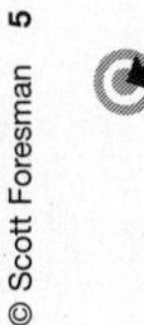

5 How did the author organize the facts presented in this book? Use details and examples from the book to support your answer.

____

____

____

____

Name ___

Summarizing

Read the book *Sheepdogs on Guard* and then answer Numbers 1 through 5.

1 Look at page 5. What is this page mostly about?

- **A.** how to protect sheep with poisons, traps, and guns
- **B.** ranchers who own sheep
- **C.** dogs that are used to guard sheep
- **D.** how sheep live in flocks

2 In what way does the author say that all sheepdogs are ALIKE?

- **F.** They are nervous and playful.
- **G.** They have an instinct to guard.
- **H.** They look like sheep.
- **I.** They act like sheep.

3 What is one reason that guard dogs are placed with sheep at a very young age?

- **A.** so they can begin learning from the other guard dogs
- **B.** so they will become loyal to the sheep
- **C.** so they will not be afraid of predators like coyotes
- **D.** so they can begin protecting the sheep right away

4 Why do ranchers use sheepdogs to guard their animals? Use details and examples from the book to support your answer.

___
___
___
___
___

5 What is this book mostly about? Use details from the book to support your answer.

___
___
___
___

Name ____________________

Summarizing

Read the story *The Mystery of the Silver Stump* and then answer Numbers 1 through 5.

1. What is the silver stump that the animals find?

   A. a special tree stump
   B. a brand-new turtle shell
   C. a silver canoe
   D. a garbage can

2. Why are the animals so interested in the silver stump?

   F. They have heard of stumps like this and want to find out how they work.
   G. They have never seen anything like it and they think it may be valuable.
   H. They want to hide it from the strangers before they return from their trip.
   I. They think the stump may be a cousin of Turtle or Raccoon.

3. If this story needed a new title, which would be BEST?

   A. Trouble at Umbagog Pond
   B. How to Get Rid of Bad Smells
   C. Never Throw Away Smelly Fish
   D. Stumps are Good for Sunning

4. How do the animals change during the story? Use details and examples from the story to support your answer.

____

____

____

5. What is this story mostly about? Use details from the story to support your answer.

____

____

____

____

Name ________________________________

Compare and Contrast

Read the story *When in Rome* and then answer Numbers 1 through 5.

1 Uncle Kronos sends the boy back in time because he wants the boy

A. to taste sow's paunch.
B. to go to a fun party.
C. to try out his new invention.
D. to learn about table manners.

2 Why do the Romans whisper when the boy eats with his hands?

F. They think he is mean.
G. He uses five fingers instead of three.
H. His hands are very dirty.
I. He is supposed to congratulate the host first.

3 What does the boy think the serviette looks like?

A. a piece of bread
B. a soup bowl
C. a towel
D. a waiter

4 How are the table manners of ancient Rome DIFFERENT from the table manners most children are taught today? Use details and examples from the story to support your answer.

____

____

____

____

5 Why is *When in Rome* a good title for this story? Use details and examples from the story to explain your answer.

____

____

____

____

Name ___

Compare and Contrast

Read the book *From the High Hills* and then answer Numbers 1 through 5.

1 What does the author say Hmong villages were like?

A. one large family
B. a tribe of barbarians
C. an army troop
D. a group of outcasts

2 Why did the Hmong first move from China to Laos?

F. The Vietnam War forced them out of their homes.
G. They thought the Chinese people were barbarians.
H. People who considered them outcasts forced them out.
I. They were mountain people who did not know how to swim.

3 What happened to the Hmong when they left Laos for Thailand?

A. They became rice farmers and raised cows and goats.
B. Some died while others were taken to refugee camps.
C. They decided to go to China instead.
D. Soldiers forced them to go back to Laos.

4 How is life DIFFERENT for the Hmong who are now in America? Use details and examples from the book to support your answer.

___

___

___

___

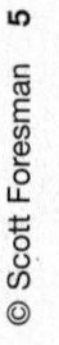

5 Describe the Hmong people. Use details and examples from the book to support your answer.

___

___

___

Name ___

Main Idea and Supporting Details

Read the story *Alone in the Arctic* and then answer Numbers 1 through 5.

1 Why is George out in the cold wilderness alone?

A. He wants to play by himself.
B. He is hunting for food.
C. He wants to build a big tower like his grandfather did.
D. He is returning from delivering medicine to an elder named Elly.

2 Why does George decide to take a shortcut across the creek?

F. He hears his grandfather's voice.
G. He is in a hurry to get home because a storm is coming.
H. He likes to ride on the ice.
I. His father told him this was the best way to get home.

3 What happens when George gets to the other side of the creek?

A. He falls and hurts himself.
B. He sees a few large slabs of ice in the creek.
C. He finds the little seal in his pocket.
D. He runs into his worried parents.

4 What does George do to help himself survive the snow storm? Use details and examples from the story to support your answer

___

___

___

5 What is the main idea of *Alone in the Arctic*? Use details and examples from the story to support your answer.

___

___

___

___

Name ______________________________

Main Idea and Supporting Details

Read the book *A Very Cool Festival* and then answer Numbers 1 through 5.

1 How did the yearly Sapporo Snow Festival begin?

A. In 1974, the city of Sapporo hosted the Winter Olympics.
B. In 1950, some high school students made snow sculptures in Odori Park.
C. The government wanted a festival that would be famous.
D. A team built a copy of Linderhoff Castle in Germany.

2 Snow sculptors buy *hokkailos* to

F. keep their boots from skidding.
G. carve the sculpture.
H. pack the snow tightly.
I. keep them warm while they work.

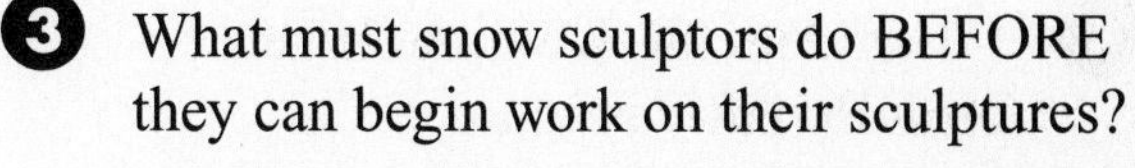

3 What must snow sculptors do BEFORE they can begin work on their sculptures?

A. bring snow down from the mountain
B. chip icicles off the edges of the sculpture
C. build a wire frame
D. carve intricate details in the sculpture

4 What kinds of sculptures are built at the Sapporo Snow Festival? Use details and examples from the book to explain your answer.

____

____

____

____

5 What is the main idea of this book. Use details from the book to explain your answer.

____

____

____

____

Name ______________________________

Predicting

Read the story *Soccer Bash* and then answer Numbers 1 through 5.

1. Corky does NOT want to have a birthday party because

   A. she does not want to grow older.
   B. she does not want to invite the new girl, Billie.
   C. she does not like sleeping at Grandpa's lodge.
   D. she does not want to miss her soccer game.

2. What happens to Corky when Billie kicks the soccer ball?

   F. She falls down and hurts herself.
   G. She gets kicked off the team.
   H. She gets hit in the face by the ball.
   I. She runs into another player.

3. Why do Corky's feelings for Billie change?

   A. Her mom says she has to be nice to Billie.
   B. She feels bad that Billie is so upset about hitting her.
   C. She gets excited about going to her birthday party.
   D. She realizes Billie's dad has a canoe.

4. How might Corky celebrate her birthday next year? Use details and examples from the story to explain your answer.

____

____

____

5. Think about how the story ends. What might happen next? Use details and examples from the story to explain your prediction.

____

____

____

____

Name ______________________________

Predicting

Read the story *Night Journey* and then answer Numbers 1 through 5.

1 What is this story mostly about?

A. a baby's birth
B. working in a hospital
C. jobs that people do at night
D. a midwife

2 What does a midwife do before a baby is born?

F. works at a hospital to learn about babies
G. talks to kindly neighbors and worried husbands
H. helps the mother take care of herself and the unborn baby
I. works with the family to get the baby's room ready

3 What would the midwife MOST likely do if her pager started beeping while she was eating dinner?

A. Get in her car and go to the drugstore.
B. Turn the pager off so she would not be disturbed any more.
C. Leave her dinner and go to help the person who was paging.
D. Finish her dinner and then call the person who was paging.

4 What will the midwife do when she gets to her office? Use details and examples from the story to support your answer.

____

____

____

____

5 What was the author's purpose in writing this book? Use details and examples from the story to explain your answer.

____

____

____

Name ______________________________

Context Clues

Read the story *The Boy and the Eagle: A Pima Folk Tale* and then answer Numbers 1 through 5.

 What does Kelihi want to do at the beginning of the story?

A. climb the mountain and look for an eagle's nest
B. hunt rabbits, quail, and lizards
C. help his father care for the beans and squash
D. ride on an eagle's back

2 When Kelihi reaches the mountaintop and looks down to the desert, what does he see?

F. an eagle
G. an eagle feather
H. his home
I. his father

 What happens after Kelihi finds the eagle's nest?

A. He takes a feather from one of the eagles and brings it to his father.
B. He tries to relax and leans back on a rock to sleep.
C. He gets very nervous and decides to climb down and go home.
D. He falls from the ledge, and an eagle rescues him and carries him home.

4 Read the first paragraph on page 8. What does *downy* mean? Use details from the story to explain how you know what this word means.

____

____

____

5 Read these sentences from the story.

"Why did I sneak away?" he said. Now Kelihi was regretting his entire adventure on the mountain.

What does *regretting* mean? Use details from the story to explain how you know what this word means.

____

____

Name ______________________________

Context Clues

Read the book *Olympics* and then answer Numbers 1 through 5.

1 How were the early Olympics DIFFERENT from today's Olympics?

A. They were very popular events.
B. They were held to honor Zeus.
C. Athletes competed for medals.
D. Sprinting was an Olympic event.

2 How did the Roman emperor Nero win every game he entered?

F. He practiced and trained every day.
G. He was the strongest and fastest man in every competition.
H. He executed anyone who tried to beat him.
I. He had the best coach.

3 Read this sentence from the book.

> **At first, women, slaves, and foreigners were *barred from competing.***

What does *barred from competing* mean?

A. They were not allowed to compete.
B. They were forced to compete.
C. They could only compete against each other.
D. They could only use special bars or poles.

4 Read page 15. Explain what *obstacles* means. Use details and examples from the book to support your explanation.

____

____

____

____

5 Why did a French baron decide to bring back the Olympic games? Use details and examples from the book to explain your answer.

____

____

____

____

Name ______________________________

Author's Purpose

Read the story *Gifts* and then answer Numbers 1 through 5.

1 What has the narrator learned from Michael?

A. how to use a computer
B. how to fly fish
C. how to get up early
D. how to send an e-mail

2 Which word BEST describes the narrator's mood in this story?

F. nervous
G. sad
H. excited
I. angry

3 Why did the author write this story?

A. to give facts about how computers work
B. to persuade readers to learn how to fly fish
C. to entertain readers with a story about two good friends
D. to express strong feelings about how hard it is when a friend moves

4 What gifts do the two friends give each other? Use details and examples to describe the gifts and explain why they are special.

____

____

____

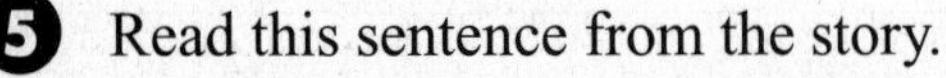

5 Read this sentence from the story.

"No one could figure out how we got to be best friends, but we were."

Why did the author have the narrator say this? Use details and examples from the story to explain your answer.

____

____

____

____

Name ______________________________

Author's Purpose

Read the book *The Great Auto Race of 1908* and then answer Numbers 1 through 5.

1 This book is

A. science fiction.
B. nonfiction.
C. a biography.
D. a folk tale.

2 Who came up with the idea for the Great Auto Race of 1908?

F. George Schuster
G. the owners of the Thomas Flyer
H. the makers of cars in France, Germany, Italy, and the U.S.
I. a newspaper in Paris and a newspaper in New York

3 Why was the German car penalized?

A. Its drivers did not stop in Vladivostok as they had been instructed.
B. The car and its drivers had ridden by train from Idaho to Seattle.
C. The car was too fast for the race.
D. The drivers used horses to pull the car.

4 What problems did Schuster have on his trip to Paris? Use details and examples from the book to explain your answer.

____

____

____

____

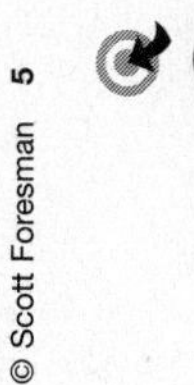

5 Why did the author write this book? Use details and examples from the book to explain your answer.

____

____

____

____

Name

Setting

Read the story *How I Settled the West* and then answer Numbers 1 through 5.

1 When does this story take place?

A. in present times
B. more than a hundred years ago
C. last week
D. at some point in the future

2 What annoying thing happens as the family is traveling west?

F. There is a flood.
G. A wheel breaks on the wagon.
H. A man tries to rob them.
I. They are attacked by coyotes.

3 What is bothering the narrator throughout the story?

A. She does not know which way to go.
B. She is very hungry.
C. She is worried about her children.
D. She misses her husband.

4 Describe the area where the family settles. Use details from the story to explain your answer.

____

____

____

____

5 How do you know this story could NOT really happen? Use details and examples from the story in your answer.

____

____

____

____

____

Name ______________________________

Setting

Read the story *Molly McGill's Great Ride* and then answer Numbers 1 through 5.

1 Where does this story take place?

A. at a peppermint factory
B. in the mayor's mansion
C. next to Molly's school
D. in the town of Mintville

2 Why does Molly want to ride on the trolley?

F. She is tired of living in Mintville.
G. She wants to meet Hamilton Gross.
H. Her father rode on it once when he was a boy.
I. Mrs. Longnotes tells her it will take her back in time.

3 Where does the trolley take Molly?

A. to another town
B. to the yo-yo factory
C. to Mintville ten years earlier
D. to Hamilton Gross's house

4 What does Molly do to get Hamilton Gross to quit lying about her father? Use details and examples from the story to explain your answer.

____

____

____

____

5 How is Molly's family DIFFERENT when she returns to the present time? Use details and examples from the story to explain your answer.

____

____

____

____

Name ______________________________

Paraphrasing

Read the book *A Thousand Miles to Freedom* and then answer Numbers 1 through 5.

1 How did Ellen and William Craft escape from their Georgia plantation?

- **A.** They snuck off in the middle of the night.
- **B.** They followed Harriet Tubman's Underground Railroad.
- **C.** William borrowed a horse and gun from the owner.
- **D.** Ellen dressed as a white man and pretended to be William's owner.

2 Which word BEST describes William and Ellen Craft?

- **F.** friendly
- **G.** brave
- **H.** dangerous
- **I.** unprepared

3 Why did Ellen put her arm in a sling?

- **A.** She thought it would make her look less like a slave.
- **B.** She was hiding supplies in the sling.
- **C.** She did not want anyone to expect her to write.
- **D.** She injured her arm while trying to escape.

4 Describe how the Crafts traveled from Macon to Philadelphia, and name the different kinds of transportation they used.

____

____

____

____

5 Why did the Crafts move to England? Include details from the book in your answer.

____

____

____

Name ______________________________

Paraphrasing

Read the book *Nelson Mandela* and then answer Numbers 1 through 5.

1 What did Nelson Mandela learn about when he was a boy?

A. why his name meant "pulling the branches of trees"
B. how the black Africans lost their land and became very poor
C. how to get a job as a policeman
D. that the African National Congress was in Johannesburg

2 What is *apartheid*?

F. a separation of the races
G. a type of prison cell
H. vowing to end unfair treatment
I. working with the government

3 Why was Mandela arrested and sent to jail so many times?

A. He refused to speak out against unfair laws.
B. He opened his own law office, which was illegal for black lawyers.
C. He lived outside of his black township.
D. He worked to change laws that were unfair to blacks.

4 Describe what life was like for Mandela while he was in prison. Use details from the book to support your answer.

____

____

____

5 What happened when Mandela ran for president in 1994? Use details and events from the book to support your answer.

____

____

____

____

____

Name ______________________________

Visualizing

Read the book *Riding the Bullet* and then answer Numbers 1 through 5.

1. What does Kenji convince his sister and grandmother to do?

   A. ride an airplane to Grandmother's house
   B. go shopping in Hiroshima
   C. buy peanuts from the snack cart
   D. take the bullet train to Hiroshima

2. How are the Nozomi 500 and a jet plane ALIKE?

   F. they both have a long, thin nose and a silver body
   G. they use the same type of fuel
   H. they hold the same number of people
   I. their lengths are the same

3. The author says, **"The two trains passed in a blur of white cars,"** to show that

   A. the trains are made up of hundreds of white connected cars.
   B. the trains were going so fast that the individual cars just looked like a blur.
   C. the colors on the train are blurry and need to be repainted.
   D. the cars were so close together that they almost crashed into each other.

4. Read page 9. What phrases does the author use to describe the way the Nozomi 500 comes into a station? Explain what these phrases mean.

____

____

____

____

5. How does Kenji feel about riding the bullet train? Use details and examples from the book to support your answer.

____

____

____

____

Name ____

 # Visualizing

Read the story *Pound Pals* and then answer Numbers 1 through 5.

1 How is this story told?

A. through a journal in which a dog has recorded his thoughts
B. through a child's report about what life is really like in a dog pound
C. as an autobiography written by a talking dog
D. through letters that have been exchanged between two dogs

2 Where does Mitzi live after she is taken from the pound?

F. at Mrs. Uptown's house
G. on the waterfront
H. on a farm
I. in the forest

 **3** Read page 4. Which sentence BEST describes Mugsy's new owner?

A. She yips, yaps, and howls like a dog.
B. She is a fancy lady who smells like soap.
C. She is a sad lady looking for a new dog.
D. She has fancy food at her house.

4 How does the author help the reader imagine what the woods are like when Mitzi is there? Use details from the story in your answer.

____

____

____

____

5 How do both dogs feel about their new homes at the end of the story? Use details and examples from the story to support your answer.

____

____

____

Name ______________________________

Context Clues

Read the story *To Your Good Health: A Russian Tale* and then answer Numbers 1 through 5.

1. Why does Larissa buy 183 pairs of shoes, 67 purses, and 48 belts in one year?

   A. She is tired of being an ordinary woman and wants special things.
   B. She keeps buying things at Pavel's store so she can see him.
   C. Her father, the czar, insists that she have all these things.
   D. Princes from around the world are coming to the palace to marry her.

2. Read the first paragraph on page 6.

   What does *decreed* mean?

   F. curiously wondered
   G. quietly thought
   H. angrily disagreed
   I. formally announced

3. Why does Pavel refuse to say **"To your good health!"** to the czar when he sneezes?

   A. He does not like the czar.
   B. He does not know how to say it correctly.
   C. He wants to hear the bells ring.
   D. He wants the czar to notice him.

4. Read page 14. What does the author mean when he says that the boars in the boar pen are *ferocious*? Use details from the story to explain your answer.

   ____
   ____
   ____
   ____

5. Why does the czar finally allow Pavel to marry his daughter? Use details and examples from the story to explain your answer.

   ____
   ____
   ____

Name ______________________________

Context Clues

Read the book *Passing Through Ellis Island* and then answer Numbers 1 through 5.

1 Read page 2. What are *immigrants*?

A. people who are poor and take many tests
B. people who are not allowed to stay in America
C. people who leave their homelands and come to live in America
D. people who leave America and go to live in other countries

2 What was it like to travel to America by boat in third class?

F. very uncomfortable
G. very fancy
H. very comfortable
I. very quiet

3 Why did the inspectors at Ellis Island make chalk marks on some people's clothing?

A. to show that the person had to return to their home country
B. to let everyone know that the person had a child
C. to indicate that the person had some sort of a problem
D. to show that the person was ready to enter the country

4 Why were some immigrants especially upset to be sent back to their homelands? Use details and examples from the book to support your answer.

____

____

____

5 Read page 13. The author says that *translators* were needed at Ellis Island. Use details from the book to explain what *translators* are.

____

____

____

____

Name ______________________________

Paraphrasing

Read the story *Papa Lincoln* and then answer Numbers 1 through 5.

1 When does this story take place?

A. in present times
B. in the early 1900s
C. on April 14, 1865
D. during the Civil War

2 Who are the most important characters in this story?

F. Mr. and Mrs. Lincoln
G. Abe Lincoln and Walt Whitman
H. Abe Lincoln and his son Tad
I. Abe Lincoln and some soldiers

3 What does Abe Lincoln say about Negro soldiers becoming officers?

A. These are difficult times. No one can predict what will happen.
B. It will never happen. People are not ready for it.
C. They can certainly do it. It will definitely happen someday.
D. They will make great soldiers. It might happen in the future.

4 What problem does Abe Lincoln have in this story? Use details from the story to explain your answer.

____

____

____

____

____

5 How do Tad Lincoln and his father feel about each other? Use details and examples from the story to explain your answer.

____

____

____

____

Name ______________________________

Paraphrasing

Read the story *Elena's Ride* and then answer Numbers 1 through 5.

 Why is Elena staying on her uncle's ranch for the summer?

A. Her mother is in school and her father has started a new job.
B. Her cousin Pepe needs help with the chores on the ranch.
C. She wants to get to know her relatives better.
D. She is interested in the ranch that has been in her family for years.

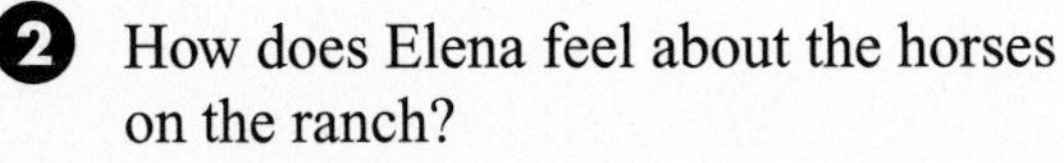
2 How does Elena feel about the horses on the ranch?

F. She wants to learn to ride them.
G. She thinks they are very interesting.
H. She thinks they are ugly.
I. She is afraid of them.

 What happens to Pepe when he climbs up the rock?

A. He gets to the top easily, but then realizes he cannot get down.
B. A loud noise frightens him and he cannot go any further.
C. Rocks crumble and fall, and Pepe slips into a mine shaft.
D. He falls from the top of the cliff and injures his leg.

4 What does Elena do when she realizes Pepe needs help? Use details from the story to explain your answer.

____

____

____

____

5 Explain why Elena is NOT afraid as she rides the horse down the mountain. Use details from the story to explain your answer.

____

____

____

Name

Theme

Read the play *The Great Bake-off* and then answer Numbers 1 through 5.

1 Why do the characters in this play decide to have a bake sale?

A. Jenna's dad says that baking is one of life's pleasures.
B. All of their parents are busy, and they like to cook.
C. They want to raise money for their class trip.
D. They are bored and want a new project.

2 Why does Jenna's dad leave the children alone in the kitchen?

F. He is busy with other work.
G. He does not like to be in the kitchen.
H. The children want to cook by themselves.
I. He has to go catch the dog.

3 What lesson do the children learn about cooking in this play?

A. Baking bread and cookies is very easy to do.
B. Peanut butter cookies are like peanut butter dog biscuits.
C. It is important to read and follow directions carefully.
D. You should clean each dish as soon as you use it.

4 Why do the children add more yeast to the bread dough? Explain why this was a bad idea. Use details and examples from the play in your answer.

____

____

____

5 Why is it a good idea for the children to have a pet fair? Use details from the play to support your answer.

____

____

____

Name ______________________________

Theme

Read the story *Clever Manka* and then answer Numbers 1 through 5.

1 When two brothers are unable to settle a dispute over land, Manka suggests that

- **A.** the brothers draw straws to see who should get the better piece.
- **B.** they share the land so that they will both be happy.
- **C.** they return to their parents and let them decide.
- **D.** one brother divide the land and the other choose his half first.

2 When the judge marries Manka, he tells her to never

- **F.** make a plan without telling him.
- **G.** return to her peasant family.
- **H.** let other people know how clever she is.
- **I.** interfere with any of his judgments.

3 What lesson does Manka teach the judge in this story?

- **A.** that living in a peasant's house is better than living in a mansion
- **B.** that people need to share all of their worldly possessions
- **C.** that he should not let his anger make him do foolish things
- **D.** that women are really smarter than men

4 Why are the judge's rulings wiser and more sound at the end of the story? Use details from the story to explain your answer.

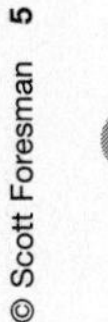

5 What lesson does this story teach? Use details and examples from the story to explain your answer.

Name ______________________________

Steps in a Process

Read the story *The Assignment* and then answer Numbers 1 through 5.

1 What problem does Tyler have at the beginning of the story?

A. His sister keeps nagging him so he cannot study for his test.
B. He has to write an essay about pioneer life on the Oregon Trail.
C. He has to complete an assignment on the Oregon Trail by Monday.
D. He needs his sister to help him with a project, and she is not cooperating.

2 Tyler decides to go to the library to

F. find books about drawing.
G. find a topic for his report.
H. learn the Dewey Decimal system.
I. find information on what the pioneers ate.

When Tyler and Nancy get to the library, which of the following do they do FIRST?

A. go to the computer terminal and type in *Oregon Trail*
B. look through the books on the shelves to find one about pioneers
C. look up their topic in the index of a book
D. find the *Oregon Trail* section in the library

4 When Tyler selects the book with the covered wagon on the front, what does Nancy tell him to do NEXT? Use details from the story to explain your answer.

____

____

____

How do Tyler's feelings about his sister change during the story? Use details from the book to explain your answer.

____

____

____

____

Name ______________________________

Steps in a Process

Read the book *Beetles* and then answer Numbers 1 through 5.

 How are all beetles ALIKE?

A. They have hard and soft wings.
B. They live in ponds and streams.
C. They glow in the dark.
D. They live for only three weeks.

 Which beetle may have developed before dinosaurs?

F. the whirligig
G. the firefly
H. the ladybug
I. the scarab

3. What happens AFTER a beetle larva is finished growing?

A. It finds a protected place and lays hundreds of eggs.
B. It uses its strong jaws to eat more and more.
C. It finds a quiet space and grows a hard case called a pupa.
D. It begins to fly and uses its flicker as a signal.

4. Describe the four stages in the development of a firefly. Use details and examples from the book to explain your description.

____

____

____

____

 What are the most important facts about water beetles? Use details and examples from the book to explain your answer.

____

____

____

____

____

Name

Plot

Read the story *Winning Tubby* and then answer Numbers 1 through 5.

1 At the beginning of the story, Liz wants to

A. write an essay to win a hamster for her classroom.
B. write a convincing essay so she will get to take Tubby home.
C. teach her dog to quit chewing on everything.
D. remember to feed and take care of her pets every day.

2 What does Liz's father tell her she should do?

F. explain exactly why the classroom needs a hamster
G. prove that she can make Tubby's life better
H. enjoy the pets that she already has
I. teach her pets new tricks

3 How does Liz feel about her essay when she brings it to class?

A. proud
B. sad
C. unsure
D. embarrassed

4 How do Liz's feelings change AFTER she sees Charlotte's essay? Use details from the story to explain your answer.

____

____

____

5 Did Liz do the right thing when she let Charlotte have the hamster? Use details from the story to support the judgment you make.

____

____

____

Name

Plot

Read the story *A Marvelous Event* and then answer Numbers 1 through 5.

1 What is known about the people who come from Don Roberto's town?

A. They tell stories that can always be proven.
B. They love fast horses.
C. They love the truth and never lie.
D. They live to be more than 100 years old.

2 Why do all the family members come and sit around Don Roberto's bed?

F. His great strength comes from rock juice.
G. They want to tell him some stories.
H. He has just turned eighty-eight years old.
I. He will not wake up and they fear he is very ill.

3 What do the family members begin to do as they sit with Don Roberto?

A. They talk to one another about how much they love him.
B. They make a plan for dividing his land.
C. They tell stories of his amazing courage and strength.
D. They talk about how sad and lonely they feel.

4 What does Don Roberto do as Doña Maria is telling a story? Use details from the story to explain what he does and why.

5 Why did the author call this story *A Marvelous Event?* Use details and examples from the story to explain your answer.

Name ______________________________

Making Judgments

Read the book *How the Cat Got His Hat: The Story of Dr. Seuss* and then answer Numbers 1 through 5.

1 Book publishers did NOT like Ted Geisel's work at first because they

A. did not like his drawings.
B. thought his books were too long.
C. thought his stories were too scary.
D. thought his stories were too silly.

2 Why did Geisel select Dr. Seuss as his pen name?

F. He always wanted to be a doctor.
G. Seuss was his middle name.
H. He thought it sounded interesting.
I. His publisher told him to use it.

3 Why did Dr. Seuss write *The Cat in the Hat*?

A. His publisher asked him to write a children's book using only 250 words.
B. His drawing of an elephant landed on top of his drawing of a tree.
C. He and his wife wanted to start their own publishing company.
D. His friend asked him to write it for his children.

4 Did Ted Geisel (Dr. Seuss) like challenges? Use details and examples from the book to explain your answer.

____

____

____

____

5 Was Dr. Seuss's work important? Use details and examples from the book to explain your answer.

____

____

____

____

Name ______________________________

Making Judgments

Read the story *A Grand Opening* and then answer Numbers 1 through 5.

1 How does Tina want Jake to help her with the opening of the flower shop?

A. put the new vases on the shelves
B. write an interesting advertisement for her to put in the newspaper
C. paint the walls and put up shelves
D. get rid of the old junk and spread the word that the shop is opening

2 How do Jake and his friends use the old cart FIRST?

F. They roll it downtown with flowers and plants in it.
G. They use it as a go cart.
H. They hang signs and banners on it.
I. They use it as a way to sell things and attract attention.

3 Why does the flower shop get very few customers on opening day?

A. The boys have taken down all their banners.
B. Everyone is at the opening of the new department store.
C. Most people are not interested in flowers.
D. Some people think Rosie does not have good flowers.

4 Was it a good idea for Jake and his friends to wheel the flower cart downtown? Use details from the story to explain your answer.

____

____

____

5 How do Jake and Tina feel about each other? Use details and examples from the story to explain your answer.

____

____

____

____

Name

Visualizing

Read the book *Pablo Picasso* and then answer Numbers 1 through 5.

1 Picasso's father FIRST realized that his son had great artistic talent when Picasso drew

A. a dolphin on the beach.
B. a flower instead of a sun in the sky.
C. with charcoal on a clean bed sheet.
D. pictures that looked cut up and rearranged.

2 Look at the painting on pages 18 and 19. What kinds of feelings does Picasso express about the bombing of Guernica?

F. wonder and amazement
G. love and happiness
H. victory and pride
I. sadness and horror

3 Why was Picasso put into the advanced classes at the art academy in Barcelona?

A. His friend died suddenly and unexpectedly.
B. His father saw that Picasso's work was much better than his own.
C. He painted two impressive human figures in one day.
D. He could not develop a style of his own yet.

4 Tell what emotions Picasso expressed through his paintings during his "Blue Period" and tell why he felt these emotions. Use details from the book to explain your answer.

____

____

5 Describe Cubism and tell why Picasso developed this style of painting. Use details and examples from the book to explain your answer.

____

____

____

____

____

Name ______________________________

 # Visualizing

Read the book *Behind the Scenes* and then answer Numbers 1 through 5.

1 What is this book mostly about?

A. a new type of special effect known as claymation
B. the tricks that producers used in creating early movies
C. the special effects that are used in movies
D. Albert E. Smith and J. Stuart Blackton's use of special effects

2 What was one of the first special effects used?

F. stop-motion photography
G. miniatures
H. claymation
I. blue screens

3 Which sentence BEST tells what a telephoto lens does?

A. It makes two things that are far apart look close together.
B. It makes two things that are close together look far apart.
C. It takes pictures faster than other lenses.
D. It makes miniature objects appear large.

4 Explain how blue screen photography works. Use details from the book in your answer.

____

____

____

____

5 Look at the picture on page 23. How would the people, the butterflies, and the dog made of clay look in the finished movie? Use details and examples from the book in your answer.

____

____

____

Answer Key

Leveled Reader Practice

Page 154

1. B
2. I
3. C
4. Robo grabs a boy's sandwich right out of his hands.
5. Possible answer: Robo needs a little more work. It cleans a student's lunch right off the table. Then it grabs a boy's sandwich right out of his hands.

Page 155

1. B
2. F
3. C
4. Grown men's lips begin to tremble, and the crowd begins to bawl like babies. When Rusty finishes, everyone jumps to their feet and cheers.
5. Possible answer: Rusty loves the Old Cowboy very much. When Rusty sees that the Old Cowboy is unable to sing, she jumps up to sing for him. The story says that if the Old Cowboy is happy, Rusty is happy.

Page 156

1. C
2. I
3. A
4. Possible answer: He is smart, adventurous, and brave. He travels to faraway planets and studies ancient cultures.
5. He is interested in the puppy because it resembles the dogs that ancient Egyptians had. He thinks that may mean that ancient Egyptians were on Artemis at one time.

Page 157

1. B
2. G
3. B
4. Possible answer: At first, he thinks Chiapas will be boring, but by the end he says it is amazing. He is excited to see Palenque and the king's tomb. He wants to know about the ruins and asks his uncle a lot of questions.
5. Possible answer: The author wrote *Chiapas* to give information about an area in Mexico and to tell an entertaining story about a boy who learns that new places can sometimes be more exciting than expected.

Page 158

1. D
2. F
3. C
4. She is very proud of Lilah. She hugs her and says she is in awe of her.
5. They select dogs that are small to mid-sized. The dogs have to be smart enough to understand when there is danger. They have to be able to jump up on their owner's bed to wake their owners.

Page 159

1. B
2. I
3. A
4. Possible answer: Ant crawls into Lion's ear to find out what is causing him pain. She sees Worm and wakes him up. When they jump out of Lion's ear, the pain goes away.
5. Possible answer: He learns that no one is ever too small to be important. The small worm causes him great pain. The tiny ant helps him when larger animals cannot.

Page 160

1. D
2. H
3. A
4. Possible answer: People began to see how good the African American players were. They decided it was time for these players to play in the major leagues.
5. Possible answer: The author wanted to give information about the Negro Leagues and let readers know about some great African American baseball players who played in these leagues.

Page 161

1. C
2. I
3. B
4. Possible answer: Carol begins running as fast as she can. The crowd is cheering so loudly that Lisa doesn't hear her coming. At the last minute, Carol sprints past her and wins.
5. Possible answer: After Yumiko's fall, Yumiko convinces Carol to keep running. Carol thinks Yumiko's encouragement helps her win the race, so she wants Yumiko with her for the special float ride.

Page 162

1. B
2. H
3. C
4. Possible answers: When she saves the little girl, Aisha realizes how important her glasses are. When she sees that her cousin is just as embarrassed about her braces, she decides the glasses are no big deal.
5. Possible answers: The author wanted to entertain readers with a story about a girl and her cousin. The author wanted to help readers remember that the way we look is not that important.

Page 163

1. A
2. I
3. C
4. Possible answer: The students do work very well together. They organize the tasks and divide them fairly. They get all the jobs done in time for the play. They all seem happy and act is if they're having fun.
5. Possible answer: The author wanted to tell a story about some fifth graders and give information about the jobs that

have to be done when preparing a play.

Page 164

1. A
2. I
3. D
4. First, she brushes away loose sand and twigs with her flippers. Next, she digs a hole with her back legs. Then she lays her eggs.
5. Possible answers: People have hunted sea turtles for food and for their beautiful shells. They have also destroyed many of the places where sea turtles live.

Page 165

1. D
2. H
3. C
4. They begin trying to push the dolphin toward the water. Other people come forward to help. The dolphin slides and splashes around. Finally, a big wave breaks and lots of water comes into the canal. The dolphin shoots down the canal and into the water.
5. Possible answers: A Dolphin Rescue, A Fish Out of Water, Teamwork Saves the Day

Page 166

1. A
2. G
3. C
4. She lists the name of the bird, the place it was sighted, the date, and the time she saw it.
5. She draws a beautiful picture of a condor in her journal. Jemma is surprised because she thought Aunt Connie just kept numbers in her journal. Also, she didn't know Aunt Connie was such a good artist.

Page 167

1. A
2. H
3. C
4. Possible answer: The author includes photographs to show pictures of the founders of the Red Cross and to show some of the different ways the Red Cross helps people.
5. Possible answer: The Red Cross supplies blood and organs for transplants, offers first-aid and CPR programs, offers swimming and water safety classes, and provides relief services after disasters.

Page 168

1. C
2. H
3. D
4. Possible answer: All of the volunteers have worked very hard. Everyone is proud of a job well done and is happy for the family that now has a home.
5. Possible answer: The author thinks Habitat for Humanity is a worthy organization that does important work. He supports this opinion by describing the work that people do and telling how the volunteers and homeowners feel about it.

Page 169

1. A
2. H
3. B
4. Possible answer: They probably thought it was very important. Evidence shows that structures inside the pyramids are aimed right at important stars. The pyramids may be the oldest star observatories.
5. First, find Orion. Next, find its belt. Then look downward to the left. The first bright star you see is Sirius.

Page 170

1. D
2. G
3. C
4. Possible answer: The author wrote this book to give facts about the history of sequoia trees and Sequoia National Park.
5. Possible answer: The author thinks it is a good idea to save the sequoias. When she says the sequoias are now protected "thanks to Muir and others," we can tell she is pleased that the trees were saved.

Page 171

1. C
2. I
3. C
4. Possible answer: No, he would not. He says it is unfortunate that some people only see it as a worthless swamp. He says that we need to protect and preserve the salt marshes for animals, fish, birds, and people.
5. Possible answer: You might see birds, ducks, shellfish, snails, mud, cord grass, geese, muskrats, sea lavender, glasswort, fiddler crabs, snowy egrets, and monarch butterflies.

Page 172

1. A
2. I
3. D
4. Possible answers: The population grew. Some businesses, such as Levi Strauss, formed. Many Native Americans lost their lives and their land.
5. Possible answer: A person needed to be brave, adventurous, and hard-working. A person had to be willing to risk his or her life to get to California and be willing to work hard digging dirt and sifting gravel to find gold.

Page 173

1. C
2. F
3. D
4. Possible answer: Anansi doesn't want to wait until the feast to try the elephant's food, so he tries to trick the elephant into letting him sample the food to prove how good it is.
5. Answers will vary, but students should cite story details that support the lesson they suggest. Possible answer: If you're too greedy, you could end up with nothing.

Page 174

1. D
2. G
3. B
4. Possible answer: Emily does not give up. She rebuilds her fort, making it stronger than it was before.

5. Possible answer: A deaf girl named Emily moves to a new school and feels very out of place. While playing in the woods one day, she decides to build a fort. A man who owns the land tears down her fort. Two girls who are nearby help her rebuild it in another place. The girls become her friends, and Emily feels much happier.

Page 175

1. C
2. H
3. A
4. Possible answer: Grandma Wingfield is a kind, honest person. She does not use her flying skills to do bad things. In fact, when Burt says he would like to fly so he could slam dunk every basketball, Grandma tells him that that would be cheating.
5. Possible answer: Burt will be able to fly because it's a family trait. His sister can fly, and Grandma says that if he's inherited the trait, his ability should show up sometime soon.

Page 176

1. B
2. I
3. C
4. Possible answer: The pictures show the danger Vitek was in. You can see Vitek's arm trapped behind his back and how far he is from the rescuers.
5. Possible answer: The author titled it in this way because the rescue really seemed impossible. Fuel was seeping all around Vitek, and there was wreckage that could come crashing down at any minute.

Page 177

1. B
2. F
3. D
4. Possible answers: They were made of logs. The whole house was one big room. A large kettle hung over the fireplace. The furniture was hard and uncomfortable. Food hung on the walls. A butter churner, spinning wheel, and horn book were in the house.
5. Possible answer: The author wanted to give information about life in Colonial America, create interest in the study of Colonial America, and show how life in Colonial America was different from life today.

Page 178

1. D
2. F
3. B
4. Possible answer: Cindy dives in the meet and does a good job. Her team is proud of her, and she is proud of herself. She now wants to become an even better diver.
5. Possible answer: If you want something badly enough, you can have it. If you work hard and don't give up, you will achieve your goals.

Page 179

1. C
2. H
3. D
4. Possible answer: Mr. Pope wants to reward Otis for being honest. He sees Otis look at a bicycle on the street, so he takes Otis to the carriage house to give him one of his bicycles.
5. Possible answer: Otis does not have to clean chimneys anymore. He can be a messenger, which is a much safer job.

Page 180

1. C
2. F
3. C
4. Possible answer: The queen leaves the colony into which she was born. She finds a new place to build a nest. She uses her mouth to dig a tunnel and strengthens the walls with dirt and saliva. As soon as her wings drop off, she lays eggs and begins guarding them.
5. Possible answer: Ants work very hard and very well together, each doing the task it was born to do.

Page 181

1. D
2. F
3. C
4. Possible answers: Thinning helps the tree grow bigger apples. Apple buds form in clusters of five. By removing four of the buds, all of the nutrients in the branch go to just one apple. So instead of getting five small apples, growers get one big one.
5. Possible answer: The author organized the facts in this book in time order. The author went through the seasons and months of the year in order, telling what happens in the apple orchard during each time of the year.

Page 182

1. C
2. G
3. B
4. Possible answer: Sheepdogs are alert and smart, and they are good at warning off predators. They are strong enough to stand up to a pack of coyotes. Ranchers on large ranches don't have enough time to check on their sheep very often.
5. Possible answer: Special dogs are used to guard sheep on ranches. These dogs are calm, loyal, and smart. Ranchers who use sheepdogs do not lose many sheep to predators.

Page 183

1. D
2. G
3. A
4. Possible answer: In the beginning of the story, the animals fight with one another over who will get to keep the strange stump. Once they realize that the stump is just garbage, they stop arguing over it.
5. Possible answer: The animals of Umbagog Pond discover a silver stump that they think is very important. They start to fight over the mysterious stump until they realize it is just a smelly garbage can.

Page 184

1. D
2. G
3. C

4. Possible answer: In ancient Rome, people laid down to eat. They didn't use forks. They ate using only three fingers on their right hands. They congratulated one another when they sneezed. They wiped their greasy fingers on bread. They considered a loud burp the height of good manners.
5. *When in Rome* is a good title because there is an old phrase that says, "When in Rome, do as the Romans do." This story is about a boy who learns the importance of following the customs of the people he is with.

Page 185

1. A
2. H
3. B
4. Possible answers: They have been exposed to modern inventions such as airplanes, cars, washing machines, and stoves. They have had to learn new ways to earn a living. People who do not understand their ways have sometimes insulted them.
5. Answers will vary, but students should cite details that support their responses. Students may say that the Hmong are patient, fair, kind, and good. They look after one another and value their traditions.

Page 186

1. D
2. G
3. A
4. Possible answers: He wraps cloth around his hurt leg. He builds a rock tower so people can find him. He scoops a hole out of the snow where he can rest and stay warm.
5. Possible answers: A boy uses his brains to survive a terrible storm in the Arctic wilderness. A boy stuck in the Arctic wilderness stays calm until he is rescued.

Page 187

1. B
2. I
3. A
4. Possible answer: Some sculptors make copies of famous palaces and temples; others create original works. Some create sculptures just for kids. Others create sculptures that simply have interesting shapes.
5. Possible answers: The Sapporo Snow Festival is an interesting and exciting event. The Sapporo Snow Festival is a lot of fun.

Page 188

1. B
2. H
3. B
4. Possible answer: Corky will probably go up to Grandpa's lodge again. Grandma will make fry bread and Grandpa will tell stories.
5. Answers will vary, but students should use story details to support their predictions. Their responses should be logical and should reflect the idea that the girls are now friends and will probably continue to be so.

Page 189

1. D
2. H
3. C
4. Possible answer: She will take care of patients in her office, teaching mothers how to take care of themselves and their unborn babies. She might even get another call telling her to go to the hospital to deliver another baby.
5. Possible answer: The author wanted to give information about being a midwife and to express opinions about the importance of a midwife's job.

Page 190

1. A
2. H
3. D
4. *Downy* means soft and fluffy. The author says the baby eagles looked like fluffy clouds.
5. *Regretting* means feeling sorry about something. Kelihi thinks his idea to climb the mountain was a bad one.

Page 191

1. B
2. H
3. A
4. Possible answer: The book says that people have overcome *obstacles* on their way to the Olympics. Then it gives examples, such as sickness and poverty. From these examples, it is clear that *obstacles* are problems.
5. Possible answers: He believed that the ancient Greeks' love of sports had made their civilization great. He believed that if people from all over the world got together to compete, they would get to know each other better. This might make war less likely.

Page 192

1. B
2. G
3. C
4. Michael gives the narrator a rod, a reel, some flies, a knife, and a fishing hat. The narrator gives Michael her old computer. The gifts are special because they will help the friends remember each other.
5. Possible answer: The author wanted to show that the narrator and Michael were very different. The narrator was a good athlete and loved computers. Michael loved to fish. Even though they had different interests, they still managed to be best friends.

Page 193

1. B
2. I
3. B
4. Possible answer: He kept getting stuck in the mud. He had to stop at garages for repairs. He got caught in a blizzard. He had to battle clouds of gnats and swollen rivers. He ran into some chickens.
5. Answers will vary, but students should support their opinions with details from the book. Most will probably say that the author wrote this book to give information about an historic event.

Page 194

1. B
2. H
3. D

4. Possible answer: It is called Paradise, Texas, and it has long, grassy meadows, sparkling waters, and trees that are so tall that the tops disappear into the clouds.
5. Answers will vary, but students should cite specific story details that could not happen. For example, a coyote would not sing with a family, a family couldn't build a house in one day, and a woman could not talk five bears into giving her their fur.

Page 195

1. D
2. I
3. C
4. She runs to the town square and begins singing a beautiful song. Hamilton Gross is so touched by the song that he breaks down and tells the truth about Hubert McGill
5. Possible answer: They live in the mayor's mansion. Her father is the mayor. Her parents do not have their boring jobs anymore. They all look much happier.

Page 196

1. D
2. G
3. C
4. They took a train from Macon to Savannah. Then they took a ship to Charleston, South Carolina. Next, they took another steamship to Wilmington, North Carolina. Then a train took them to Fredericksburg, Virginia. There they took a ship to Washington, and then a train to Baltimore. Finally, they took a train to Philadelphia.
5. Possible answer: A law was passed that allowed slave owners to come north to get their escaped slaves. The Crafts did not want to be captured and taken back to Georgia, so they left the country.

Page 197

1. B
2. F
3. D
4. Possible answer: He lived in a cell with one small window covered with iron bars. He did not have much to eat, and he had to spend his days crushing stones into gravel. He could have one visitor every six months.
5. Possible answer: Millions of people stood in line so they could vote for Mandela. Since apartheid had begun, people had not been given this opportunity. They were determined to wait until they had their chance. Mandela won the election and officially became the president on May 10, 1994.

Page 198

1. D
2. F
3. B
4. Possible answer: He says it "swoops in like a seabird landing," which means that it comes in very quickly and somewhat suddenly. He also says it arrives in a "hissing whoosh," which tells the sound the train makes as it stops.
5. Students should understand that Kenji is very excited about riding the bullet train. They should cite specific details that support this idea, such as his desire to convince the others to take the train and his thrill when the two trains pass each other.

Page 199

1. D
2. H
3. B
4. Possible answer: The author describes the woods as a "symphony of sounds." He writes about the "chirping, chittering, cooing, whistling, buzzing, and humming" that Mitzi hears while she is there.
5. Answers will vary but should be well supported by specific story details. Most students will probably conclude that both animals are content at the end of the story.

Page 200

1. B
2. I
3. D
4. Possible answer: The story says the boars were not sweet little pigs. They had sharp tusks and angry red eyes, so *ferocious* must mean fierce or vicious.
5. Possible answer: When Pavel refuses to take all the gold and treasure, the czar realizes how much Pavel loves his daughter. Then he allows him to marry her.

Page 201

1. C
2. F
3. C
4. Possible answer: Some had left their home countries to escape from war, hunger, or hatred. They desperately wanted to stay to make a new home for their families.
5. Possible answer: The author says that most of the people who arrived at Ellis Island did not speak English and that is why translators were needed. Translators must be people who can speak more than one language and tell people what is being said.

Page 202

1. D
2. H
3. C
4. Possible answers: He's very concerned about the war in which his country is involved. He's preparing for an important speech. He thinks that all people should be treated equally. He knows that some people disagree with him, so he is unsure of what will happen.
5. Answers will vary but should be well supported by story details. Most students will probably say that Tad Lincoln and his father are very close. They spend a lot of time talking together about things that are important to the boy.

Page 203

1. A
2. I
3. C
4. Possible answer: She yells Pepe's name and waits for him to answer. When he says he's okay, she grabs the horse's reins and leads him to a rock so she can climb up on his back. Then she races down the hill to get help.

5. Possible answer: She is not thinking about her own fear. She is worried about her cousin, and she is determined to get help for him quickly.

Page 204

1. C
2. I
3. C
4. Possible answer: They think it will make the bread get bigger. This is a bad idea because it is not what the recipe tells them to do. Later, when they bake the bread, it grows too big for the oven.
5. It is a good idea because the children made plenty of dog biscuits to sell. They can also make money for their class trip by being pet sitters and dog walkers.

Page 205

1. D
2. I
3. C
4. Possible answer: He begins to listen to his wife because she is a very clever woman.
5. Possible answers: Sometimes you can learn a lot by listening to other people. Even if you are very important, there may be people who are smarter than you.

Page 206

1. C
2. I
3. A
4. She tells him to use the index to find out what pages in the book tell about food the pioneers ate.
5. Possible answer: At the beginning of the story, Tyler thinks Nancy is a pest. By the end of the story, he realizes she is pretty smart. He is grateful to have a little sister who knows more than he does about some topics.

Page 207

1. A
2. H
3. B
4. First, the firefly is an egg. Then a soft wormlike larva hatches out of the egg. It eats and grows for one to two years. In the spring, the larva grows a hard pupa shell. Then after a few weeks, an adult firefly comes out of the pupa.
5. Possible answer: Water beetles live in ponds and streams. Their back legs are flat and covered with little hairs. Their back legs work like little paddles. They have breathing holes on their sides. They eat insects, snails, and even small fish.

Page 208

1. B
2. G
3. A
4. Possible answer: When she reads Charlotte's essay, she starts to feel bad. She decides that Charlotte needs Tubby more than she does.
5. Answers will vary but should be supported by story details. Most students will probably say that Liz did the right thing.

Page 209

1. C
2. I
3. C
4. He wakes up to correct a mistake she has made in a story. He wants to make sure his family and friends know the true story.
5. Possible answer: It was a miracle that Don Roberto woke up. Everyone thought he was going to die. Also, all of the stories told about Don Roberto had him doing amazing and marvelous things.

Page 210

1. D
2. G
3. A
4. Possible answer: Yes, he probably did. When a publisher asked him to write a book using only the 250 words he listed, Geisel did it using only 220. He also accepted a challenge to write a story using only 50 different words.
5. Answers will vary but should be well supported with details from the book. Many students will probably say his work was important because millions of people have enjoyed his books and learned from them.

Page 211

1. D
2. I
3. B
4. Answers will vary, but students should cite specific story details that support the judgments they make. Most students will say it was a good idea because it brought customers into the store.
5. Answers will vary, but students should support their judgments with story details. Most will say that Tina and Jake are very close. Tina lets Jake be involved in the opening of her store, and Jake is willing to work hard to help the store become a success.

Page 212

1. A
2. I
3. C
4. Possible answer: He was feeling sad and lonely because his best friend had died.
5. In a cubist painting the subject is chopped up into cubes and rearranged. Picasso wanted to paint the world in new and different ways. He liked showing more than one side of an object at a time. Cubism was an interesting way to show the weight and volume of objects on a flat canvas.

Page 213

1. C
2. G
3. A
4. Possible answer: First, you film a person against a blue background with a camera that filters out blue light. Another camera films the location you want. Then the two images are combined. This makes the person look like he or she is in the location you filmed.
5. Possible answer: The clay figures would look like they were moving smoothly and realistically. You would not see the person moving the figures.

Scott Foresman Leveling System

Stage	Language Structure	Illustrations (Art and Photos)	Vocabulary, Concepts, Content, and Genre	Text Format and Features (Book Length, Size, and Layout)	Phonics and Word Study
Beginning Independent Readers (K, 1.1)	repetitive patterns with one word substitutions, rhyme, and repetition	simple illustrations, consistent picture-to-text sequence	familiar objects and/or common experiences, many words are pictured	single line of text per page; large, clear type size and typeface; small number of words per selection	one syllable words or high frequency words predominate
Early/Novice Leveled Readers Grade 1: 1A–30A	memorable repetitive language patterns throughout, predictable forms	strong support for text, consistent picture-to-text sequence	easily understood concepts, short words	short selections with few characters; single line of text per page; large, clear type size and typeface; small number of words per selection	focus on consonants, rhyming patterns, phonograms, and phonetically regular words; greater use of high frequency words
Novice/Developing Leveled Readers Grade 1: 1B–30B Grade 2: 31A–60A	some repeated language, consistent sentence structure	pictures reinforce overall meaning	short words, words with similar visual patterns	short selections with few characters, one to two lines of text per page, clear and consistent type size and typeface	focus on consonants, rhyming patterns, phonograms, and phonetically regular words; greater use of high frequency words
Developing/Fluent Leveled Readers Grade 1: Level C Grade 2: 31B–60B Grade 3: 61A–90A	mix of speech and language patterns, some sentence variety	some text support to reinforce meaning, moderate picture-to-text match	story-like but short episodes, stories become more complex with several characters	more lines of text per page, consistent arrangement of text on page	focus on short vowels, long vowels, consonant blends, and digraphs

Scott Foresman Leveling System

Stage	Language Structure	Illustrations (Art and Photos)	Vocabulary, Concepts, Content, and Genre	Text Format and Features (Book Length, Size, and Layout)	Phonics and Word Study
Fluent Leveled Readers Grade 2: Level C Grade 3: 61B–90B Grade 4: 91A–120A	greater variety in sentence structure, some examples of compound sentences	illustrations reinforce overall meaning, convey setting and atmosphere	more story-like with longer events, several characters, some specialized vocabulary, increase in content-area words, photos add support for nonfiction selections	longer selections with varied genres and literary styles, increase in nonfiction selections	focus on inflected endings, compound words, plurals, *r*-controlled vowels, and long and short vowels
Fluent/Proficient Leveled Readers Grade 3: Level C Grade 4: 91B–120B Grade 5: 121A–150A	written language forms and literary language predominate, greater variety in sentence structure, many more compound sentences	few illustrations to reinforce overall meaning and convey setting and atmosphere	more specialized topics and vocabulary, increase in number of vocabulary words, photos add support for nonfiction selections	longer selections with varied genres and literary styles, increase in nonfiction selections	emphasis is on multisyllabic words
Proficient Leveled Readers Grade 4: Level C Grade 5: 121B–150B Grade 6: 151A–180A	well-developed events, more examples of literary language, greater variety in sentence structure, many compound sentences	varied styles to support overall meaning; convey setting, atmosphere, and/or mood; partial pages with illustrations	more specialized topics and vocabulary, increase in number of vocabulary words	smaller type size fits full page, longer selections with varied genres and literary styles, increase in nonfiction selections	many examples of multisyllabic words
Proficient Leveled Readers Grade 5: Level C Grade 6: 151B–180B Grade 6: Level C	well-developed events, more examples of literary language, greater variety in sentence structure, many compound sentences, more sophisticated language structures	partial pages with illustrations, minimum picture support	increase in number of vocabulary words, challenging vocabulary incorporated	smaller type size fills full page; complex stories that describe setting, characters, problem(s), and resolution(s) in more detail	many examples of multisyllabic words

Observation Checklist

Student's Name ______________________ **Date** __________

Behaviors Observed	Always (Proficient)	Usually (Fluent)	Sometimes (Developing)	Rarely (Novice)

Reading Strategies and Skills

Uses prior knowledge and preview to understand what book is about				
Makes predictions and checks them while reading				
Uses context clues to figure out meanings of new words				
Uses phonics and syllabication to decode words				
Self-corrects while reading				
Reads at an appropriate reading rate				
Reads with appropriate intonation and stress				
Uses fix-up strategies				
Identifies story elements: character, setting, plot structure, theme				
Summarizes plot or main ideas accurately				
Uses target comprehension skill to understand the text better				
Responds thoughtfully about the text				

Reading Behaviors and Attitudes

Enjoys listening to stories				
Chooses reading as a free-time activity				
Reads with sustained interest and attention				
Participates in discussion about books				

General Comments

Taking a Running Record

A running record is an assessment of a student's oral reading accuracy and oral reading fluency. Reading accuracy is based on the number of words read correctly. Reading fluency is based on the reading rate (the number of words read per minute) and the degree to which the student reads with a "natural flow." Note: After Grade 3, some teachers do not take running records to assess oral reading.

How to Measure Reading Accuracy

1. Choose a grade-level text of about 80 to 120 words that is unfamiliar to the student.
2. Make a copy of the text for yourself. Make a copy for the student or have the student read aloud from a book.
3. Give the student the text and have the student read aloud. (You may wish to tape-record the student's reading for later evaluation.)
4. On your copy of the text, mark any miscues or errors the student makes while reading. See the running record sample on page 9, which shows how to identify and mark miscues.
5. Count the total number of words in the text and the total number of errors made by the student. Note: If a student makes the same error more than once, such as mispronouncing the same word multiple times, count it as one error. Self-corrections do not count as actual errors. Use the following formula to calculate the percentage score, or accuracy rate:

$$\frac{\text{Total Number of Words} - \text{Total Number of Errors}}{\text{Total Number of Words}} \times 100 = \text{percentage score}$$

Interpreting the Results

- A student who reads **98–100%** of the words correctly is reading at an **independent level** and may need more challenging texts.
- A student who reads **91–97%** of the words correctly is reading at an **instructional level** and will likely benefit from guided instruction.
- A student who reads **90% or less** of the words correctly is reading at a **frustrational level** and may benefit most from targeted instruction with lower-level texts and intervention.

See the Scott Foresman Leveling System on pages 200 and 221 to help you select materials that are appropriate for the student's reading level.

How to Measure Reading Rate

1. Follow Steps 1–3 above.
2. Note the exact times when the student begins and finishes reading.
3. Use the following formula to calculate the number of words per minute (wpm), or reading rate:

$$\frac{\text{Total Number of Words Read}}{\text{Total Number of Seconds}} \times 60 = \text{words per minute}$$

Interpreting the Results

An appropriate rate is roughly equal to the student's age × 10, plus or minus 10. For example, a 9-year-old student should be reading 80–100 words per minute.

Progress Report

Student's Name ______________________________

At the top of the chart, record the book title, the accuracy rate, and the reading rate at which the student reads the Leveling System. See page 223 for taking a running record to calculate accuracy and reading rates. At the bottom of the chart, record the date you took the running record. In the middle of the chart, write *F, I, ID* across from the appropriate stage to indicate whether the student is reading at a frustrational level (below 90% accuracy), an instructional level (91–97% accuracy), or an independent level (98–100% accuracy). See the Scott Foresman Leveling System on pages 220–221 to find the stage at which the Leveled Reader is leveled. Note: After Grade 3, some teachers do not take running records to assess oral reading.

Book Title, Accuracy Rate, Reading Rate												
STAGE	**Proficient**											
	Fluent/Proficient											
	Fluent											
	Developing/Fluent											
	Novice/Developing											
	Early/Novice											
	Beginning											
Date												